Charles G. Finney
Principles of Holiness

Selected messages on biblical holiness
by one of America's greatest evangelists

Compiled & Edited by
Louis G. Parkhurst, Jr.

BETHANY HOUSE PUBLISHERS
MINNEAPOLIS, MINNESOTA 55438
A Division of Bethany Fellowship, Inc.

Published by Bethany House Publishers
A Division of Bethany Fellowship, Inc.
6820 Auto Club Road, Minneapolis, MN 55438

Printed in the United States of America

Library of Congress Cataloging in Publication Data

Finney, Charles Grandison, 1792–1875.
    Principles of holiness.

    Includes bibliographical references.
    1. Sermons, American. 2. Theology—Addresses,
essays, lectures. I. Parkhurst, Louis Gifford, 1946–
II. Title.
BV4253.F44   1984   252'.058   83–25769
ISBN 0871234033

CHARLES G. FINNEY

This picture of Finney was taken from the 1847 edition of his *Systematic Theology*. It was painted by F. R. Spencer in 1835, and made into a wood engraving by J. W. Paradise for printing in the book. It was "Entered according to Act of Congress in the year 1835 by H. F. Brayton in the Clerk's Office of the District Court of the Southern District of New York" and published by Van Nostrand & Dwight, 146 Nassau Street, New York.

CHARLES G. FINNEY was one of America's foremost evangelists. Over half a million people were converted under his ministry in an age that offered neither amplifiers nor mass communications as tools. Harvard Professor Perry Miller affirmed that "Finney led America out of the eighteenth century." As a theologian, he is best known for his *Revival Lectures* and his *Systematic Theology.*

LOUIS GIFFORD PARKHURST, JR., is pastor of First Christian Church of Rochester, Minnesota, and teaches Ethics/ Philosophy at Minnesota Bible College. He garnered a B.A. and an M.A. from the University of Oklahoma and an M.Div. degree from Princeton Theological Seminary. He is married and the father of two children.

ACKNOWLEDGMENTS

I wish to thank Jack Key for use of the facilities of the Mayo Clinic Library to photocopy the lectures from *The Oberlin Evangelist*. I thank Jim Martin, also of the Mayo Clinic, who reproduced the photo of Finney from *Systematic Theology* for use in this book. Gordon Olson, of Bible Research Fellowship, kindly loaned me the 1847 edition of *Systematic Theology* for study and use of Finney's picture. Help was also provided by Bob and Kathy Lytle, who are co-workers in the Christian Life Study Center. My wife and family, with their patience and love, have continued to encourage these labors and ministry. My faithful co-laborers in the First Christian Church of Rochester have supported my continued efforts to research and write in the area of Finney's theology, and we have rejoiced together in seeing Finney's principles work in our lives. The staff of Bethany House Publishers, under the leadership of Gary and Carol Johnson, continue their labor of love and perfection in publishing these series on Finney, for which thousands are grateful. Finally, I will never be able to repay the debt I owe Harry Conn, Gordon Olson, and Francis Schaeffer for their personal prayers and encouragement in my labors for the truth of Scripture as empowered by the Spirit.

—L. G. Parkhurst, Jr.

BOOKS BY CHARLES G. FINNEY
Published by Bethany House Publishers

CONTENTS

INTRODUCTION

More than anything else today, we need reformation, revival, and renewal in our churches—and in our lives. No one in nine-teenth-century America was more successful in bringing these blessings to the churches than was Charles G. Finney. God wants to bestow these blessings upon us. He greatly desires to pour out His Spirit into our lives and into our churches, with pentecostal power, but *we* are not fulfilling the conditions He has set for revival and renewal; therefore, He cannot wisely bless us. Until we reform our preaching, teaching, and living, until we seek holiness by faith in Christ, we will not see revival, and renewal will only be cosmetic.

Francis Schaeffer has defined reformation and revival most succinctly: "Reformation is a return to the sound doctrine of the Bible. Revival is the practice of that sound doctrine under the power of the Holy Spirit." Church renewal can be nothing less than *both* reformation and revival in a fellowship of love.

Yet, we will not see revival until Christians are convicted by the holiness of the Father, Son, and Holy Spirit, who, by the light of their standard, reveal to us personally our awesome need for holiness. Charles Finney knew this, and he worked for holiness in the church as much as he worked for personal revival. Our preaching and practice of the Christian life are not going to man-ifest the power of God until we take seriously our need for holy living in the presence of God.

We must study the holiness teaching of Finney for ourselves. Nothing is more apt to move us into the depths of Finney's theo-logical thinking than study of his lectures and sermons. They

11

help us to understand a theology that will bring renewal, because they show us from many different angles how he applied the central ideas of his teaching. For this reason, *Principles of Holiness* is a remarkable collection—especially when added to *Principles of Victory* and *Principles of Liberty*.[1] When studied carefully, these lectures and sermons should lead each person, who is committed to obeying God to the limits of his understanding, to seek a holy life for the sake of God's reputation and His work in the world.

Principles of Holiness contains nineteen lectures and sermons by Charles Finney, taken from two different sources. Thirteen lectures (Chapters 3-15 in this book) are the series, "Holiness of Christians in the Present Life," published in *The Oberlin Evangelist* in 1843. This was an important year in the life of Finney, as Timothy Smith has pointed out in his introduction to a collection of Finney's lectures, *The Promise of the Spirit*.[2] Chapters 3-15 as well as three sermons on God's character ("Joy in God," "The Benevolence of God," and "Revelation of God's Glory") from 1843 provide the necessary context to understand the experience of refreshing which Finney had that year. Finney wrote that in 1843 his "mind was exceedingly exercised on the question of personal holiness." Indeed, exercised enough to print his thirteen lectures. Finney also wrote that after the time of refreshing, his preaching took on a noticeable change; even his congregation noticed it. That change is demonstrated in the three sermons about God's character, in which Finney's focus moves from holiness in the Christian's life to the wonderful joy and peace of knowing God truly and trusting in Him.

In the year of 1843, God revealed himself to Finney in a deeper way. Not in the sense of a second work of grace, but in the sense of a new *revelation of himself*—another in a whole series of revelations to Finney. Finney makes this clear in the three sermons included here, and in the autobiographical account "Total Commitment" in *Answers to Prayer*.[3] Finney did not directly insist that people seek a second work of grace or have a "second crisis," but he did insist that they always seek new revelations of God to their souls for the sake of fulfilling their calling.

In "Revelation of God's Glory" (the final sermon printed in 1843), we see Finney's experience compared with that of Moses.

We should especially compare his autobiographical account of 1843 with the sermon itself. Speaking of Moses, he says, "He had subsequent and frequent manifestations of God's presence and power as circumstances required." And he concludes from Moses' experiences, "A principle of divine administration is here developed; namely, God will furnish such grace and manifestations of His goodness as the circumstances demand and their demands require." Finney knew the quest for a second crisis, or second work of grace, could possibly be nothing more than pure selfishness. He was concerned that holy living promote the glory of God. For this reason, he exhorts us to seek times of spiritual refreshing and fresh fillings of the Holy Spirit *for Christ's sake*, not ours: "Whatever we find ourselves in need of for the success of *His work*, to which He has called us, we have a right to go and ask for, with perfect confidence, and complete assurance, and we should not let go our suit till the request is granted." Speaking of his life he says, "Always, yes, always, when I have gone to God, as Moses did, with the prayer, 'Show me Thy glory,' He has never denied me, never, *never* [italics are Finney's]." Rather than promoting a second work of grace, Finney challenges, "Brethren, is it not true that we need new manifestations of God? One revelation brings need of new and more glorious revelations." After mature reflection, Finney wrote of his conversion experience: "Of this experience I said nothing, that I remember, at the time, to anybody; that is, of this experience of justification [and so far as I could see, of present sanctification]."[4] From felt need in 1843, for greater effectiveness in his work, Finney called to the Lord for an even greater manifestation of himself to him, and he made a searching re-committal of all he had and was, and the Lord refreshed his soul, empowering him for the great work of teaching, writing and publishing his *Systematic Theology*, and other works.

The other three lectures in *Principles of Holiness* are from Finney's *Lectures to Professing Christians*.[5] These lectures ("Christian Perfection I and II" and "Rest of the Saints") show the continuity of Finney's thought over seven years, from 1837-1843. Timothy Smith makes special mention of these three lectures on holiness (but does not include them) in *The Promise of the Spirit*, along with mention of "Sanctification by Faith" and "Love Is the Whole of Religion," which I included in *Principles of Victory*. The lectures entitled "Christian Perfection" refer to the attainability of holiness and demonstrate from Scripture that God expects us to be holy; therefore, we can be holy.

What is holiness, holy living, sanctification, or Christian perfection, according to Finney? Certain points from *Principles of Holiness* answer the question:

1. "Holiness is that state of the will or heart which consists in the voluntary consecration of the whole being to God. Sin is the exact opposite of this, and consists in the consecration of the will or heart, of the whole being, to the gratification of self. This is selfishness."

2. "Entire conformity of heart and life to all known truth is holiness, and nothing short of this is or can be."

3. "With all Christians, holiness is the rule and sin is the exception."

4. "The Christian is benevolent, while the sinner is selfish. These are ultimate states of mind, and will manifest themselves in both by a natural necessity."

5. "The Christian is influenced by reason, and the sinner by mere feeling."

6. "Sanctification is nothing else than delivering up the mind to the truth and promises of God."

When I began my study of Finney, I focused first on prayer in *Principles of Prayer*.[6] We are to pray, not to extract blessings in some impersonal way from a grudging God, but to develop a deeper personal relationship with Him. He helps us develop that relationship by blessing us in many ways through prayer, sometimes immediately and sometimes over a period of time, depending on our state of commitment to Him, and on what is best for His Kingdom. *Principles of Victory* and *Principles of Liberty* showed that salvation is not a technicality to get us to heaven, but a relationship with God. Our new relationship with God through Christ should free us from slavery to sin and the law, so we can live in God's will from now through eternity. *Principles of Holiness* focuses on God's plan to fit us for greater service for Him and others. We will abhor sin all the more, and will desire to live a completely holy life, once we have seen how sin hinders our witnessing for God in every way, and how sin distorts our representation of the character of God—even so-called hidden sin. Holy living, then, is not practiced to assure us of heaven, for that is selfishness and salvation by works of the law; holy living is practiced so we can reveal the character of God to the world in the hope of saving some and bringing Him the glory He deserves.[6] *Answers to Prayer* demonstrates how these principles were worked out in Finney's life, and how some perished for refusal to come to God in Christ.

I believe the church desperately needs the message of Charles Finney—each of us needs it. We need to make his message part of our souls, because it is true to Scripture, and because it will bring reformation, revival, and renewal. We need to be mastered by the same Holy Spirit and truth that mastered Finney, so that we can preach, teach, and live in a way that will meet the spiritual needs of those in the twentieth century.

For the sake of His Kingdom,
L. G. Parkhurst, Jr.
Pentecost 1983

Notes

1. Published by Bethany House Publishers (Minneapolis, Minnesota, 1981, 1983), these are Finney's sermons on the Book of Romans.
2. Published by Bethany House Publishers in 1980, these sermons and lectures on Christian Holiness were published first in *The Oberlin Evangelist* in 1839.
3. Finney's *Answers to Prayer* challenge us with a practical application of his *Principles of Prayer* and include probing questions for individual and group study. See the chapter on "Total Commitment" in *Answers to Prayer*, pp. 94-101 (Minneapolis: Bethany House Publishers, 1983).
4. *Ibid*, p. 24.
5. Published in London by Milner and Company in 1837, these are lectures XIX, XX, pp. 214-241, and XXIV, pp. 276-285. "Holiness of Christians in the Present Life" were published in *The Oberlin Evangelist* from January 4 through August 16, 1843.

6. Published by Bethany House Publishers in 1980, these are 40 daily devotionals on how to pray effectively.
7. For another very good, brief study of holiness from Finney's perspective, see *Holiness and Sin* by Gordon C. Olson (Minneapolis: Men for Missions, 1971).

1

CHRISTIAN PERFECTION I*

Matthew 5:48

"Be ye therefore perfect, even as your Father which is in heaven is perfect."

The Savior says in verses 43-48, "Ye have heard that it hath been said, Thou shalt love thy neighbour, and hate thine enemy. But I say unto you, Love your enemies, bless them that curse you, do good to them that hate you, and pray for them which despitefully use you and persecute you; that ye may be the children of your Father which is in heaven: for he maketh his sun to rise on the evil and on the good, and sendeth rain on the just and on the unjust. For if ye love them which love you, what reward have ye? do not even the publicans the same? And if ye salute your brethren only, what do ye more than others? do not even the publicans so? Be ye therefore perfect, even as your Father which is in heaven is perfect."

In speaking on Christian perfection, I plan to follow this order:

> I. *I shall show what is not to be understood by this requirement, "Be ye therefore perfect"; or, what Christian perfection is not.*

Lectures to Professing Christians by C. G. Finney (London: Milner and Company, 1837), Lecture XIX, pp. 214-229.

II. *Show what is the perfection here required.*
III. *Show that this perfection is duty.*
IV. *Show that it is attainable.*
V. *Answer some of the objections commonly urged against the doctrine of Christian perfection.*

I. *What Christian perfection is not.*

It is not required that we should have the same natural perfections God has.

God has two kinds of perfections, natural and moral. His natural perfections constitute His nature, essence, or constitution. They are His eternity, immutability, omnipotence, etc. These are called natural perfections, because they have no moral character. They are not voluntary. God has not given them to himself, because He did not create himself but existed from eternity in full possession of all these natural attributes. All these God possesses in an infinite degree. These natural perfections are not the perfection here required. The attributes of our nature were created in us, and we are not required to produce any new natural attributes, nor would it be possible. We are not required to possess any of them in the degree God possesses them.

The perfection required in the text is not perfection of knowledge, even according to our limited faculties.

Christian perfection, as here required, is not freedom from temptation, either from our constitution or from things about us. The mind may be severely tried with the animal appetites, and yet not sin. The Apostle James says, "Every man is tempted, when he is drawn away of his own lust, and enticed." The sin is not in the temptations, but in yielding to them. A person may be tempted by Satan, by the appetites, or by the world and yet not have sin. All sin consists in unlawful *voluntary consent* to the desires.

Neither does Christian perfection imply a freedom from what ought to be understood as Christian warfare.

The perfection required is not the infinite moral perfection which God has; because man, being a finite creature, is not capable of infinite perfections. The perfection of God is infinite perfection, God being infinite in himself. But this is not required of us.

II. *What is the Christian perfection here required.*

Christian perfection is perfect obedience to the law to God. The law of God requires perfect, disinterested, impartial benevolence—love to God and love to our neighbor. It requires that we be motivated by the same feeling, and act on the same principles, upon which God acts. It requires us to leave self out of the question as uniformly as He does, to be as much separated from selfishness as He is—in a word, to be in our measure as perfect as God is. Christianity requires that we should do neither more nor less than the law of God prescribes. Nothing short of this is Christian perfection. This is being just as morally perfect as God. Everything is here included: to feel as He feels, to love what He loves, to hate what He hates, and to do so for the same reasons that He does.

God regards every being in the universe according to its relative value. He regards His own interests according to their relative value in the scale of being, and no more. He exercises the same love toward himself that He requires of us, and for the same reason. He loves himself supremely, with both the love of benevolence and the love of complacency, because He is supremely excellent. And He requires us to love Him as perfectly as He loves himself. He loves himself with the love of benevolence, or regards His own interest, and glory, and happiness, as the supreme good, because it is the supreme good. And He requires us to love Him in the same way. He loves himself with infinite complacency, because He knows that He is infinitely worthy and excellent, and He requires the same of us. He also loves His neighbor as himself, not in the same degree that He loves himself, but in the same proportion, according to his relative value. From the highest angel to the smallest worm, He regards their happiness with perfect love, according to their worth. It is His duty to conform to these principles as much as it is our duty. He can no more depart from this rule than we can without committing sin; and for Him to do it would be worse than for us to do it since He is greater than we. God is infinitely obligated to do this. His very nature, not depending on His own volition, but uncreated, binds Him to this. And He has created us moral beings in His own image, capable of conforming to the same rule with himself. This rule requires us to have the same character with Him, to love as impartially, with as perfect love—to seek the good of others with as single an eye as He does. This, and nothing less than this, is Christian perfection.

III. *Christian perfection is a duty.*

This is evident from the fact that God requires it, both under the law and under the gospel.

The command in the text, "Be ye therefore perfect, even as your Father which is in heaven is perfect," is given under the gospel. Christ here commands the very same thing that the law requires. Some suppose that much less is required of us under the gospel than was required under the law. It is true that the gospel does not require perfection as the condition of salvation. But no part of the obligation of the law is discharged. The gospel holds those under it to the same holiness as those under the law.

I argue that Christian perfection is a duty, because God has no right to require anything less.

God cannot discharge us from the obligation to be perfect, as I have defined perfection. If He were to attempt it, He would give license to sin. He has no right to give any such license. While we are moral beings, there is no power in the universe that can discharge us from the obligation to be perfect. Can God discharge us from the obligation to love Him with all our heart, and soul, and mind, and strength? That would be saying that God does not deserve such love. And if He cannot discharge us from the whole law, He cannot discharge us from any part of it, for the same reason.

If anyone contends that the gospel requires less holiness than the law, I would ask him to say just how much less it requires.

If we are allowed to stop short of perfect obedience, where shall we stop? How perfect are we required to be? Where will you find a rule in the Bible to determine how much less holy you are allowed to be under the gospel than you would be under the law? Shall we say each one must judge for himself? Then I ask, is it your duty to be any more perfect than you are now? Probably all would say, "Yes." Can you lay down any point at which, when you have arrived, you can say, "Now I am perfect enough; it is true, I have some sin left, but I have gone as far as it is my duty to go in this world"? Where do you get your authority for any such notion? No. All who truly seek piety, the more pious they are, the more strongly they feel the obligation to be perfect as God is perfect.

IV. *Christian perfection is attainable or feasible in this life.*

It may be fairly inferred that Christian perfection is attainable from the fact that it is commanded.

Does God command us to be perfect as He is perfect, and still shall we say it is an impossibility? Are we not always to infer, when God commands a thing, that there is a natural possibility of doing what He commands? I remember hearing an individual say that he would preach to sinners that they ought to repent because God commands it; but he would not preach that they could repent because God has nowhere said that they can. What consummate trifling! Suppose a man were to say he would preach to citizens that they ought to obey the laws of the country because the government had enacted them, but he would not tell them that they could obey because it is nowhere in the statute book enacted that they have the ability. It is always to be understood that when God requires anything of men, they possess the necessary faculties to do it. Otherwise God requires impossibilities and sends sinners to hell for not doing what they were in no sense able to do.

That there is natural ability to be perfect is a simple matter of fact.

There can be no question of this. *What is perfection? It is to love the Lord our God with all our heart, and soul, and mind, and strength, and to love our neighbor as ourselves.* That is, it requires us not to exert the powers of somebody else, but our own powers. The law itself goes no further than to require the right use of the powers you possess. So it is a simple matter of fact that you possess natural ability, or power, to be just as perfect as God requires.

Objection. Here some may object that if there is a natural ability to be perfect, there is a moral inability, which comes to the same thing. For inability is inability, call it what you will, and if we have moral inability, we are as truly unable as if our inability was natural.

Answer 1. There is no more moral inability to be perfectly holy than there is moral inability to be holy at all. So far as moral ability is concerned, you can as well be perfectly holy as you can be holy at all. The true distinction between natural ability and moral ability is this: Natural ability relates to the powers and faculties of the mind; moral ability relates only to the will. Moral inability is nothing other than unwillingness to do a thing. So it is explained by President Edwards, in his treatise on the will,* and by other writers on the subject. If you ask whether you have moral ability to be perfect and mean by it, whether you are willing to be perfect, I answer no. If you were willing to be perfect, you would be perfect; the perfection required is only a perfect conformity of the will to God's law, or willing right. If you ask then, "Are we able to will right?" I answer that the question implies a contradiction, in supposing that there can be such a thing as a moral agent unable to choose, or will. President Edwards says expressly, in his chapter on Moral Inability—as you may see, if you will read it—that strictly speaking, there is no such thing as moral inability. If inability to do a thing means real inability, it implies a willingness to do it, but a lack of power. To say we are unable to will is absurd. It is saying we will and yet are unable to will at the same time.

Answer 2. But I admit and believe that there is desperate unwillingness in the case. And if this is what you mean by moral inability, it is true. There is an obstinate unwillingness in sinners to become Christians, and in Christians to become perfect, to come up to the full perfection required both by the law and gospel. Sinners may strongly wish or desire to be rid of all their sins, and may pray for it, even with agony. They may think they are willing to be perfect, but they deceive themselves. They may feel willing to renounce their sins as a whole, or as an abstract idea, but taken in detail, one by one, there are many sins they are unwilling to give up. They wrestle against sin in general, but cling to it in the detail.

I have known cases of this kind where individuals break down in such a manner that they think they never will sin again; then

---

*See Jonathan Edwards, *Freedom of the Will* (New Haven: Yale University Press, 1957); Henry Philip Tappan, *A Review of Edwards' "Inquiry into the Freedom of the Will"* (New York: John S. Taylor, 1839); and Charles Finney, *Principles of Liberty,* p. 176.

perhaps in one hour, something will come up and they are ready to fight for the indulgence, and need to be broken down again and again. Christians actually need to be hunted from one sin after another before they are willing to give them up; and after the hunt they are unwilling to give up all sins. When they are truly willing to give up all sin, when they have no will of their own, but merge their own will entirely in the will of God, then their bonds are broken. When they yield absolutely to God's will, then they are filled with the fullness of God.

After all, the true point of inquiry is this: Have I any right to expect to be perfect in this world? Is there any reason for me to believe that I can be so completely subdued that my soul shall burn with a steady flame, and I shall love God wholly, up to what the law requires? That is an undeniable duty. But the great query is: Is it attainable? Yes, I believe it is.

So much has been said within a few years about Christian perfection, and individuals who have entertained the doctrine of perfection have run into so many wild notions, that it seems as if the devil had anticipated the movements of the church and created such a state of feeling that the moment the doctrine of the Bible respecting sanctification is crowded on the church, people cry, "Why, this is perfectionism." But I will say despite the errors into which some of those called perfectionists have fallen, the Bible does teach Christian perfection, and the Bible doctrine on the subject is what nobody needs to fear, but what everybody needs to know. I disclaim, entirely, the charge of maintaining the peculiarities, whatever they be, of modern perfectionists. I have read their publications and have much knowledge of them as individuals, and I cannot assent to many of their views. But the doctrine that Christian perfection is a duty is one which I have always maintained. I have become more convinced of it these last few months, and that it is attainable in this life. Many doubt this, but I am persuaded it is true on various grounds. *Christian perfection is attainable because:*

1. *God wills it.*

The first doubt in many minds is this: "Does God really will my sanctification in this world? He says He does. The law of God is itself as strong an expression as He can give of His will on the subject, and it is backed up by further declaration. The gospel is but a republication of the same will in another form. How can God express His will more strongly on this point than He has in the text, "Be ye therefore perfect, even as your Father which is in heaven is perfect"? In 1 Thess. 4:3, we are told expressly, "For this is the will of God, even your sanctifcation."* If you examine the Bible carefully, from one end to the other, you will find that it is everywhere just as plainly taught that God wills the sanctification of Christians in this world as it is that He wills sinners should repent in this world. And if we go by the Bible, we might just as readily question whether He wills that men should repent as whether He wills that Christians should be holy. Why should He not reasonably expect it? He requires it. What does He require? When He requires men to repent, He requires that they should love God with all the heart, soul, mind, and strength. What reason have we to believe that He wills they should repent at all, or love Him at all, if that is not a reason for believing that He wills they should love Him perfectly? Strange logic, indeed!—to teach that He wills it in one case, because He requires it, and not admit the same inference in the other. No man can show from the Bible that God does not require perfect sanctification in this world, nor that He does not will it, nor that it is not just as attainable as any degree of sanctification.

I have studied the Bible with special reference to this point, and thought I would note on my card, where I have the plan of my discourse, the passages that teach this doctrine. But I found they were too numerous to include, and that if I collected them all, I should do nothing else this evening but stand and read passages of Scripture. If you have never looked into the Bible with this view, you will be astonished to see how many more passages speak of deliverance from sin than deliverance from the punishment of sin. The passages that speak only of deliverance from punishment are as nothing in comparison with the others.

2. *All the promises and prophecies of God regarding sanctification of believers in this world are to be understood regarding their perfect sanctification.*

What is sanctification but holiness? When a prophecy speaks of the sanctification of the church, are we to understand that it is

---

*"It is God's will that you should be holy" (NIV).

to be sanctified only partially? When God requires holiness, are we to understand that as partial holiness? Surely not. By what principle, then, will you understand partial holiness when He promises holiness? We have so long understood the Scriptures with reference to the existing state of things that we lose sight of the real meaning. But if we look only at the language of the Bible, I defy any man to prove that the promises and prophecies of holiness mean anything short of perfect sanctification, unless the requirements of both the law and gospel are to be understood as a partial obedience, which is absurd.

3. *Perfect sanctification is "the great blessing" promised throughout the Bible.*

The Apostle Peter says we have exceeding great and precious promises, and tells us what their use is. "Whereby are given unto us exceeding great and precious promises: that by these ye might be partakers of the divine nature, *having escaped the corruption that is in the world through lust*" (2 Pet. 1:4). If that is not perfect sanctification, I beg to know what is. It is a plain declaration that these "exceeding great and precious promises" are given so that believing and appropriating them, we might become partakers of the divine nature. And if we will use them for that purpose, we may become perfectly holy.

Let us look at some of these promises in particular. I will begin with the promise of the Abrahamic covenant. The promise is that his posterity should possess the land of Canaan, and that through him, by the Messiah, all nations should be blessed. The seal of the covenant, circumcision, which is a type of holiness, shows us the principal blessing intended. It was *holiness*. So the Apostle tells us in another place, Jesus Christ was given that He might sanctify unto himself a peculiar people.

All the purifications and other ceremonies of the Mosaic ritual signified the same thing: they all pointed to a Savior to come. Every ordinance of purifying the body was set forth with reference to the purifying of the mind, or holiness.

Under the gospel, the same thing is signified by baptism—the washing of the body representing the sanctification of the mind.

In Ezek. 36:25, this blessing is expressly promised as the great blessing of the gospel: "Then will I sprinkle clean water upon you, and ye shall be clean: from all your filthiness, and from all your idols, will I cleanse you. A new heart also will I give you, and a new spirit will I put within you: and I will take away the stony heart out of your flesh, and I will give you an heart of flesh. And I will put my spirit within you, and cause you to walk in my statutes, and ye shall keep my judgments, and do them."

So it is in Jer. 33:8: "And I will cleanse them from all their iniquity, whereby they have sinned against me; and I will pardon all their iniquities, whereby they have sinned, and whereby they have transgressed against me." But it would take up too much time to quote all the passages in the Old Testament prophecies that represent holiness to be the great blessing of the covenant. I desire you all to search the Bible for yourselves, and you will be astonished to find how uniformly the blessing of sanctification is held up as the principal blessing promised to the world through the Messiah.

Who can doubt that the great object of the Messiah's coming was to sanctify His people? Just after the Fall it was predicted that Satan would bruise Christ's heel, but that He should bruise Satan's head. And the Apostle John tells us that "for this purpose the Son of God was manifested, that he might destroy the works of the devil" (1 John 3:8). He has undertaken to put Satan under His feet. His object is to win us back to allegiance to God, to sanctify us, to purify our minds. As it is said in Zech. 13:1, "In that day there shall be a fountain opened to the house of David and to the inhabitants of Jerusalem for sin and for uncleanness."

And Dan. 9:24 says, "Seventy weeks are determined upon thy people and upon thy holy city, to finish the transgression, and to make an end of sins, and to make reconciliation for iniquity, and to bring in everlasting righteousness, and to seal up the vision and prophecy, and to anoint the Most Holy." But it is in vain to name the multitude of these texts. The Old Testament is full of it.

In the New Testament, the first account we have of the Savior tells us He was called "Jesus: for he shall save his people from their sins" (Matt. 1:21). So it is said, "He was manifested to take away our sins" (1 John 3:5), and "to destroy the works of the devil." In Titus 2:13-14, the Apostle Paul speaks of the grace of God, or the gospel, as teaching us to deny ungodliness: "Looking for that blessed hope, and the glorious appearing of the great God and our Saviour Jesus Christ; who gave himself for us, that he might redeem us from all iniquity, and purify unto himself a peculiar people, zealous of good works." And in Eph. 5:25-27 we learn that "Christ also loved the church, and gave himself for it; that he might sancity and cleanse it with the washing of water by the word, that he might present it to himself a glorious church, not having spot, or wrinkle, or any such thing; but that it should be holy and without blemish." I only quote these few passages to illustrate that the object for which Christ came is to sanctify the church to such a degree that it should be absolutely "holy and without blemish." So in Rom. 11:26-27, "And so all Israel shall be saved: as it is written, There shall come out of Sion the Deliverer, and shall turn away ungodliness from Jacob: for this is my covenant unto them, when I shall take away their sins." And in 1 John 1:9, it is said, "If we confess our sins, he is faithful and just to forgive us our sins, and to cleanse us from all unrighteousness." What is it to "cleanse us from *all* unrighteousness" if it is not perfect sanctification? I presume all of you, if there is such a thing promised in the Bible as perfect sanctification, wish to know it. Now, what do you think? In 1 Thess. 5:23, the Apostle Paul prays a very remarkable prayer: "And the very God of peace sanctify you wholly; and I pray God your whole spirit and soul and body be preserved blameless unto the coming of our Lord Jesus Christ." What is that? "Sanctify you wholly." Does that mean perfect sanctification? You may think it does not mean perfect sanctification in this world. But the Apostle says that not only your whole soul and spirit but your "body be preserved blameless." Could an inspired apostle make such a prayer if he did not believe the blessing prayed for to be possible? But he goes on to say in the very next verse, "Faithful is he that calleth you, who also *will do it*." Is that true, or is it false?

4. *The perfect sanctification of believers is the very object for which the Holy Spirit is promised.*

To quote the passages that show this would take up too much time. The whole tenor of Scripture respecting the Holy Spirit proves it. The whole array of gospel means, through which the Holy Spirit works, is aimed at this and adapted to the end of sanctifying the church. All the commands to be holy, all the promises, all the prophecies, all the ordinances, all the providences, the blessings and the judgments, all the duties of religion are the means which the Holy Spirit is to employ for sanctifying the church.

5. *If it is not a feasible duty to be perfectly holy in this world, then it will follow that the devil has so completely accomplished his design in corrupting mankind that Jesus Christ is at fault, and has no way to sanctify His people but by taking them out of the world.*

Is it possible that Satan has gained the advantage so that God's kingdom cannot be reestablished in this world, and that the Almighty has no way but to back out and take His saints to heaven before He can make them holy? Is God's kingdom to be only partially established, and will it always be that the best saints shall one-half of their time be serving the devil? Must the people of God always go drooping and drivelling along in religion, and live in sin till they get to heaven? What is meant by a stone cut out of a mountain without hands that is to fill the earth if it does not mean that there is yet to be a universal triumph of the love of God in the world?

6. *If perfect sanctification is not attainable in this world, it must be either from a lack of motives in the gospel or a lack of sufficient power in the Spirit of God.*

It is said that in another life we may be like God, for we shall see Him as He is. But why not here, if we have faith which is the "substance of things hoped for, and the evidence of things not seen"? There is a promise to those who "hunger and thirst after righteouness" that "they shall be filled." What is it to be "filled" with righteousness but to be perfectly holy? And are we never to be filled with righteousness till we die? Are we to go through life hungry and thirsty and unsatisfied? So the Bible has been misunderstood, but it does not read so.

V. *Common objections to Christian perfection.*

1. "The power of habit is so great that we ought not to expect to be perfectly sanctified in this life."

Answer. If the power of habit can be so far encroached upon that an impenitent sinner can be converted, why can it not be absolutely broken so that a converted person may be wholly sanctified? The greatest difficulty, surely, is when selfishness has entire control of the mind and when the habits of sin are wholly unbroken. This obstacle is so great, in all cases, that no power but that of the Holy Ghost can overcome it, and so great, in many instances, that God himself cannot, consistently with His wisdom, use the means necessary to convert the soul. But it is possible to suppose that after He has begun to overcome it—after He has broken the power of selfishness and the obstinacy of habit, and actually converted the individual—God has sufficient resources to sanctify the soul altogether!

2. "Many physical difficulties have been created by a life of sin that cannot be overcome or removed by moral means."

Answer. This is a common objection. Men feel they are burdened with appetites and physical influences impossible to overcome by moral means. The Apostle Paul, in Romans 7, describes a man in great conflict with the body. But in the next chapter he speaks of one who had gained victory over the flesh. "And if Christ be in you, the body is dead because of sin; but the spirit is life because of righteousness. But if the Spirit of him that raised up Jesus from the dead dwell in you, he that raised up Christ from the dead shall also quicken your mortal bodies by his Spirit that dwelleth in you" (Rom. 8:10-11). This quickening of the body does not refer to the resurrection of the body, but to the influence of the Spirit of God upon the body—the sanctification of the body.

You will ask, "Does the Spirit of God produce a physical change in the body?" I will illustrate it by the case of the drunkard. The drunkard has brought upon himself a diseased state of the body, an unnatural thirst, which is insatiable and so strong that it seems impossible he should be reclaimed. But very likely you know cases in which they have been reclaimed, and have entirely overcome this physical appetite. I have heard of cases where drunkards have seen the sin of drunkenness in such a strong light that they abhorred strong drink and forever renounced it with such a loathing that they never had the least desire for it again.

I once knew an individual who was a slave to the use of tobacco. At length he became convinced that it was sin for him to use it, and the struggle against it finally drove him to God in such an agony of prayer that he got the victory at once over the appetite, and never had the least desire for it again. I am not giving you philosophy but *facts*. I have heard of individuals who were mastered by certain appetites, but in time of revival were subdued into perfect stillness, and these appetites have ever after been as dead as if they had no body. I suppose the mind may be so occupied and absorbed with greater things that it does not give a thought to the things that would revive the vicious appetite. If a drunkard goes by a bar or sees people drinking and allows his mind to think upon it, the appetite will be awakened. The wise man, therefore, tells him to "look not upon the wine when it is red." But there is no doubt that any appetite of the body may be subdued if a sufficient impression is made upon the mind to break it up. I believe every real Christian will be ready to admit from his own experience that this is possible. Have you not, beloved, known times when one great absorbing topic has so filled your mind and controlled your soul that the appetites of the body remained, for the time, perfectly neutralized? Now, suppose this state of mind were to continue, to become constant, would not all these physical difficulties be overcome, which some speak of as standing in the way of perfect sanctification?

3. "The Bible is against this doctrine, where it says, there is not a just man on the earth that liveth and sinneth not."

Answer. Suppose the Bible does say that there is not one on earth; it does not say there *cannot* be one. Or, it may have been true at that time, or under that dispensation, that there was not one man in the world who was perfectly sanctified; and yet it may not follow that at this time, or under the gospel dispensation, there is no one who lives without sin. "For the law made nothing perfect, but the bringing in of a better hope did" (Heb. 7:19). The better hope, the gospel, did make something perfect.

4. "The apostles admit they were not perfect."

Answer. I know the Apostle Paul says in one place, "Not as though I had already attained, either were already perfect" (Phil. 3:12). But it is not said that he continued so till his death, or that he never did attain to perfect sanctification; and the manner in which he speaks in the remainder of the verse looks as if he expected to become so: "But I follow after, if that I may apprehend that for which also I am apprehended of Christ Jesus." Nor does it appear true that in this passage he is speaking of perfect sanctification, but rather of perfect knowledge.

And the Apostle John speaks of himself as if he loved God perfectly. But whatever may be the truth about the actual character of the apostles, it does not follow because they were not perfect, no others can be. They clearly declare it to a be a duty, and that they were aiming at it just as if they expected to attain it in this life. And they command us to do the same.

5. "But is it not presumption for us to think we can be better than the apostles and early Christians?"

Answer. What is the presumption in the case? Is it not a fact that we have far greater advantages for religious experience than the early churches. The benefit of their experience, the complete Scriptures, the state of the world, the near approach of the millennium—all give us the advantage over the early believers. Are we to suppose the church is always stationary in regard to religious experience and never to go ahead in anything? What scripture is there for this? Why should not the church be always growing better? It seems to be the prevailing idea that the church is to be always looking back to the early saints as the standard. I suppose the reverse of this is a duty, and that we ought to be always aiming at a much higher standard than theirs. I believe the church must go far ahead of the early Christians before the millennium can come. I do not refer here to the apostles, because it does not clearly appear, but it seems evident that they became fully sanctified.

6. "But so many profess to be perfect, who are not so, that I cannot believe in perfection in this life."

Answer. How many people profess to be rich who are not? Will you therefore say you cannot believe anybody is rich? Fine logic!

7. "So many who profess perfection have run into error and fanaticism that I am afraid to think of it."

Answer. I find in history that a sect of perfectionists has grown out of every great and general revival that ever took place. And this is exactly one of the devil's masterpieces to counteract the effects of a revival. He knows that if the church were brought to the proper standard of holiness, it would be a speedy death blow to his power on earth. So he takes this course to defeat the efforts of the church to elevate the standard of piety, by frightening Christians from marching right up to the point and aiming at living perfectly conformed to the will of God. And so successful has he been that the moment you begin to push the church to be holy, and give up all their sins, somebody will cry out, "Why, this leads to perfectionism"; they thus give it a bad name and put it down.

8. "But do you really think anybody ever has been perfectly holy in this world?"

Answer. I have reason to believe there have been many. It is highly probable that Enoch and Elijah were free from sin before they were taken out of the world. And in different ages of the church there have been numbers of Christians who were intelligent and upright, and had nothing that could be said against them, who have testified that they themselves lived free from sin. I know it is said, in reply, that they must have been proud, and that no man would say he was free from sin for any other motive but pride. But I ask, why may not a man say he is free from sin, if it is so, without being proud, as well as he can say he is converted without being proud? Will not the saints say it in heaven to the praise of the grace of God which has thus crowned His glorious work? And why may they not say it now from the same motive? I do not myself profess now to have attained perfect sanctification, but if I had attained it, if I felt that God had really given me the victory over the world, the flesh and the devil and made me free from sin, would I keep it a secret, locked up in my own breast, and let my brethren stumble on in ignorance of what the grace of God can do? Never! I would tell them that they might expect complete deliverance if they would only grasp the arm of help which Christ reaches forth to save His people from their sins.

I have heard people talk like this, that if a Christian really was perfect, he would be the last person that would tell of it. But would you say of a person who professed conversion, "If he was really converted, he would be the last person to tell of it"? On the contrary, is it not the first impulse of a converted heart to say, "Come and hear, all you that fear God, and I will declare what He has done for my soul!"? Why, then, should not the same desire exist in one who feels that he has obtained sanctification? Why all these suspicions, and refusing to credit evidence? If anyone gives evidence of great piety—if his life is irreproachable, and his spirit not to be complained of, if he shows the very spirit of the Son of God, and if such a person testifies that after great struggles and agonizing prayer God has given him the victory, and his soul is set at liberty by the power of divine grace—why are we not bound to receive his testimony just as much as when he says he is converted? We always take such testimony. And now, when he says he has gone further, and has the victory over all sin, and that Christ has actually fulfilled His promise in this respect, why should we not credit this also?

I have recently read Mr. Wesley's *Plain Account of Christian Perfection,* a book I never saw until lately.* I find some expressions in it to which I should object, but I believe it is the expression rather than the sentiments. And I think, with this qualification, it is an admirable book, and I wish every member of this church to read it. I would also recommend the memoir of James Brainerd Taylor, and I wish every Christian would get it and study it.** I have read most of it three times within a few months. From many things in that book, it is plain that he believed in the doctrine that Christian perfection is a duty, and that it is attainable by believers in this life. There is nothing published which shows that he professed to have attained it, but it is manifest that he believed it to be attainable. But I have been told that much which is found in his diary on this subject, as well as some things in his letters, were suppressed by his biographers as not suitable for the eye of the church in her present state. I believe if the whole could come to light, it would be seen that he was a firm believer in this doctrine. These books should be read and pondered by the church.

I have now in my mind an individual who was a member of the church, but very worldly, and when a revival came he opposed it at first. But afterward he was awakened, and, after an awful conflict, he broke down and has ever since lived a life of most devoted piety, laboring and praying incessantly, like his

---

*See *A Plain Account of Christian Perfection As Believed and Taught by The Rev. Mr. John Wesley, from the Year 1725 to the Year 1777* in *The Works of The Rev. John Wesley, A.M.* (London: Wesleyan Conference Office, 1865), Vol. XI, pp. 351-438.

**See *Memoirs of James Brainerd Taylor* (New York: American Tract Society, 1833), and Charles Finney, *Principles of Liberty,* p. 51.

blessed Master, to promote the kingdom of God. I have never heard this man say he thought he was perfect, but I have often heard him speak of the duty and feasibility of being perfectly sanctified. And if there is man in the world who is so, I believe he is one.

People have the strangest notions on this subject. Sometimes you will hear them argue against Christian perfection on the ground that a man who was perfectly holy could not live, could not exist in this world. I believe I have talked just so in time past. I know I have talked like a fool on the subject. Why, a saint who was perfect would be more alive than ever, to the good of his fellowmen. Could not Jesus Christ live on earth? He was perfectly holy. It is thought that if a person was perfectly sanctified and loved God perfectly, he would be in such a state of excitement that he could not remain in the body, could neither eat nor sleep, nor attend to the ordinary duties of life. But there is no evidence of this. The Lord Jesus Christ was a man subject to all the temptations of other men. He also loved the Lord His God with all His heart and soul and strength. And yet it does not appear that He was in such a state of excitement that he could not both eat and sleep and work at His trade as a carpenter, and maintain perfect health of body and perfect composure of mind. And why does a saint who is perfectly sanctified need to be carried away with uncontrollable excitement, or killed with intense emotion, any more than Jesus Christ? There is no need of it, and Christian perfection implies no such thing.

REMARKS

We can see now why there is no more perfection in the world.

1. Christians do not believe that it is the will of God, or that God is willing they should be perfectly sanctified in this world.

They know He commands them to be perfect, as He is perfect, but they think He is secretly unwilling and does not really wish them to be so. "Otherwise," they say, "why does He not do more for us to make us perfect?" No doubt God prefers their remaining as they are to using any other means or system of influences to make them otherwise. For He sees that it would be a greater evil to introduce a new system of means than to let them remain as they are. Where one of the evils is unavoidable, He chooses the lesser of the two evils. And who can doubt that He prefers their being perfect in the circumstances in which they are to their sinning in these circumstances? Sinners reason just like those who protest religion. They say, "I don't believe He wills my repentance; if He did, He would make me repent." Sinner, God may prefer your continued impenitence, and your damnation, to using any other influences than He does to make you repent. But for you to infer from this that He does not wish you to yield to the influences He does use is strange logic! Suppose your servant should reason so and say, "I don't believe my master means I should obey him, because he doesn't stand by me all day to keep me at work." Is that a just conclusion? Very likely the master's time is so valuable that it would be a greater evil to his business than for that servant to stand still all day.

So it is in the government of God. If God were to bring all the power of His government to bear on one individual, He might save that individual; while at the same time, it would so materially derange His government that it would be a vastly greater evil than for that individual to go to hell. In the same way, in the case of a Christian, God has furnished him with all the means of sanctification, and required him to be perfect, and now he turns around and says, "God does not really prefer my being perfect; if He did, He would make me so." This is just the argument of the impenitent sinner—no better in one case than the other. The plain truth is, God does desire, of both, that in the circumstances in which they are placed, they should do just what He commands them to do.

2. The greater part of the church does not really expect to be any more pious than they are.

3. Much of the time the church does not even desire perfect sanctification.

4. Many are satisfied with their hunger and thirst after righteousness and do not expect to be filled.

Here let me say that hunger and thirst after holiness *is not holiness*. The desire of a thing is not the thing desired. If they hunger and thirst after holiness, they ought to give God no rest until He comes up to His promise that they shall be filled with holiness, or made perfectly holy.

5. They overlook the great design of the gospel.

Too long has the church been in the habit of thinking that the great design of the gospel is to save men from the punishment of sin; whereas its real design and object is to deliver men *from sin*. But Christians have taken the other ground and think of nothing but that they are to go on in sin; and all they hope for is to be forgiven, and when they die to be made holy in heaven. Oh, if they only realized that the whole framework of the gospel is designed to break the power of sin and fill men on earth with all the fullness of God, how soon there would be one steady blaze of love in the hearts of God's people all over the world!

6. The promises are not understood and not appropriated by faith.

If the church would read the Bible and lay hold of every promise there, she would find them exceeding great and precious. But now the church loses its inheritance and remains ignorant of the extent of the blessings she may receive. If I had time I could lead you to some promises which, if you would only get hold of and appropriate, you would know what I mean.

7. They seek it by the law, and not by faith.

How many are seeking sanctification by their own resolutions and works, their fastings and prayers, their endeavors and activity, instead of taking hold of Christ, by faith, for sanctification as they do for justification. It is all work, work, work, when it should be by faith in "Christ Jesus, who of God is made unto us wisdom, and righteousness, and *SANCTIFICATION*, and redemption" (1 Cor. 1:30). When they take hold of the strength of God, they will be sanctified. Faith will bring Christ right into the soul, and fill it with the same spirit that breathes through himself. These dead works are nothing. It is faith that must sanctify; it is faith that purifies the heart. That faith, which is the substance of things hoped for, takes hold of Christ and brings Him into the soul to dwell there, the hope of glory, that the life which we live here should be by the faith of the Son of God. It is from ignorance or disregard of this that there is so little holiness in the church.

8. They do not have the right kind of dependence.

Instead of taking scriptural views of their dependence and seeing where their strength is and realizing how willing God is to give His Holy Spirit to them that ask, now and continually, and thus grasping and holding onto the arm of God, they sit down in unbelief and sin to wait God's time and call this depending on God. Alas, how little is felt. After all this talk about dependence on the Holy Spirit, how little of it is really felt; how little there is of the giving up of the whole soul to His control and guidance, with faith in His power to enlighten, to lead, to sanctity, to kindle the affections, and to fill the soul continually with all the fullness of God!

2

CHRISTIAN PERFECTION II*

Matthew 5:48

"Be ye therefore perfect, even as your Father which is in heaven is perfect."

In speaking from these words previously, I pursued the following order: (1) I showed what is implied in being perfect; (2) what Christian perfection is; (3) that it is a duty; (4) that it is attainable in this life; (5) answered some objections, and then gave some reasons why so many persons are not perfect.

My object here is to mention some additional causes which prevent the great body of Christians from attaining perfect sanctification. As a matter of fact, we know that the church is not sanctified, and we ought to know the reasons. If the defect is in God, we ought to know it. If He has not provided a sufficient revelation, or if the power of the Holy Spirit is not adequate to sanctify His people in this world, we ought to understand it so as not to perplex ourselves with idle endeavors. And if the fault is in us, we ought to know it, and the true reasons ought to be understood, lest by any means we should charge God foolishly, even in thought, by imagining that He has required of us that which He has furnished us no adequate means of attaining.

In this lecture, I will discuss:

Ibid., Lecture XX, pp. 230-241.

I. *The first general reason which I shall mention for persons not being sanctified is that they seek sanctification "by works" and not "by faith."*

II. *Another reason so many persons are not sanctified is this: They do not receive Christ in all His relations as He is offered in the gospel.*

I. *The first general reason which I shall mention for persons not being sanctified is that they seek sanctification "by works" and not "by faith."*

The religion of works assumes a great variety of forms, and it is interesting to see the ever-varying shifting forms it takes.

1. One form is where men are aiming to live so as to render their damnation unjust. It matters not, in this case, whether they deem themselves Christians or not, if they are in fact trying to live so as to render it unjust for God to send them to hell. This was the religion of the ancient Pharisees. And there are many in the present day whose religion is purely of this character. You will often find them out of the church and perhaps ready to confess that they have never been born again. Yet they speak of their own works in a way that makes it manifest that they think themselves too good to be damned.

2. Another form of the religion of works is not so much aiming to render it unjust in God to damn, but seeking by works to recommend oneself to the mercy of God. People know they deserve to be damned, and will forever deserve it. But they also know God is merciful. They think that if they live honest lives and do many kind things to the poor, it will so recommend them to the general mercy of God and He will not impute their iniquities to them, but will forgive their sins and save them. This is the religion of most modern moralists. Living under the gospel, they know they cannot be saved by their works, and yet they think that if they go to meetings, help to support the minister, and do this and that and the other kind of good works, it will recommend them to God's mercy sufficiently for salvation. So far as I understand the system of religion held by modern Unitarians, this must be their system, whether or not they understand or admit it to be so. They set aside the atonement of Christ and do not expect to be saved by His righteousness. And I know not on what they do depend but this: They seem to have a kind of sentimental religion, and on this, with their morality and their liberality,

they depend to recommend them to the mercy of God. On this ground they expect to receive the forgiveness of their sins and to be saved.

3. Another form of the religion of works is endeavoring to prepare oneself to accept Christ.

People understand that salvation is only through Jesus Christ. They know that they cannot be saved by works, nor by the general mercy of God, without an atonement, and that the only way to be saved is by faith in Christ. But they have heard of the experience of others who went through a long process of distress before they submitted to Christ and found peace in believing. And they think a certain preparatory process is necessary, that they must make a great many prayers, run here and there to attend meetings, lie awake many nights, suffer so much distress, perhaps fall into despair, and then they shall be in a situation to accept Christ. This is the situation of many convicted sinners. When they are awakened, and get so far as to find that they cannot be saved by their own works, then they set themselves to prepare to receive Christ.

Perhaps some of you are in just this case. You dare not come to Christ just as you are, when you have made so few prayers, attended so few meetings, felt so little distress, and done so little and been so little engaged in God's work. And so, instead of going right to Christ for all you need, as a poor lost sinner, throwing yourself unreservedly into His hands, you set yourself to lash your mind into more conviction and distress in order to prepare yourself to accept Christ. Such cases are just about as common as convicted sinners are. How many there are who abound in such works and seem determined they will not fall down at once at the feet of Christ! It is not necessary to go into an argument here to show that they are growing no better by all this process. There is no love to God in it, no faith, and no religion. It is all mere mockery of God and hypocrisy and sin. There may be much feeling, but it is of no use. It brings them in fact no nearer to Christ; and after all, they have to do the very thing at last which they might have done just as well at first.

Now suppose an individual should take it into his head that this is the way to become holy. Every Christian can see that it is absurd, and that however he may multiply such works, he is not beginning to approach holiness. The first act of holiness is to believe, to take hold of Christ by faith. And if a Christian, who is awakened to feel the need of sanctification, undertakes to go through a preparatory process of self-created distress before he applies to Christ, it is just as absurd as for an awakened sinner to do it.

4. Another form of the religion of works is performing works to beget faith and love.

The last mentioned class includes individuals preparing to come to Christ. Here we suppose them to have come to Christ, that they have accepted Him, and are real Christians; but having backslidden they set themselves to perform many works to beget faith and love, or to beget and perfect a right state of feeling. This is one of the most common and most subtle forms in which the religion of works shows itself today.

Now, this is absurd. It is an attempt to produce holiness by sin. For if the feelings are not right, the act is sin. If the act does not proceed from faith and love, whatever they may do is sin. How idle to think that a person by multiplying sins can beget holiness! And yet it is perfectly common for persons to think they can beget holiness by a course of conduct that is purely sinful. For certainly, any act that does not spring from love already existing is sinful. The individual acts not from the impulse of faith that works by love and purifies the heart, but he acts without faith and love with a design to beget those affections by such acts as these.

It is true, when faith and love exist and are the motive to action, practicing them through action has a tendency to increase them. This arises from the known laws of mind by which every power and every faculty gains strength by exercise. But the case supposed is where individuals have left their first love, if ever they had any, and then set themselves, without faith or love, to bustle about and warn sinners, or the like, under the idea that this is the way to wake up, or to become holy, or to get into the state of feeling God requires. It is really most unphilosophical, absurd and ruinous to think of waking up faith in the soul, where it does not exist, by performing outward acts from some other motive. It is mocking God to pretend that by doing things from wrong motives, one can produce a holy frame of mind. By and by,

I shall show where the deception lies, and how it comes to pass that any persons should ever dream of such a way of becoming sanctified. The fact is too plain to be proved that pretending to serve God in such a way, so far from having any tendency to produce a right spirit, is in fact grieving the Holy Ghost and insulting God.

So far as the philosophy of the thing is concerned, it is just like the conduct of convicted sinners, except for one difference. The sinner, in spite of all his wickedness, may by and by learn his own helplessness, and actually renounce all his own works, and feel that his continued refusal to come to Christ, so far from being a preparation for coming, is only heaping up so many sins against God. But it is otherwise with those who think themselves to be already Christians, as I will explain later.

It is often remarked by careful observers in religion that many persons who abound in religious acts are often the most hardened and the furthest removed from spiritual feeling. If performing religious duties was the way to produce religious feelings, we should expect that ministers and leaders in the church would always be the most spiritual. But the fact is, that where faith and love are not in exercise, in proportion as persons abound in outward acts without the inward life, they become hardened, cold, and full of iniquity. They may have been converted, but have backslidden; and so long as they are seeking sanctification in this way—by multiplying their religious duties, running around to protracted meetings, or warning sinners, without any spiritual life—they will never find it, but will in fact become more hardened and stupid. Or if they get into an excitement in this way, it is a spurious superficial state of mind that has nothing holy in it.

II. *Another reason so many persons are not sanctified is this: They do not receive Christ in all His relations as He is offered in the gospel.*

1. Most people are entirely mistaken here, and they will never go ahead in sanctification until they learn that there is a radical error in the manner in which they attempt to attain it. Suppose an individual is convinced of sin. He sees that God might in justice send him to hell, and that he has no way in which he can make satisfaction. Now tell him of Christ's atonement; show him

how Christ died to make satisfaction so that God can be just and yet the justifier of them that believe in Jesus. He sees it to be right and sufficient, exactly what he needs, and he throws himself upon Christ, in faith, for justification. He accepts Him as his justification, and that is as far as he understands the gospel. He believes, and is justified, and feels the pardon of his sins.

Now, here is the very attitude in which most convicted sinners stop. They take up with Christ in the character in which, as sinners, they most feel the need of a Savior—as the propitiation of their sins, to make atonement and procure forgiveness—and there they stop. After that it is often exceedingly difficult to get their attention to what Christ offers beyond. Say what you will in regard to Christ as the believer's wisdom, righteousness, sanctification, and all his relations as a Savior from sin—they do not feel their need of Him sufficiently to make them really throw themselves upon Him in these relations. The converted person feels at peace with God; joy and gratitude fill his heart; he rejoices in having found a Savior that can stand between him and his Judge. He may have really submitted, and for a time he follows on in the way of obedience to God's commandments. But, by and by, he finds the workings of sin in his members—unsubdued pride, his old temper breaking forth, and a multitude of enemies assaulting his soul, from within and without—and he is not prepared to meet them. Thus far he has taken up Christ and regarded Him, mainly in one of His relations, that of a Savior to save Him from hell.

If I am not mistaken, the great mass of professing Christians lose sight, almost altogether, of many of the most interesting relations of which Christ assures believers. When the convert finds himself thus brought under the power of temptation, and drawn into sin, he needs to receive Christ in a new relation, to know more of the extent of His provision, to make a fresh application to Him, and give a new impulse to His mind to resist temptation. This is not fully apprehended by many Christians. They never really view Christ under His name Jesus, because He saves His people from their sins. They need to receive Him *as a king*, to take the throne in their hearts, and rule over them with absolute and perfect control, bringing every faculty and every thought into subjection. The convert thus falls under the power of temptation because he has not submitted his own will to Christ, as a king, in everything, as perfectly as he ought, but is, after all, exercising his own self-will in some particulars.*

2. There is a multitude of what are called sins of ignorance, which need not be. Christians complain that they cannot understand the Bible, and there are many things concerning which they are always in doubt. They need to receive Christ as wisdom, to accept Him in His relation as the source of light and knowledge. Who of you now attach a full and definite idea to 1 Cor. 1:30, which says we are "in Christ Jesus, who of God is made unto us wisdom, and righteousness, and sanctification, and redemption"? What do you understand by it? It does not say He is a justifier, a teacher, a sanctifier, and a redeemer. It says, He is wisdom, righteousness, sanctification, and redemption.

What does that mean? Until Christians find out *by experience*, how can the church be sanctified? The church is just like a branch plucked off a vine. Jesus said, "Except ye abide in me," you cannot bear fruit. Suppose a branch had power voluntarily to separate itself from the vine, and then should undertake to bring forth fruit—what would you think? So it is with the church; until Christians will go to the Eternal Source of sanctification, wisdom, and redemption, it will never become holy. If they would become, by faith, absolutely united with Him, in all those offices and relations in which He is offered, they would know what sanctification is.

When the church shall once take hold of Christ in *all* His relations, as here described, she will know what it is, and will see that He is the light and the life of the world. To be sanctified by Him, she must so embrace Him as to receive from Him those supplies of grace and knowledge which alone can purify the soul and give the complete victory over sin and Satan.

3. I will mention some reasons why Christians do not receive Christ in all His relations.

(1) They may not have those particular convictions that are calculated to make them deeply feel the necessity of a Savior in those relations.

---

*See a forthcoming book by Charles G. Finney, presently untitled (Minneapolis: Bethany House Publishers, 1984), for a devotional study of the Christian's various relations to Christ.

If an individual is not deeply convicted of his own depravity, and has not learned intimately his own sinfulness, and if he does not know experientially, as a fact, that he needs help to overcome the power of sin, he will never receive Jesus Christ into his soul *as a king*. When men attempt to help themselves out of sin, and feel strong in their own strength to cope with their spiritual enemies, they never receive Christ fully nor rely on Him solely to save them from sin. But when they have tried to keep themselves by resolutions and oaths to obey God, and find that, after all, if left to themselves, there is nothing in them but depravity, then they feel their own helplessness, and begin to inquire what they shall do. The Bible teaches all this plainly enough, and if people would believe the Bible, converts would know their own helplessness and their need of a Savior to save from sin at the outset. But, as a matter of fact, they neither receive nor believe the Bible on this subject until they have set themselves to work out a righteousness of their own, and thus have found out by experiment that they are nothing without Christ. Therefore they do not receive Him in this relation until after they have perhaps spent years in these vain and self-righteous endeavors to do the work of sanctification themselves. Having begun in the Spirit, they are trying to be made perfect by the flesh.

(2) Others, when they see their own condition, do not receive Christ as a Savior from sin, because they are, after all, unwilling to abandon all sin.

They know that if they give themselves up entirely to Christ, all sin must be abandoned, and they have some idol which they are unwilling to give up.

(3) Sometimes, when persons are deeply convinced, and anxious to know what they shall do to get rid of sin, they do not apply to Christ in faith, because they do not know what they have a right to expect from Him.

There are many who seem to suppose they are under a fatal necessity to sin and there is no help for it; they think they must drag along this load of sin until their death. They do not absolutely charge God foolishly, and say in words that He has made no provision for such a case as this. But they seem to suppose that Christ's atonement being so great as to cover all sins, and God's mercy being so great, if they do go on in sin all their days, as they expect they will, He will forgive all at last, and it will be just about as well in the end as if they had been really sanctified. They do not see that the gospel has made provision sufficient to rid us forever of the commission of all sin. They look at it as merely a system of pardon, leaving the sinner to drag along his load of sin to the very gate of heaven, instead of a system to break up the very power of sin in the mind. Consequently they make very little account of the promises.

Oh, how little use do Christians make of those exceeding great and precious promises in the Bible, which were given expressly for this purpose, that we might become partakers of the divine nature! Here God has suited His promises to our predicaments and we have only to draw upon Him for all we want, and we shall have whatever we need for our sanctification. Hear the Savior say, "What things soever ye desire, when ye pray, *believe* that ye receive them, and ye shall have them" (Mark 11:24).

The fact is, Christians do not really believe much that is in the Bible. Now, suppose you were to meet God, and you knew it was God himself speaking to you, and He should hold out a book in His hand and tell you to take that book, and that the book contains exceeding great and precious promises of all that you need, or ever can need, to resist temptation, to overcome sin, and to make you perfectly holy, and fit you for heaven. And then He tells you that whenever you are in want of anything for this end, you need only take the appropriate promise and present it to Him at any time, and He will do it. Now, if you were to receive such a book directly from the hand of God, and knew that God had written it for you with His own hand, would you not believe it? And would you not read it a great deal more than you now read the Bible? How eager you would be to know all that was in it. And how ready to apply the promises in time of need! You would want to learn it all by heart, and often repeat it all, that you might keep your mind familiar with its contents, and always be ready to apply the promises you read! Now, the truth is, the Bible is that book. It is written just so, filled with just such promises, so that the Christian, by laying hold of the right promise, and pleading it, can always find all he needs for his spiritual benefit.

Christ is a complete Savior. All the promises of God are in Him Yea, and in Him Amen, to the glory of God the Father. That is, God has made promises in the second person of the Trinity, in the person of Jesus Christ, and made them all certain through Him. Now, Christians should understand these promises, believe them, and in every circumstance of need apply them for sanctification. Suppose they lack wisdom. Let them go to God and plead the promise. Suppose they cannot understand the Scriptures, or the path of duty is not plain. The promise is plain enough; they may take that. Whatever they lack of wisdom, righteousness, sanctification, and redemption, only let them go to God in faith and take hold of the promise, and if He does not prove false, they will assuredly receive all they need.

(4) Another reason why many do not receive Christ in all His relations is that they are too proud to relinquish all self-dependence or reliance on their own wisdom and their own will.

How great a thing it is for the proud heart of man to give up its own wisdom, knowledge, will, and everything to God. I have found this the greatest of all difficulties. Doubtless all find it so. The common plea is, "Our reason was given us to be exercised in religion, but what is the use if we may not rely on it or follow it?" But there is one important discrimination to be made, which many overlook. *Our reason was given us to use in religion; it is not in the proper province of reason to ask whether what God says is reasonable, but to show us the infinite reasonableness of believing that ALL which God says must be true, whether or not we in our ignorance and blindness can see the reasonableness of it.* And if we go beyond this, we go beyond the proper province of reason. But how unwilling the proud heart of man is to lay aside all its own vain wisdom, and become like a little child, under the teaching of God! The Apostle says, "If any man think that he knoweth any thing, he knoweth nothing yet as he ought to know" (1 Cor. 8:2). There is a vast meaning in this. He that does not receive Christ alone as his wisdom, knows nothing in religion to any purpose. If he is not taught by Jesus Christ, he has not learned the first lesson of Christianity. So again, "Neither knoweth any man the Father, save the Son, and he to whomsoever the Son will reveal him" (Matt. 11:27). The individual who has learned this lesson, feels he has not one iota of knowledge in religion that is of any value unless he is taught by Jesus Christ. For it is written, "And they shall be all taught of God" (John 6:45).

REMARKS

1. You see what kind of preaching the church now needs.

The church needs to be searched thoroughly, shown their great defects, and brought under conviction, and then pointed to where their great strength lies. With their everlasting parade of dead works, they need to be shown how poor they are. "Thou sayest, I am rich, and increased with goods, and have need of nothing; and knowest not that thou art wretched, and miserable, and poor, and blind, and naked" (Rev. 3:17). Until Christians are shown their poverty, and the infinite emptiness and abominable wickedness of their dead works, and then shown just where their help is, and that it is by *faith alone*, they can never be sanctified; the church will go further and further from God until it will have only the form of godliness, denying the power thereof.

2. When you see the Christian character defective in any particular, you may always know that the individual needs to receive Christ more fully in the very relation calculated to supply this defect.

The defect, whatever it be, in the character of any believer, will never be remedied until he sees the relation of Christ to that part of his character and by faith takes hold of Christ and brings Him in to remedy that defect. Suppose a person is naturally penurious and selfish, reluctant to act in a disinterested manner; he will never remedy that defect until he receives Christ as his pattern and the selfishness is driven out of his heart by saturating his very soul with the infinite benevolence of the Savior. So it is with regard to any other defect; he will never conquer it until he sees that the infinite fullness of Christ is answerable to that very want.

3. You see the necessity of ministers being persons of deep experience in religion.

It is easy for even a carnal mind to preach so as to bring sinners under conviction. But until the tone of sanctification is greatly raised among ministers, it is not to be expected that the piety of the church will be greatly elevated. Those Christians who have experienced these things should therefore be much in prayer for ministers that the sons of Levi may be purified, that the leaders of Israel may take hold of Christ for the sanctification of their own hearts, and then they will know what to say to the church on the subject of holiness.

4. Many seek sanctification by works, but they do not know they are seeking in this way.

They profess they are seeking sanctification only by faith. They tell you they know very well it is in vain to seek it in their own strength. Yet the results show they are seeking by works, not by faith. It is of importance that you know whether you are seeking sanctification by works or by faith. All seeking of it by works is absurd and never will lead to any good results. How will you know if you are seeking sanctification by works or by faith?

Consider again the case of a convicted sinner. "Sinner, how are you seeking salvation?" The sinner replies, "By faith, of course; everybody knows that no sinner can be saved by works." "No, you are seeking salvation by works." How shall I show it to him? "Sinner, do you believe in Christ?" "I do." "But does He give you peace with God?" "Oh, no, not yet; but I am trying to get more conviction, and to pray more, and be more in earnest in seeking, and I hope He will give me peace if I persevere." Every Christian sees at a glance that with all his pretensions to the contrary, this man is seeking salvation by works. And the way to prove it to him is exceedingly simple. It is evident he is seeking by works, because he is relying on the accomplishment of certain preparatory steps and processes before he exercises saving faith. He is not ready now to accept Christ; he is conscious he is not, but thinks he must bring himself into a different state of mind as a preparation, and it is at this that he is aiming. That is works. No matter what state of mind he aims at as preparatory to his coming to Christ, if it is anything that must precede faith, or any preparatory process for faith, and he is trying without faith to get into a proper state of mind to have faith, it is all the religion of works.

How common is just such a state of mind among Christians who profess to be seeking sanctification. You say you must mortify sin, but the way you go about it is by a self-righteous preparation, seeking to recommend yourself to Christ as worthy to receive the blessing, instead of coming right to Christ, as an unworthy and ruined beggar, to receive at once, by faith, the very blessing you need. No efforts of your own will make you any better. Like a person in a horrible pit of miry clay, every struggle of your own sinks you deeper into the clay. You have no need of any such thing, and all your endeavors, instead of bringing you any nearer to Christ, are only pulling you down into the filth, further and further from God. It is not even the beginning of help.

The sinner, by his preparatory seeking, gains no advantage. There he lies, dead in trespasses and sins, as far removed from spiritual life, or holiness, as ever a dead corpse was from natural life, until at length, ceasing from his own works, he comes to the conviction that there is nothing he can do for himself but go *now*, just as he is, and submit to Christ. As long as he thinks there is something he must do first he never feels that now is God's time of salvation. And as long as the Christian is seeking sanctification in the way of works, he never feels that now is God's time to give him the victory over sin.

5. Multitudes deceive themselves in this matter, having seen the manner in which certain old-fashioned antinomian churches were roused up, who were dragging along in death.

Where a church has been found that has been fed on dry doctrine until the members are about as stupid as the seats they sit on, the first thing necessary is to rouse them up to do something, and that very fact perhaps would bring such a church under conviction and lead them to repentance. It is not because there is any religion in these doings of those who profess religion in such a state; it shows them their deficiencies, their unfitness to be members of the church, and awakens their consciences. So it is, sometimes, when a careless sinner has determined to pray. Everybody knows there is no piety in such prayers, but it calls his attention to the subject of religion and gives the Holy Spirit an opportunity to bring the truth full upon his conscience. But if you take a man who has been in the habit of praying from his childhood, whose formal prayers have made him as cold as a stone, praying will never bring that man under conviction until you show him what is the true character of his prayer and *stop* his ungodly and heaven-daring praying.

In many cases, where a church has sunk down in stupidity, the most effectual way to rouse its members has been to set them to warning sinners of their danger. This would get the attention of the church to the subject of religion and perhaps bring many of its people to repentance. Hence, many have formed a general rule stating that the way for a church to wake up is always to go to work and warn sinners. They do not discriminate here between the habits of different churches and the different treatment they consequently require. Whereas, if you examine a "working church," where they have been in the habit of enjoying revivals and holding protracted meetings, you will find no difficulty rousing up the church to act, bustle about and make a noise. But as a general rule, unless there is great wisdom and faithfulness in dealing with the church, every succeeding revival will make their religion more and more superficial; their minds will be more hardened instead of being convicted by their efforts. Tell such a church they are self-righteous, and that there is no Holy Ghost in their bustling, and they will be affronted and stare at you, "Why, don't you know that the way to wake up is to go to work in religion?" Whereas, the very fact that activity has become a habit with them shows that they require a different course. They need first to be thoroughly probed and searched and made sensible of their deficiencies, and brought humble and believing to the foot of the cross for sanctification.

When I was an evangelist, I labored in a church that had enjoyed many revivals, and it was the easiest thing in the world to get the church to go out and bring in sinners to the meetings; the impenitent would come in and hear, but there was no deep feeling and no faith in the church. The minister saw that this way of proceeding was ruining the church, that each revival brought about in this manner made the converts more and more superficial, and unless we came to a standstill and got more sanctification in the church, we should defeat our object. We began to preach with that view, and the church members writhed under it. The preaching ran so directly across all their former notions about the way to promote religion that some of them were quite angry. They would run about and talk but would do nothing else. After a terrible state of things, many of them broke down and became as humble and as teachable as little children.

Multitudes in the churches insist that the way to sanctification is to go to work, and they think that by the energy of mere friction that they can produce the warm love of God in their hearts. This is all wrong. Mere driving about and bustle and noise will never produce sanctification—and least of all, when persons have been accustomed to this course.

6. You who are in the habit of performing many religious duties, and yet fall short of holiness, can see what is the matter.

The truth is, you have gone to work to wake up instead of at once throwing yourself on the Lord Jesus Christ for sanctification, and then going to work to serve Him. You have gone to work for your life instead of working from a principle of life within, impelling you to the work of the Lord. You have undertaken to get holiness by a lengthened process, like that of the convicted sinner who is preparing to come to Christ. But the misfortune is that you have not half the perseverance of the sinner. The sinner is driven by the fear of going to hell, and he exerts himself in the way of works till his strength is all exhausted, and all his self-righteousness is worked up, and then, feeling that he is helpless and undone, he throws himself into the arms of Christ. But you have not so much perseverance, because you have not so much fear. You think you are a Christian and that however you may come short of sanctification, yet you are safe from hell and can go to heaven without it. And so you will not persevere and put forth your efforts for holiness by works until you have used up all your self-righteousness and are driven to Christ as your only hope for sanctification. This is the reason why convicted Christians so generally fall short of that submission to Christ for holiness, which the convicted sinner exercises for forgiveness.

You say to the sinner who is seeking salvation by works, "Why don't you yield up all your self-righteous efforts, and come right to Christ for salvation? He is ready to receive you *now*!" And why don't you do so too? When will you learn the first lesson in religion—that you have no help in yourself without Christ, and that all your exertions without Christ, for sanctification, are just as fruitless as are those of the wretch in the horrible pit and miry clay, who is struggling to get himself out?

7. The growth of works in the church is not a certain sign of growth in holiness.

If the church grows in holiness, it will grow in works. But it does not follow that growth in works always proves growth in holiness. It may be that works of religion may greatly increase, while the power of religion is actually and rapidly declining. It often happens in a church that when a revival of religion begins to lose its power, the church may be willing to do even more than before—in works—but it will not arrest the decline unless they get broken down before God.

Oh, that I could convince the whole church that they need no other help but Christ and that they should come at once to Christ for all they want and receive Him as their wisdom, righteousness, sanctification, and redemption. How soon would all their wants be supplied from His infinite fullness!

3

PROVE ALL THINGS*

1 Thessalonians 5:21

"Prove all things; hold fast that which is good."

In regard to this text, I remark:

1. It enjoins the duty of fundamental and thorough inquiry on religious subjects. It requires us to know the reason of our faith and practice so that our piety may not be superstition, but the result of intelligent conviction arising from thorough investigation.

2. In order to fulfill this requirement, the mind must be free from prejudices on religious subjects. So long as prejudices exist in any mind, it is impossible to examine religious opinions with a spirit of obedience toward this subject. All its views will be perverted in the proportion it is uncandid and prejudiced.

3. This precept assumes the fact of our ability to "prove all things." The ability to comply with any requirement is always implied in the requirement. Otherwise the command is unjust.

The Oberlin Evangelist: Vol. V, No. 1, January 4, 1843. (All succeeding references to *The Oberlin Evangelist* are from Vol. V; therefore, only the No. and date will be given in the following notes on each sermon. The following series of sermons was titled "Holiness of Christians in the Present Life," and comprised 13 sermons, all of which are included here in chapters 3-15. They are published as a series in book form for the first time in this volume.)

4. This precept implies the necessity of correct information on religious subjects. The sentiment that our opinions are immaterial seems to prevail among men, but it is plainly a mistake. Men can never be expected to remain rooted and grounded in the truth any further than the truth of their opinions will allow. All observation and experience prove this, and so does the Bible.

5. This command is given to all, not merely to ministers, but to lay people. Each is required to examine for himself, and to call no man master, so as to receive his *"ipse dixit"** as authoritative. It requires each one to know for himself the reasons of his faith.

6. The great mass of mankind doesn't love to think closely. They would prefer to do almost anything else. They are like schoolboys who shun the labor of study and go to be taught without having studied their lesson. What they are told they forget before the next recitation.

7. I shall address myself, in this lecture, to those, and only those, who will take the trouble to think. To address others would be a waste of time and strength. Those who will not think cannot be saved.

8. I will neither spend my time nor endanger your souls by random exhortation and appeal, but will strive to follow the spirit of the text.

9. My object is not controversy; I hope wholly to avoid its spirit, and, as far as possible even its form. On the contrary, it will be my object as far as possible to present what I honestly believe to be the truth for the consideration of the honest and truth-loving person.

10. There is but little obedience to the requirement in the text, and as a consequence great ignorance and error prevail on many questions of fundamental importance. There are very few who can give any rational account of what constitutes sin and holiness, moral obligation, or human responsibility.

11. The terms which represent the attributes of Christian character, or what are commonly called the Christian graces, are almost never rightly defined. The definitions scarcely ever represent the right idea of love, faith, repentance, self-denial, and humility. It is manifest that but few know how to define them.

**"ipse dixit"* [Latin, "he himself said it"]: an assertion made but not proved.

Why? Because they have not complied with the requirement of the text. And because these attributes of holiness are not rightly defined, they are misunderstood, and the result is that they are not exhibited in the lives of Christians. We see one picture drawn in the Bible and quite another in real life. The former is beautiful and glorious; the latter—how sadly deformed. Why? Because the mass is mistaken, mistaken as the result of incorrect views respecting the nature of true piety.

12. The distinction between natural and revealed theology should be understood and appreciated. Indeed, it is fundamental to an understanding of the Bible, for the Bible both assumes the truths of natural theology and our understanding of them—truths such as our existence, the existence of God, our moral agency, natural ability, and the distinction between right and wrong. We do not and cannot therefore rightly understand the Bible unless we understand the fundamental truths of natural theology, which are taken for granted in the Bible.

13. Natural theology consists in those truths that we may learn from the book of nature. God has presented us with two books—that of nature and that of revelation, and they are equally authentic, and mutually confirmatory of each other.

14. The Bible not only assumes, and in various ways confirms the truths of natural theology, but adds many truths not discoverable by unaided reason, but which are recognized as truths as soon as suggested.

15. Many err in supposing that because a truth is seen to be true in the light of its own evidence, therefore it might have been discovered without inspiration. There are plainly multitudes of truths revealed in the Bible which men could never otherwise have discovered, but which, now that they are discovered, are seen to be perfectly reasonable. It is one thing to apprehend and recognize truth when made known, but quite another thing to discover it.

I request your prayers and attention while I proceed to show:

    I. *How we know anything.*
    II. *How we know everything we know.*
    III. *Some things we know about ourselves, the truth, and our knowledge, of which are taken for granted by inspiration.*

I. *How we know anything.*

Consciousness is a condition of all knowledge. It is the mind's recognition of its own existence, choice, thoughts, and feelings. It is a knowledge of ourselves in the phenomena of our minds. The mind does not first observe its phenomena, and thence infer its own existence; for to attempt to prove this would be to assume as doubtful that which is absolutely certain and which must be so regarded in order to attempt proof or inferences. The mind absolutely affirms its own existence, and consciousness testifies to this affirmation, saying, "I exist, I think, I feel, I will." Consciousness gives both the *I* and its phenomena; that is, its choices, thoughts, and feelings, together with their freedom or necessity. Without consciousness, knowledge would be impossible, for there is no other way of obtaining knowledge. *How* and *what* could one know without knowing that he knows? What knowledge would that be, of which you have no knowledge?

II. *How we know everything we know.*

1. As our existence and all our mental acts and states are given us by consciousness, it is plain that we know by consciousness everything which we do know. For example, suppose I have a sensation: how do I know that I have it? By consciousness. So it is with all our emotions, desires, choices, judgments, affirmations, denials, hopes, fears, doubts, joys and sorrows. They are all given us by consciousness. I am now speaking what every man knows to be true.

2. Everything outside us is known to us only as it makes an impression upon our minds, which impression is revealed to us by consciousness.

3. What we know by consciousness we know with certainty; that is, we know that our existence, acts, thoughts, and feelings are realities.

4. Consciousness is, therefore, the highest possible evidence. We do, and cannot but, rely upon it as conclusive. If I think, feel, or act, I know that I think, feel, or act, and know it absolutely. It is impossible from our very constitution to doubt its testimony.

5. But we should carefully distinguish between what is revealed to us by our consciousness and inferences drawn from such revelations. We may mistake the *cause* of a sensation but

not the sensation. When God spoke to Christ from heaven, the people who heard were conscious of the sensation upon the auditory nerve. Here was no mistake. But they mistook its *cause*. They said, it thundered. So, in forming our various judgments and opinions, we *may mistake*, but when consciousness testifies that we do judge or form an opinion, in this we cannot be mistaken.

III. *Some things we know about ourselves, the truth, and our knowledge, of which are taken for granted by inspiration.*

1. We know that we exist, and we know it so certainly that to ask for evidence is absurd. It would be to assume as *doubtful* that which must be assumed as *absolutely true* in order to prove anything true.

2. We know that we perform certain mental acts and are the subjects of certain mental states. For example, we know that we originate choices and volitions and are the subjects of thought and feeling.

3. Hence, we know that we possess certain faculties and capacities, that is, we are capable of acts, thoughts, and feelings.

4. We know that these faculties, as also their products, are capable of being classified. All men naturally classify them. They never confuse thinking with feeling, feeling with willing, nor willing with either of them. No child does this. Nor do they confuse the power of thinking, or of feeling with that of willing, or with one another.

5. Hence, all men fully understand the thing intended by these terms, although they may not understand the terms employed by philosophers to represent the natural faculties. They know themselves to possess those faculties which we call intelligence, sensibility, and free will. We *think, feel,* and *will*; and therefore, we know we have the faculties of thinking, feeling, and willing, and mental philosophy is nothing else than an analysis of what all men are conscious of. Under the general term "intelligence" we include consciousness, reason, and understanding. All thoughts, affirmations, intuitions, judgments, and inferences are the product of the intelligence.

6. We are conscious of our own liberty in the sense of having ability to choose in any direction in view of motives—to choose or

refuse any object of choice. We know this with absolute certainty. This is an intuition of reason revealed by consciousness, and however men may deny their own freedom in theory, yet they always act upon the assumption that mankind is free.

7. We are conscious that we can voluntarily control some of our capabilities, and some we cannot. For example, consider the voluntary and involuntary muscles. If I will to move my arm, it moves in obedience to my will, but if I will that my heart shall cease to beat, it still continues to beat wholly regardless of my will. In like manner, we know that some of our capabilities are *directly* under the control of the will, and some *indirectly*.

8. We know by consciousness that voluntary muscular action is directly necessitated by our will—that there is a necessary connection between volitions and outward action. Some have made freedom to consist in doing as we please or as we will, but everyone knows there is no freedom in this, for when I will to move my arm or to perform any other outward action, the action takes place by a natural necessity. While the volition exists, the outward action must be.

9. We also know by consciousness that thought and feeling are only indirectly subject to the will. Suppose, for instance, you wish to transfer your thoughts from one object to another. You cannot do this directly, and yet you are conscious that you can indirectly do so through the attention. Hence, by directing the attention to any given subject upon which you wish to think, thought is the necessary result. So if you abstract the attention from an object upon which you do not wish to think, you thus indirectly detach the thoughts from it. Even children know this with absolute certainty. So with feeling of every kind. We are conscious that we cannot directly feel by willing to feel. Suppose, for example, we wish to call into being the feelings of love, hope, fear, joy, or sorrow. We are conscious that we cannot, by direct willing, create these feelings, or even modify them. But, nevertheless, we are conscious that we can indirectly regulate the feelings to a great degree. For example, if we wish to experience the emotions produced by the beautiful, we turn our attention to a beautiful object, and the emotions arise of course. On the contrary, by turning our attention to an offensive object, we can indirectly produce disagreeable emotions in our own minds. The

same law operates respecting all religious feelings. They can to a very great degree be regulated indirectly by the will through the attention, but never directly.

10. We know by consciousness that whatever we can do at all, we can do by willing, and that whatever act or state is not connected with the action of our will is impossible to us by a natural necessity. Suppose, for example, I will to move, but suddenly the nerves of voluntary motion are paralyzed, so that they will not obey my will. Then to move is impossible for me. The same is true of thoughts and feelings. If I will to expel certain thoughts and feelings from my mind, and to produce others, I separate my attention from those objects on which it rests and direct it to other objects. This course will universally change the existing thoughts and feelings, but if it should not, then to change them is impossible for me. The same is true of everything else. Whatever we cannot accomplish by willing, we cannot accomplish at all. This is universal experience.

11. We are conscious of possessing in our intelligence a faculty called "reason," or the intuitive faculty, by which we perceive and affirm truths which carry with them their own evidence. This faculty gives us, when certain conditions are fulfilled, all necessary, absolute and universal truths. It is so infallible and uniform in its affirmations that whenever the terms of a proposition are understood, every reason in the world will affirm the same things—for example, mathematical truths, as two and two equal four, or things which are equal to the same thing are equal to one another. These affirmations are so absolute that the mind cannot doubt them.

12. Among these self-evident truths are all the first principles of morals such as:

(1) That there is such a thing as right and wrong, and that the difference between them is fundamental.

(2) That the existence of these implies moral law.

(3) That men have moral character.

(4) That moral character implies moral obligations.

(5) That moral character implies moral law and moral agency.

(6) That moral agency implies natural ability.

(7) That natural ability implies the existence of intelligence,

sensibility and free will; that is, that moral agents actually know, feel, and will. The mind does not call for proof of these things, but affirms them as absolute verities, and the Bible therefore assumes them as true. It assumes that moral agents do actually know, feel, and will.

(8) That moral character does not and cannot belong in the constitution of either body or mind, since it is impossible that a moral being should be either praiseworthy or blameworthy for his constitution. But moral character is necessarily either praiseworthy or blameworthy. It cannot thus belong to the constitution.

(9) That the constitutional appetites, desires and passions can have no moral character in themselves since they are in themselves involuntary—for example, consider the appetite for food. Suppose yourself hungry and in the presence of food. The appetite will naturally demand it from the very constitution, and can therefore in itself have no moral character. The same is true of desires and passions whenever you are in the presence of objects adapted to awaken them.

(10) This intuitive faculty affirms that on the will's consenting to gratify any of these appetites, desires, or passions under forbidden circumstances, there is sin. For example, when Eve saw the fruit, her appetite naturally craved it. In this there was nothing wrong, but when she consented to gratify her appetite, even though it was prohibited, this was supreme selfishness. Had it not been prohibited, the gratification would have been proper, but being prohibited, it was sin. It is the same respecting the gratifying of any desire or passion whatever.

(11) This intuitive faculty asserts that moral character cannot belong to any involuntary act or state of mind whatever, nor to any outward actions. If I stab a man, the moral character of the act does not belong to the dagger, nor to the hand which held it, nor to the muscles of the arm, nor to the volition which impelled the arm, but to the intention.

(12) It also asserts that moral character cannot belong to the states of the sensibility—that is, to the various emotions or feelings—for these are necesary, nor to the states of the intelligence. There is no moral excellence in the perception of truth. Devils, wicked men and good men alike perceive truth, and doubtless

think correctly on many subjects, and their reason affirms moral truths, but there is no virtue in this.

(13) It also asserts that moral character cannot belong to volitions as distinguished from choices, for choice or intuition necessitates volition, for the time being.

(14) But it does assert that *moral character belongs to the ultimate intention of the mind.* Intention is the choice of an end. The ultimate intention is the last end chosen—that for which everything else is chosen or done. I will illustrate the difference between ultimate and proximate intention. Suppose a young man is employed, and you inquire what he is working for. He says, to get money. This is one end. But ask again why he wants money. He says, to buy books. This is another end. Ask again why he wants books. He says, to get knowledge. This is another end. But continue the inquiry; why does he want knowledge? He says, to preach the gospel. This is still another end. But you may ask further, why does he want to preach the gospel? He replies, to do good—because the good of the universe is valuable in itself. This is the last end—the *ultimate* intention, and all the previous ends are only *means* to this or what are called proximate ends. But in this case the whole moral character of all the process belongs plainly to the ultimate intention. In this, all ethical philosophers worthy of note at the present day agree. It is plainly the doctrine of the Bible, and thus the Bible and natural theology are precisely at one. The truth is, even children understand that character consists in ultimate intention. "Pa," says the child in self-justification, "I didn't *mean* to do it." And the question between the child and his parent is about the intention. So it is in courts of justice. They always inquire for the intention. In short, all men, whatever may be their theory, understand and act upon the truth of this doctrine. If a physician gives medicine with an intent to cure, he would be universally acquitted of blame, even though instead of curing the disease, it should take the life of a patient. In fact, this doctrine is so certain that the Bible could not be believed if it disagreed with it.

4

NATURE OF TRUE VIRTUE*

Galatians 5:14

"For all the law is fulfilled in one word, even this; Thou shalt love thy neighbour as thyself."

In this lecture I propose to show:

    I. *What is intended by the term love.*
    II. *That the thing intended is the whole of virtue.*

I. *What is intended by the term love.*

It is of the utmost importance to understand the Bible's meaning of the term love. It is represented in the text, and the Bible generally, as the substance of all religion, and the only preparation for heaven. What, then, can be more important?

1. I remark, then, in the first place, that the love required in the text is not what is generally called natural affection or the love of kindred. This is manifest first in the fact that natural affection is involuntary. It is true, the will is employed in acting out this love, but the thing generally intended by natural affection is the strong constitutional impulses experienced by parents toward their offspring, brothers and sisters toward one another, etc. Second, this natural affection is common to both saints and

---

Ibid., No. 2, January 18, 1843. Finney also cites *Romans 13:8-10.*

sinners, and certainly nothing can be religion which is common both to the ungodly and the saints. And third, I may add that it is practiced by brutes.

2. This love is not complacency or esteem. Complacency is that pleasant emotion, or state of the sensibility which is experienced when we see anything which, from the laws of our constitution, is naturally pleasing to us. For example, if you contemplate beautiful natural scenery, you experience a pleasing emotion, or delight, from the very nature of your constitution. It is precisely the same in contemplating moral beauty. Men are so constituted that whenever they contemplate a virtuous character, provided it does not in any way conflict with their selfishness, they delight in it—a pleasurable emotion always springs up of course. Now this complacency, or esteem of virtuous character, is perfectly involuntary, and therefore, can have no virtue in it. This we know by consciousness, which I defined in my last lecture to be the mind's knowledge of its own existence, acts, and states, and of the liberty or necessity of these acts and states. By consciousness, then, we know that this complacency in the character, either in God or any other virtuous being, is involuntary; this complacency is the natural and necessary result of the mental constitution when it is brought into certain relation to such characters. Again, this complacency cannot be true virtue, or the love required in the Bible, because it can be properly exercised only toward the virtuous, whereas the love which the Bible requires is to be exercised toward all. We are not required to exercise complacency toward sinners, and it would plainly be unjust and absurd if we were, since to delight in a sinful character is impossible. But the text requires *universal* love. Therefore the love which it requires and complacency cannot be identical. Again, complacency is common to real saints and to the self-deceived and impenitent. Much evil is done by denying that sinners have this feeling of complacency toward God and His law, when the fact is they know that they have. Whenever they see the character of God aside from His relation to themselves, they cannot avoid it. It arises by a natural necessity from the mental constitution. The wickedest devil in hell would experience it if he could view the character of God aside from its relations to himself. It is absurd to deny that even that mind would feel thus, for if it would not, it must be in-

consistent with itself, which cannot be. Furthermore, complacency in virtuous character is consistent with the highest degree of wickedness. It is related of a certain infidel that he would go into ecstasies in contemplating the character of God. And who has not heard the wicked insist that they do love God and have found it almost impossible to convince them that they did not love Him with any virtuous love? Why? Because they are conscious of these emotions of complacency toward Him and mistake it for real benevolence.

3. The love required in the text is not what is commonly called fondness, for this is a mere emotion and therefore involuntary. I do not know what else to call a certain development of the mind toward God. Persons often exhibit a fondness toward God, the same as toward any other being. They love Him because He loves them, just as sinners peculiarly love those who do them a good turn. And they do not distinguish between this and true religion, but immediately after the strongest exhibition of it, take advantage of a neighbor in trade or exhibit selfishness in some other form.

The truth is, it often consists with the most fiendish wickedness as well as the highest irreverence. Persons in this state of mind often seem, in conversing about God in their prayers to Him, and in every way, to regard and treat Him merely as an equal. I have often thought how infinitely insulting their conduct must be to Him. Again, this fondness is consistent with any degree of self-indulgence. In direct connection with its exercise, persons often show themselves to be the perfect slaves of their appetites and passions. They undoubtedly feel their fondness, but do they love? They say they love, but is their love benevolence? Is it religion? Can that be religion which puts no restraint on the appetites and passions, or only curbs some of them, while it cleaves the more tenaciously to others? Impossible!

4. The love intended in the text is not synonymous with desire. Persons say they desire to love God and to love their neighbor as themselves. No doubt they do, but there is no religion in this since desire is constitutional and has no moral character. Sinners have the desire and remain sinners still, and everyone knows that they are consistent with the highest wickedness. Besides, as it is *mere desire*, it may exist forever and do no good.

Suppose God had from all eternity merely desired to create a universe and make it happy. If He had never gone further than that, what good would it have done? So it will not do for us to say to our neighbors, "Be warmed, and be fed," but not give them those things essential to their well-being. Unless we really will what we desire, it will never effect any good.

5. The love required in the text is not pity or compassion. This is wholly constitutional, and men are strongly exercised with it in spite of themselves. It is related of Whitefield that he often appealed to men with such power in behalf of his orphan house that he induced those to give liberally who had beforehand determined not to give, nor to be influenced by him. The truth is, his mighty appeals aroused the constitutional susceptibility of pity to such a pitch that they had to give out of self-defense. They were brought to such agony that they had to give to relieve it.* But so far was this mere excitement from being virtuous that perhaps those very persons whom it induced to give their money called themselves a thousand fools for having done so after the excitement subsided.

6. Nor is the love required in the text delight in the happiness of mankind. We are so constituted as naturally to delight in the happiness of others whenever no selfish reason prevents it. It is this same constitutional tendency which produces such abhorrence of whatever is unjust and injurious—for example, how men's feelings of indignation swell and boil on witnessing acts of injustice. Suppose, in a court of justice, a judge perverts justice, shamefully wronging the innocent and clearing the guilty. How would the spectators feel?

There was a case some time ago in one of our cities, where a man had been guilty of a flagrant outrage. But when it was brought before the court, the judge insulted and abused the sufferer and showed a disposition to clear the guilty. This so aroused the indignation of the spectators that they could hardly be restrained from seizing and wreaking their vengeance on him. And these were persons who made no pretentions about religion. So men universally, whether virtuous or not, abhor a liar, or the character of the devil.

---

*This was exactly the experience of Benjamin Franklin, *His Autobiography* in *The Harvard Classics* (New York: P.F. Collier & Son, 1909), Vol. 1, pp. 101-104.

Whoever contemplated the character of the devil? On the contrary, men universally, whether virtuous themselves or not, admire and delight in virtuous characters. For example, consider the Jews in Christ's time. How they admired and manifested their delight in the character of the prophets who had formerly perished by the violence of their contemporaries. Now, how was this? Why, they saw the true character of those prophets without allowing such a relation to their selfishness as to annoy them, and their constitutional delight was naturally awakened in this way. But at the same time they were treating Christ in the same manner as their fathers treated those prophets, and for the same reason. So now Whitefield, Wesley, and Edwards are admired and praised by multitudes, who, if they had lived in the days of those men, would have cried as loud as their contemporaries did, "Away with them!" Now, why is this? Because the relations of the characters of these men to the world are now changed and do not directly cross the track of their selfishness as they did while living.

The same principle is manifested in respect to human freedom. For example, some years ago, during the struggle of the Greeks for their freedom, what enthusiasm prevailed—what earnestness to go and help them! The government could scarcely control the waves of excitement in their favor. But those very men, who were so enthusiastic in behalf of the Greeks, would now hiss at any effort to remove slavery from this country! Now, why is this? Because, I say again, men are so constituted that when no selfish reason exists to prevent it, men naturally delight in happiness, and sympathize with the suffering. But there is no virtue in this. It is mere natural emotion which is consistent with the highest wickedness.

7. The love required is not goodwill to any particular individuals. "Do not even sinners love those that love them?" They love their friends and allies, and so do fallen spirits for all I know, but there is no benevolence in this.

8. This love, then, must be benevolence. But what is benevolence? Benevolence is *willing the good of being.* The attributes of benevolence are:

(1) *Voluntariness.* It belongs to the will, and not to the sensibility.

(2) *Disinterestedness.* By this I mean that the good of being is not willed for the sake of its reflex influence upon self, but for its own sake. Benevolence is recognizing the good of being as valuable in itself, and willing it for that reason. The willing *terminates* on the good willed.

(3) *Universality.* Benevolence goes out toward all beings. It admits of no exceptions. Wherever there is a being capable of happiness, benevolence wills its happiness according to its perceived value and for its own sake. Such is God's benevolence. It is universal, embracing in its infinite bosom all beings from the highest archangel to the sparrow which falls to the ground. He views and really wills the happiness of every being as good. Indeed, universality is essential to the very nature of benevolence, for if good is willed on its own account, benevolence will of course cover all good known.

(4) *Unity.* Benevolence is a simple principle. It is the whole heart—an unmixed general choice, as the good of being is a unity—it is a single end, and benevolence is the choice of this one end.

(5) *Choice.* Benevolence is a choice as distinguished from *volition.* This choice of an end always of course necessitates volitions to accomplish the end, but these executive volitions have no character in themselves, and all virtue or vice belongs to the choice or intention which they are designed to execute. We know this by consciousness.

It is a choice also as distinguished from desire, emotion, or feeling. As I said in the former lecture, we are conscious that all the states of the sensibility—all desires, emotions, and passions —are involuntary, and therefore without moral character. Benevolence, then, cannot either wholly or partly consist in these.

(6) *Activity and efficiency.* Benevolence being *choice*, must be efficient. Choice necessitates volition. For example, suppose I intend to go to the post office as soon as possible. While this choice remains, it of course necessitates all the volitions necessary to its execution. Its very nature is activity.

(7) *Aggressiveness.* Of course if benevolence is willing the good of being, it wills the destruction of whatever prevents that good, and continually makes encroachments in every direction upon every form of wickedness however fortified. It will not only

sally out against such sins as licentiousness, intemperance, and profanity, but also every form of selfishness, however popular it may be.

(8) *A disposition, or ultimate intention. Intention* is the choice of an end. Benevolence is the choice of the highest good of being, and being the ultimate choice, as was illustrated in the last lecture, it is of course a disposition to promote good to the utmost.

(9) *Directed supremely to God, of course.* Benevolence, as we have already said, is willing the good of being for its own sake. Of course, then, it is willing the good of every being according to its perceived value. It is agreed that the correct definition of virtue *is a disposition to regard things according to their perceived relative value.* Now everyone must perceive that the happiness of God is the greatest good in the universe, and therefore benevolence must, as a matter of course, will it supremely.

(10) *Directed equally to men.* I do not mean to say that the happiness of every man is equal to the happiness of every other man or that they are equally valuable. The happiness of a man is of more value than the happiness of a beast. It would therefore be unjust to regard them as equal. So some men are of more value than others. For example, the life of Washington was of more value than that of any private soldier; therefore, if either of them must be sacrificed, it should be the less valuable. But what I mean to say is that the good of every being is to be regarded according to its relative value as you understand it.

(11) *Impartiality.* Benevolence also regards the good of enemies as well as of friends. The Savior insists on this as essential to virtue.

9. That this love is benevolence is generally agreed, and it is also agreed that this is the only form of love which is voluntary or can reasonably be commanded. This, and no other kind of love, is voluntary, as everyone knows by his own consciousness. We are conscious that our emotions are all produced indirectly, not directly. If a parent, for example, wishes to *feel* about his family, he must direct his attention to them. The result will be that he will *feel* about them by a natural necessity, and his feelings will take the form of whatever attitude he views them in. And while his attention is fixed upon them, he cannot but feel. So it is with every

form of love except benevolence. Hatred is produced and perpetuated in the same way. An individual conceives himself injured by another and keeps his attention upon it; the more he views it, the more emotions of hatred or indignation are felt, so that when urged to give it up, he says he cannot. And it is true that while he keeps his eye upon that particular thing—while his mind broods over it—he cannot. He can however, turn his attention elsewhere and thus indirectly remove his feelings of hatred or indignation.

10. The love required in the text must be benevolence as it is required toward all beings. This is clear from what we have already said.

11. God's love to us must be benevolence. It could not be complacency, for instead of feeling complacent toward sinners, He must abhor their character. It was benevolence, then, which made the Atonement, and all the provisions of salvation.

12. No other kind of love would do any real good. Without it God would never have made the Atonement, nor have done anything else to secure the salvation of sinners, nor would any other moral being. No other love than benevolence can, in the nature of things, be universal which consists in willing universal good for its own sake.

13. Benevolence is naturally and universally obligatory, and therefore must be virtue. The good of being is valuable; therefore to will, it must be virtue. To deny this is to talk stark nonsense. It is to deny that we are to treat things as they are, or according to their nature.

14. Therefore the law of God must require it, and would be unjust if it did not. It cannot be otherwise than unjust not to require all moral beings to act according to the nature and relations of things.

15. Nothing else need be required of moral beings, as everything else possible to us necessarily follows its exercise. This follows from the fact that it consists in choice. If I will right, this will secures corresponding volitions, muscular movements, desires, and feelings as a matter of course; and whatever willing will not secure is impossible to me. To produce the right emotions, I have only to fix my attention on the right objects. If, therefore, I will rightly, then the whole man will be right of course. That such

is the influence of the will we know by consciousness.

16. In short, nothing more nor less *can be justly required.* That nothing less can be required is a certain intuition of every moral being in the universe. Ask whomever you will if everyone ought to be required to will the universal good of being, and if he understands the terms of your proposition, he will immediately cry out, "Yes, yes," from the deepest recesses of his soul. That nothing more can be required is equally intuitive. Whenever it is asserted that men can be required to do anything beyond the power of their will, the nature of every moral being cries out against it as false. This is right, and nothing else is right.

II. *Benevolence is the whole of virtue.*

1. We have seen that this love is disposition or intention.

2. We know that intention necessitates corresponding states and acts.

3. Virtue cannot consist in the outward act, nor in necessitated mental acts. It must, therefore, consist in benevolence, and this the Bible teaches in many ways.

(1) In the text, it is asserted that love is the fulfilling of the law, and that law is fulfilled in one word, even this, *"Thou shalt love thy neighbour as thyself."*

(2) Love is the spirit of the whole law as epitomized by Christ. *"Thou shalt love the Lord thy God with all thy heart, and with all thy soul, and with all thy strength, and with all thy mind, and thy neighbour as thyself"* (Luke 10:27).

(3) Love is the spirit of every precept of the Bible. It asserts, "For if there be first a willing mind, it is accepted according to that a man hath, and not according to that he hath not" (1 Cor. 8:12). It says a right intention obeys the very spirit of the Bible. If we intend right, the will is taken for the deed. Suppose my intention is to do all the good I possibly can, but I am confined to a sickbed so that I can accomplish but little; nevertheless, I am virtuous. On the other hand, the Bible teaches that if people intend wrong, their moral character is as their intention, whatever they may do. Even if good should result from their actions, there is no thanks to them, because they did not intend it.

4. All the attributes of Christian character are only modifications of benevolence, but this will appear more fully later.

REMARKS

1. It may be said that the Bible represents our words, thoughts, and outward actions as virtuous. Answer:

(1) The Bible makes all virtue, strictly speaking, to consist in love, and it cannot be inconsistent with itself.

(2) Words, thoughts, and outward actions are and can be virtuous only in the sense of their being manifestations of benevolence.

(3) The same may be said in regard to words, thoughts, and actions that are called wicked. The Bible says that "the plowing of the wicked is sin" (Prov. 21:4). Words, thoughts, and actions are holy or sinful in no other sense than that they indicate the state of the will. A word! What is a word? A breath—a motion of the atmosphere on the drum of the ear. Can this have moral character in itself? No, but it may be an index of the state of him who utters it.

2. It is infinitely important to understand that *benevolence always and necessarily manifests itself*; consisting in choice, it is naturally impossible that it should not.

3. See the spurious nature of any religion which does not manifest itself in efforts to do good. Such religion is mere antinomianism. It may be some kind of happiness, but religion it is not.

4. All the attributes of Christian character must belong to the will, just as all God's moral attributes are only modifications of benevolence. They are not modifications of emotion but of will. His justice in sending the wicked to hell is as much a modification of benevolence as is His mercy in taking the virtuous to heaven. He does both for the same reason: because the general good equally demands both. So with all that the true Christian does.

5. How false and dangerous are the usual definitions of these attributes? For example, love is spoken of as a mere feeling. Hence, religion is represented as, at one time, smothered embers, scarcely in existence, at another, in a slight glow, which may be fanned until it breaks out into flame. Now this is not the love which the Bible requires, since it is nothing but mere feeling; and even if legitimately produced, it is only the natural and constitutional *result* of religion and not religion itself.

Repentance is also spoken of as mere *sorrow for sin*, but instead of this, it does not consist in feeling at all. It is *a change of mind*. As we say, when we have made up our mind to do one thing, and then change it and do the opposite, we say in popular language, "I changed my mind." This is the simple idea of repentance. It is an act of the will, and sorrow follows it as a result.

Faith is often represented as the conviction of the intellect. But this cannot be faith, for the Bible everywhere represents faith as a virtue, and it must, therefore, be an act of the will, and no mere belief whatever. It is a *committing* of the soul to God. The Bible says Christ did not commit himself to certain persons, for He knew what was in them; that is, He did not trust or exercise faith in them. The word rendered "commit" here is the same as that rendered "faith." Peter refers to committing the keeping of one's soul to Him in well doing, as unto a faithful Creator (1 Pet. 4:19). When the mind apprehends the true meaning of the characteristics and relations of Christ to the world, this is often mistaken for faith. But the devil may have as good a faith as that. This is a mere perception of truth by the intellect, and is, as a condition, indispensable to faith, but it is no more faith itself than an act of the intellect is an act of the will.

Humility is often understood as a sense of guilt and unworthiness. Now, Satan is doubtless humble if this is humility, and so is every convicted sinner, by a natural necessity. But *humility is a willingness to be known and esteemed according to your true character*. These illustrations show how dangerous are the prevalent mistakes respecting the attributes of Christian character.

6. There is no such thing as religion, *not in exercise*. Persons often talk as though they had some true religion about them, although they are conscious of exercising none. They have a good enough religion to be sure, but it is not in operation just now. Now this is a radical mistake.

7. How many persons are living on frames and feelings, and yet remain perfectly selfish.

8. Many are satisfied with no preaching but such as fans into existence certain happy emotions. These are a kind of religious gourmets. Whenever we preach so as to lay bare the roots of selfishness and detect its secret workings, they are not fed. They say, "This is not the gospel; let us have the gospel." But what do they mean by the gospel? Why simply that class of truths that create

and fan into a flame their emotions. And those who most need to be searched are often most unwilling to endure the probe. They make their religion to consist in emotions, and if these are taken away, what have they left? Hence, they cling to them with a death grasp. Now let me say that these emotions have not one particle of religion in them, and those who want simply that class of truths which fan them into existence are mere religious gourmets and their view of the gospel is sheer antinomianism. If the world were full of such religion, it would be none the better for it.

9. Religion is the cause of happiness, but is not identical with it. Happiness is a state of the sensibility and of course involuntary, while religion is benevolence and therefore powerful action.

10. Men may work without benevolence, but they cannot be benevolent without works. Many persons wake up occasionally, bluster about, get up protracted meetings, and make mighty efforts to work themselves into a right state of feeling by dint of mere friction. But they never get a right spirit that way and their working is mere legality. I do not mean to condemn protracted meetings nor special efforts to promote religion, but I do condemn a legal engaging in these things. But while persons may work without benevolence, it is also certain that if they are benevolent they will work. It is impossible that benevolence should be inactive.

11. *If all virtue consists in the ultimate intention, then it must be that we can be conscious of our spiritual state.* We certainly can tell what we are aiming at. If consciousness does not reveal this, it cannot reveal anything about our character. If character consists in ultimate intention, and if we cannot be conscious what this intention is, it follows necessarily that we can know nothing whatever about our own character.

12. We can see what we are to pursue in our hours of self-examination. Our inquiry should not be how we *feel*, but for what end we live—what is the aim of our life.

13. How vain is religion without love. Those who have such a religion are continually lashed by conscience to the performance of duty. Conscience stands like a taskmaster who, scourge in hand, points to the duty and says it must not be omitted. The heart shrinks back from its performance, but still it must be done or worse evil endured. The hesitating soul drags itself up by reso-

lution to fulfill the letter of the requirement, while there is no acquiescence in his spirit. Thus a miserable slavery is substituted for the cheerful obedience of the heart.

14. Finally, benevolence naturally fills the mind with peace and joy. The mind was made to be benevolent, and whenever it is so, it is in harmony with itself, with God and the universe. It wills just as God wills, and therefore it naturally and cheerfully acts out His will. This is its choice. It is like some heavenly instrument whose chords are touched by some angelic hand which makes music for the ear of God. But on the other hand, a selfish man is necessarily, from the very nature of mind, a wretched man. His reason and conscience continually affirm his obligations to God and His universe, to the world and the church. But he never wills in accordance with it, and thus a continual warfare is kept up within. His mind is like an instrument untuned and harsh. Instead of harmony, it renders only discord, and makes music only fit to mingle with the wailings of the damned.

5

SELFISHNESS*

Hosea 10:1

"Israel is an empty vine, he bringeth forth fruit unto himself."

In this passage, the Lord complains of the selfishness of Israel, and it is my purpose to show:

I. *What selfishness is not.*
II. *What selfishness is.*
III. *That selfishness and holiness cannot coexist in the same mind.*
IV. *Several evidences of selfishness.*
V. *That one form of selfishness is as inconsistent with salvation as another.*

I. *What selfishness is not.*

1. It is not a desire for happiness or dread of misery. This is perfectly constitutional in all moral beings. It is involuntary as we know by consciousness, and is, therefore, destitute of all moral character.

2. Selfishness is not the desire for esteem. This desire, to whatever degree it may exist as mere desire, is constitutional, in-

---

Ibid., No. 3, February 1, 1843.

voluntary, and without moral character.

3. It does not consist in the desire of any personal good, nor in the dread of any personal evil. These are perfectly natural, and have no character.

4. Neither does selfishness consist in any constitutional appetite, passion, impulse, or in what are generally called propensities. Some persons speak of selfish propensities, as though our propensities had moral character, and we were blamable for them. But this is absurd. There is no such thing as a *selfish* propensity. All the appetites, passions, and impulses are natural and are naturally excited whenever we come into contact with the objects adapted to excite them. Propensities are wholly the products of the sensibility, and have neither voluntariness nor moral character about them so far as they themselves are concerned.

5. Nor does selfishness consist of any kind or degree of mere desire as distinguished from choice or willing. As I have often said, everyone knows the difference between desire and willing, by his own consciousness. For example, I may desire to go to Europe, and strongly desire it, and yet never will to go. For desire does not *govern the conduct; will does.*

II. *What selfishness is.*

1. Man, as I have before said, possesses three cardinal faculties: intelligence, sensibility and will. This we know by consciousness.

2. The will is *influenced* by motives addressed to it, either through the sensibility—that is, by constitutional desires and impulses; or through the intelligence—that is, by truth and obligation to comply with it, as perceived by the intellect. There is no other way but by motives in which will can be influenced, and it must of necessity choose between the gratification of the impulses of the sensibility and the dictates of the intelligence.

3. The law of God is revealed and imposed by the reason. Man is, in a certain sense, his own lawgiver; as Paul expressed it, he "is a law to himself." If the grand principle of the law of God did not lie revealed in our reason, we could never be influenced by any outward precepts and could never perceive obligation, simply because we should have no standard of either truth or

morality. We could not know whether the Bible is the Word of God or a lying fable, because we should have no possible way of testing it. In short, if our reason did not reveal and impose the great principle of the law of God, all religion and morality would be to us naturally impossible. All precept and instruction, therefore, are valid to moral beings only because when addressed to them, reason recognizes their truth and imposes obligation to conform to them. Whatever the reason does not thus recognize as true cannot be obligatory. *All the commands and truth of God are addressed to moral beings through their reason.* I should perhaps say here, that by " reason" I mean that power of the mind which affirms all necessary and absolute truth—in other words, the intuitive faculty. *All moral influences, then, come to the will through the reason, and all virtue consists in the conformity of the will to its requirements.*

4. The sensibility always invites the will to seek gratification from the objects which awaken its susceptibilities. For example, the appetite for food is awakened by the perception of its appropriate object. And whenever the appetite is awakened, and to whatever degree, it is impulsive to the will. The impulse will be strong or weak in proportion to the degree in which the susceptibility is excited, and in proportion to its strength will impel the will to consent to the gratification. So it is with all the appetites, desires, and passions. We know that this is true by our own consciousness.

5. There are then two, and only two, directions and occasions of human action between which the will must make its election.

(1) The law of the reason requires the exercise of benevolence—that is, of supreme love to God and equal love to our neighbor. The law requires that benevolence should be the ultimate intention, or supreme choice of the will.

(2) The sensibility invites to gratification irrespective of the law of the reason. The sensibility is naturally blind. It impels towards every object which awakens its susceptibilities, for its own sake—because it will afford gratification, and for no other reason. Now every man knows by his own consciousness that such are the relations of his reason and his sensibility to his will, and that he is under the necessity of choosing between them.

The way is now prepared to state directly what selfishness is.

6. Selfishness consists in willing the gratification of the sensibility—in the mind's consecrating itself to demands of the sensibility in opposition to the law of the reason. It is a disposition to gratify self instead of seeking a higher and holier end. It is a state of the *will*, as distinguished from the sensibility.

7. Selfishness must then always consist in what I called in the last lecture, an ultimate intention. The ultimate end chosen by the mind is self-gratification. This, in some form or other, is preferred to everything else. It is not selfishness to have a capacity for gratification, nor is the gratification itself selfishness. Beasts have a sensibility like men, and when the demands of their awakened susceptibilities are met they are gratified, but there is no selfishness in them, nor are they capable of selfishness, because they have no reason to impose on them a higher law than the mere impulses of their sensibility. These impulses are, however, regulated in them by instinct. But moral beings have a higher faculty which reveals to them a higher end of life, and imposes on them obligation to choose it. It requires them to regard all personal gratification as a *means*, and not an end, and therefore to be held in perfect subordination to the law imposed by the reason. The Bible only repeats the demands of every man's own reason, when it says, "Whether therefore ye eat, or drink, or whatsoever ye do, do all to the glory of God" (1 Cor. 10:31). That is, hold all your appetites, desires, and passions with a steady rein and under perfect control. Now, selfishness consists in preferring self-gratification to the demands of this higher faculty— making personal gratification an *end, the ultimate end of life.*

8. This is just what the Bible calls the *"carnal mind,"* "walking after the flesh." That is, *the carnal mind consists in the mind's choosing the gratification of the sensibility as the end of pursuit.* I have said already that every object of desire is desired for its own sake, because it is capable of affording gratification. Selfishness therefore consists in *choosing* desired objects because they *are desired, or to gratify self*—not as a *means* to the glory of God.

III. *Selfishness and holiness cannot coexist in the same mind.*

1. In the preceding lecture, I showed that holiness, or true

virtue, consists wholly in disinterested benevolence; in willing every interest according to its perceived relative value. Benevolence must be a supreme choice, or ultimate intention; for if it wills every interest according to its perceived value, there is nothing else in the universe which it can will. If *every good is willed for its own sake according to its perceived value*, it is naturally impossible to will anything beyond that, or aside from it. To say that you can is a contradiction. It is the same as to say that you can will every interest according to its perceived value and not will it at the same time.

2. Now what is selfishness? As we have already seen, under the previous head, it is also an ultimate intention. In other words, it is the preference of self-gratification over the law of the reason, that is, to benevolence. Instead of willing every good according to its perceived value, it is willing one good more than all other goods. Whenever an individual prefers his own gratification to the demands of his own reason, he does it in the face of the law of God and in defiance of His authority.

3. But these are, self-evidently, opposite choices and therefore cannot coexist in the same mind. Is it possible that there can be two supreme, ultimate conflicting choices in exercise by the same mind at the same time? This cannot be.

I may add that benevolence and selfishness regard and treat every perceived interest in the universe in an order exactly the opposite of each other. *Benevolence regards God's interests first, and aims at His glory as the supreme good; next, the well-being of the universe; then of this world; afterwards of its own nation; then of its own community; next of its own family; and lastly of itself.* Now selfishness exactly reverses all this. The selfish man places self first, and regards his own interest as supreme; then he regards the interest of his family and special friends, but only so far as supreme devotion to himself on the whole prompts; next, he regards his own community or city in opposition to all other communities and cities, whenever their interests clash; then he regards his own nation, and is what men call very patriotic, and would sacrifice the interests of all other nations, just as far as they interfere with his own; and so he progresses until finally God and His interests find the last place in his regards. That this is so is a simple matter of fact, as everybody knows. How, then, is it possible that these two *opposite* choices should coexist in the same mind? Who can believe it?

IV. *Several evidences of selfishness.*

1. A lack of zeal for God's interests. Men are always zealous for that which they supremely choose, and if they are not zealous for God's honor, it proves that it is not the object of their supreme regard. To deny this is absurd.

2. The absence of pain and indignation when His interests are disregarded. If they willed the supreme good, it would be impossible to witness His commands and authority set at nought without the keenest sense of pain and indignation.

3. More zeal and labor in promoting self-interest than the interest of God is an evidence of selfishness. It proves by demonstration that your own interests are preferred to His. Men universally manifest the most zeal in behalf of that in which they are most interested.

4. If, therefore, persons think they have piety, while they are more zealous in promoting self-interest than the interest of God, they are deceived, and are probably mistaking mere desire for religion. Let me here remind you that the will necessarily governs the conduct, while desire does not. I may strongly desire to go to Ohio and never go; but if I really will to go there I go of necessity, unless my volition is overcome by superior force. So if a man is really benevolent, he prefers the interest of God and His universe to his own, and manifests a zeal accordingly.

5. Where persons pay more attention to their own personal interests than to the eternal interests of others, it is evidence that they are selfish. They certainly are not regarding things according to their relative value.

6. The absence of the spirit of prayer is an evidence of selfishness. In a world like this, prayer is the very breath of benevolence. How can a benevolent man walk through the streets and mingle in society without his spirit being stirred within him, vesting itself in earnest prayer? It cannot be! What! Thousands around us, jostling us at every step, in all their sins, already suffering many evils, the consequences of transgression, exposed to eternal death! Who that believes there is any help in God for them can avoid prayer? Certainly none but those who are su-

premely selfish.

7. Another evidence of selfishness is *spiritual epicureanism*. There is a certain class of persons who are always wanting something to make them happy, and whatever measures or preaching will not secure this result, they of course reject. Now what state of will does this indicate? Why, a selfish state to be sure. They do not want to have their minds enlightened and their duty pointed out, because this renders them unhappy; they delight to sit and have their emotions fanned until their sensibility is all in a glow, and the preaching which does that is to them the only gospel. Now this is nothing but a refined selfishness.

8. When persons are more zealous to defend their own reputation and character than the cause and honor of God, they evidence selfishness. There are multitudes even of those who profess religion, who, if men should say anything against their character, or if in any way their reputation was about to suffer, would be thrown into agony, lie awake all night, and wet their pillow with tears. But if they should hear a ribald infidel rail against God and cover His character all over with foul reproaches, it would scarcely catch a passing notice. Now why is this? Plainly because they prize their own character more than the honor of God and are supremely selfish.

9. Unwillingness to make personal sacrifices to promote a higher good is another evidence of selfishness. This needs no illustration.

10. Another evidence of selfishness is the dominion of any appetite or passion over the will. There are some who pretend to be religious who habitually gratify certain appetites and passions which they admit to be wrong. Ask them if they do not believe it to be wrong; they say, "Yes, but I cannot overcome it." And believe me, that is a selfish man; that is the very definition of selfishness. It is preferring self-gratification to the known will of God. It is what the Apostle means by "minding the flesh."

11. A lack of interest in the prosperity of others is another evidence. Selfish men do not know what they lose by neglecting to interest themselves in the good of others. The benevolent man enjoys the happiness of others; thus all the well-being of the universe, of which he is the spectator, contributes to his own enjoyment. Myriads of streams of happiness pour into his own bosom.

Why? Because the prosperity of others is the very thing on which his heart is set, and it is a contradiction to say that he will not be gratified in witnessing the realization of that which he supremely chooses. Whenever, therefore, an individual manifests a lack of interest in the happiness of others, it proves that he does not really will it, and is therefore supremely selfish.

12. Another evidence of selfishness is a disposition to envy and murmur if others possess what you do not. What state of mind is that? It cannot bear to see anybody live in a better house, have better accommodations, superior endowments, or richer vehicles. Instead of rejoicing in their good, their mind laments that they are not on the same level. Selfishness says, "Let no one have more than I." Now this must be supreme selfishness. How would benevolence feel and talk? Plainly, it would rejoice in their good, and its language would be, "I thank God that others possess these good things if I do not."

13. A spirit of speculation is another evidence of selfishness. By this I mean a disposition to seek bargains at the expense of others. Now, would benevolence represent the article above its real value—would it attempt to get rich by taking advantage of others? I have been amazed whenever I have thought of the mania which swept like an epidemic over all the length and breadth of the land some years ago. It was the great object to make money by speculation. Christians, and even ministers, rushed headlong into the general scramble after money. When asked why they did so, they replied that they wished to make money for God; in plain English, they wished to promote the glory of God by trampling upon His law. Why, the principle is as absurd as to become a pirate to get money to give to a Bible society. Suppose a man should turn pirate, and go out upon the high seas to run down and destroy every vessel that came in his way under pretense of getting money to give to a Bible society! And when remonstrated, suppose he should urge the importance of sending abroad the Bible, and that he could make more money by piracy in order to accomplish this object than in any other way! Who would give him credit for any benevolence in this? To attempt to justify speculation on the ground of acquiring means to spread the gospel is to put on an impudent face and baptize rebellion against God with the name of holiness. *Rob your neighbor to give to God!*

14. Squandering time and money to gratify artificial appetites is another evidence of selfishness. There are certain appetites which must be gratified—things desired which are necessary to our existence and usefulness and the gratification of which is proper under appropriate circumstances. To expend money for the gratification of these is to make a proper use of it, so long as it is done in accordance with the dictates of reason. Such are all the constitutional appetites which are really such. But when they are not natural, but artificial, their gratification can be nothing else but selfishness. To illustrate, take the appetite for fiery spirits, tobacco, or any other unnatural stimulant.

15. An unwillingness to bear your part in making public improvements is another evidence of selfishness. Suppose roads are to be made or churches to be built or anything else to be done which is essential to the public good, what else can it be but selfishness to stand back from bearing your part in the labor and expense necessary to accomplish it? I have sometimes seen cases of this kind; a church has become deeply involved in debt, and certain individuals seem to want to leave it. They show peculiar anxiety to change their associations when it is obvious that they only wish to avoid doing their part toward paying the debt.

16. When self-interest must be appealed to in order to excite to action, it is evidence of selfishness. When a man is benevolent, all that is necessary to move the deep foundations of his moral being is to lay before him some real good to be achieved. It is enough for him to have his intelligence enlightened. But in vain do you attempt to move the selfish man by appeals to his benevolence. If you wish to move him, you must exhibit an entirely different class of motives, such as take deep hold on his sensibility. If he is one who professes religion, perhaps it will be impossible to move him until you can shake his hope. With such persons duty must be brought into such relation as to appear the lesser of two evils, they must endure; and then their very selfishness leads them to perform it. Or it must be so placed before them so that its performance will advance their own special interests. For example, suppose a church is to be built. If you are obliged to go to a man for assistance and tell him how it will increase the value of his own property or in some other way promote his own peculiar interests, you may be sure that man is supremely selfish. It is the

same with this class of persons as it respects their eternal interests. Nothing will move them so effectually to any kind of religious effort as a representation of the personal good which will accrue to them in the future world. In short, the only way in which you can influence such men is by appealing either to their hopes or their fears.

17. Increasing expenditures as your income increases instead of doing more good demonstrates selfishness. During the great speculation, it was my lot to talk with men very frequently upon the principles by which they were actuated in driving after wealth. They all said they were seeking to do good with it. But I observed that with hardly an exception, they increased their expenditures, number of vehicles, buying coaches, fine horses, and rich furniture in proportion to their increased wealth, so that they were no more able to do good than before. It would be the same if their wealth were increased by thousands, and this uniform result proves that the principle which they adopted was radically wrong. The truth is, you may as well talk of stealing for God as of speculating for Him. The one is just as consistent as the other.

18. A disposition to suspect others of selfishness is characteristic of selfishness. This is an almost universal characteristic of selfish minds, never of a benevolent one. It is for this reason that selfish men so generally deny that there is any such thing as disinterested benevolence. Mankind is disposed to regard others in the light of their own character. This might be illustrated by the case of Satan and Job. Job was an upright man and served God disinterestedly. But Satan, being supremely selfish, did not believe it. He said, "Doth Job serve God for nought?" (Job 1:9), intimating that the only reason for Job's apparent obedience was the personal advantage which would accrue to him for it. And even when he had stripped him, by the permission of God, of almost all he held dear, and Job remained unmoved, he still intimates that his only reason for doing so was a selfish one. "Skin for skin, yea, all that a man hath will he give for his life. But put forth thine hand now, and touch his bone and his flesh, and he will curse thee to thy face" (2:45). The truth is, a benevolent man is naturally unsuspicious—"thinketh no evil." But show me a suspicious man, one who is always attributing the worst motives

to others, and I will show you a man who is himself supremely selfish.

19. An unwillingness to do as you would be done unto is another evidence of selfishness. I gave very high offense to certain persons in one of our cities not long ago by pressing this thought. Suppose yourself and family to be enjoying all the blessings of liberty. Suppose you have a wife whom you dearly love, and children upon whom you have centered the affections of your heart, but in a woeful day, they are pulled away from your embrace and plunged into slavery. How would you feel? How would you talk? Would you say that you have nothing to do with slavery? Nothing to do with it! Would you say it is nothing to you? Nothing to you! You may be sure that in that case you would bring up no plea of the delicacy of the subject as an excuse for refusing to interest yourself in their behalf and to condemn the outrageous system by which they were oppressed. In this way everyone may learn his duty toward those who are enslaved in this nation. Put yourself and your family in their place and inquire how you would wish others to regard your condition and to act in reference to it. Now notice, their duty in the circumstances supposed is your own in your present circumstances. Suppose it were now, as it was some years ago, that the Algerines were enslaving our fellow citizens—how would it be regarded by this nation? It would be the signal for instant war. Thousands would press forward to enlist in the work of vengeance upon the oppressors, and if they could not otherwise accomplish the rescue of those in bondage, they would wade through an ocean of blood and desolate with fire and slaughter their whole territory. But alas! The winds of heaven may come over from the south, laden with the groans of thousands of our fellowmen, daily suffering the wrongs of slavery in its worst forms, and with thousands scarcely a feeling is enlisted in their favor. Is that loving their neighbor as they love themselves? Is this the religion of Jesus Christ? My soul, come not into the secret of such religion as that! And stranger still, multitudes even attempt to make the Bible sanction and authorize this accursed system. They say the Bible has really authorized it as an institution. But who can believe it? What! The same God who uttered the fiery law, requiring man to love his neighbor as himself and pronouncing death on all who will

not comply with the requisition, authorize and sanction a system which tramples on this law at every step by which one man seizes his brother,

"Chains him and tasks him,
And exacts his sweat with stripes, that mercy,
With a bleeding heart, weeps when she sees inflicted
On a beast."

Who does not regard such a supposition, when fairly stated, as downright blasphemy? And who would not reject the Bible as a gross deception if it really did thus contradict itself and falsify its author?

20. Another proof of selfishness is covetousness. Some cannot bear to see others have what they have not without coveting it and often to such a degree that they can scarcely keep their hands from it. Wherever this spirit exists, it demonstrates supreme selfishness.

21. Selfishness is displayed by a disposition to get the best seat in church or the prominent place in assemblies. For example, in churches where they sell their seats, you will see them striving to get the best seat, the best cushion and the most convenient location, and if they fail they are more distressed than if a soul were lost. Often when churches are formed, instead of trying to secure a house best adapted to the service of God and instead of trying to promote the conversion of sinners, they put themselves out to get the best house and the best organ and the best choir and the best minister, and then sit down to be preached to heaven. But how shall a minister preach to them? He will utterly fail to do them any good and to save them from death if he does not put his finger into their very eyes and rebuke their horrible selfishness.

V. *One form of selfishness is as inconsistent with salvation as another.*

Remember that selfishness consists in obeying the propensities, appetites, passions and desires. This devotion to self-gratification develops itself in a great variety of ways without changing its character. With one, this propensity predominates; with another, that one. One, for example, is a gourmet. His desire for pleasant dishes predominates over everything else, and he values money only as it contributes to his gratification. Another is a miser and is entirely too devoted to the desire of wealth to be a gourmet. Indeed, he thinks his ruling passion contemptible. One is fond of dress and values money only as it contributes to the gratification of this desire. This is his form of selfishness. He thinks of it all year and labors with his eye on self-gratification in this form. Another is fond of power or influence to such an extent as to wonder that any can be fond of such a trifling gratification as dress affords. But he is as much enslaved by his desire of power as the other by his devotion to dress and is equally selfish. Again, some are so fond of reputation as to do anything public sentiment requires rather than to lose popularity. This is their form of selfishness. Their reputation is preferred to the well-being of the universe. But others have such a large development of some appetite or passion as to sacrifice reputation for it. For example, the drunkard regards his appetite for intoxicating drinks above everything else, and his character weighs not a straw when brought into competition with this. Now each of these different forms of selfishness is a violation of the law of God—one just as much so as the other. They all lord it over the will. And yet, those devoted to one form take great credit to themselves because they are not devoted to all others. The truth is, in all cases the sin lies in the indulgence of any appetite, desire or propensity, in opposition to the law of love.

REMARKS

1. It does not matter which of the propensities prevail over the will in order to constitute selfishness. None of them has moral character in itself. To prefer the indulgence of any one of them to higher interests is what constitutes sin. It is minding the flesh. It is enmity with God.

2. If we are asked why we have these propensities if they are not to be gratified, I answer:

(1) Those which are natural are given to serve and not to rule us. For example, without an appetite for food we would never take it, but it is essential to our existence, and therefore the appetite serves to secure life. So the desire for knowledge. Were

there not a constitutional desire for knowledge, who would ever seek it? But knowledge is essential to our highest good. The desire for it, therefore, serves to secure this essential to our well-being.

(2) Further, these propensities are given not only to serve us but to afford us gratification. The benevolence of God gave us these constitutional propensities so that we might find pleasure in that which is for our well-being. Were we destitute of appetites, desires, passions, and susceptibilities, we should be as incapable of pleasure or pain, gratification or happiness as a marble statue. Had the human race remained innocent, the gratification of these susceptibilities would doubtless have afforded them exquisite pleasure. That we possess them, therefore, must be regarded as a proof of the divine benevolence toward us, notwithstanding the fact that they render us liable to various and strong temptations.

(3) Many of the propensities that are most despotic, God never gave. They are wholly artificial, produced by a voluntary perversion of those which are natural. Such perversions include the use of intoxicating drinks or tobacco, and various narcotics.

3. Indulgence in any form of selfishness is utterly inconsistent with salvation. It is sin, and the Bible declares that without holiness no man will see the Lord.

4. A man who is selfish in his business can no more go to heaven than a pirate can. How should he? They are both living for the same end, self-gratification, in different forms, and are both therefore directly opposed to the will of God.

5. A vain man or a vain woman can no more be saved than a licentious man or a licentious woman. The former prefers the gratification of his vanity to the end of life which the law of God requires, while the latter prefers the self-gratification afforded him in this grosser form.

6. There is so little discrimination regarding the nature of sin that endless delusions prevail. For example, while it is known that drunkenness, licentiousness, theft, robbery, murder, and the like, are utterly inconsistent with salvation, various other forms of sin are regarded as consistent with a profession of religion. But the truth is, as I have said before, a man who is selfish in his business or who practices selfishness in any other form, however

slight it may seem, can no more be saved than a drunkard can. Why cannot a drunkard be saved? Or the licentious man, or the thief? Because he is selfish. So, it must be with any other man who is selfish, whatever may be the cloak his selfishness has put on. If a man were drunk but once a week, he would be excommunicated as hopelessly lost; but, he may be habitually greedy, vain, or gourmet, and yet be regarded as a good Christian in the estimation of the church. If any church should continue the drunkard in its communion, it would bring upon itself the frown of Christians universally, and yet persons indulging in various forms of selfishness are to be found in almost every church and regarded as true Christians. Scarcely anyone suspects he will not be saved. Now this must be delusion. But why does this error persist? It is because there is so little discrimination respecting the nature of sin. The truth is, if any appetite, desire, or propensity whatever rules the will, the man is on the way to death.

7. To suppose religion to consist in obeying any feeling whatever, merely as feeling, is a most ruinous error. And yet multitudes know no other religion than this. They suppose happy feelings to be religion and generally do just as they *feel*, irrespective of the demands of their reason. These persons have never yet apprehended the true idea of religion—namely, that it consists in the entire consecration of the will to the law of God, as it is regarded and imposed by their reason. Feeling is not that to which the will should bow, for it is blind; but reason, as it perceives the law of God with its intuitive eye, should be heeded in its faintest whisper respecting the application of that law.

8. Selfishness was the first sin of man—that is, his first sin consisted in preferring his own gratification to the will of God. Now, see whether I have given the right definition of sin. The first pair were placed in the garden in which were many trees bearing an abundance to supply their wants, but in the midst was one upon which God laid a prohibition. It is an important question why God laid this restraint. It is a question which is often asked, and it is important that it should receive a right answer.

The design undoubtedly was to teach them that they must control their sensibility—that they must keep their appetites, desires, and passions in subjection to the law of reason. Learning this lesson was of vast importance, one they should learn as soon as possible before their sensibility had such a development—that is, before their appetites, desires, and passions should acquire such strength, during their ignorance of the tendency to gratify them—as to render it certain they never would deny themselves of their gratification when they came to see its tendency. For this reason God prohibited their eating the fruit of one particular tree. Here Satan stepped in, and being well aware of the relation of the sensibility to the will, and of both to reason, he suggested to Eve that God was selfish in laying restraint upon the constitutional propensities, and then presented such considerations before her mind as awakened two of the strongest of them, the appetite for food and the desire for knowledge. This placed the demands of her reason, which echoed the prohibition of God, and the demands of her constitutional desires in opposition. Between these her will was compelled to choose. And in that evil hour she preferred the gratification of these appetites to the will of God, and thus, as one writer stated, "Brought death into the world, and all our woe."

This was the first sin. Observe now, these constitutional appetites were perfectly innocent in themselves, but the sin consisted in her consenting to their gratification in opposition to the requirement of God.

9. Selfishness is the first sin of every human being. Children come into the world in perfect ignorance both of the law of God and of the tendency of their sensibility. Now, what is the process by which they sin. See the little child. At first he can scarcely turn his head or open his eyes. He is hardly conscious of anything. Soon his sensibility begins to develop, and foremost his appetite for food. As soon as you give him anything, no matter what, he puts it right into the mouth. Gradually other appetites are awakened, equally constitutional, and therefore without moral character. At what age his reason begins to develop, we cannot know. But it is doubtless very early. But as soon as it is developed and affirms obligation, its very next is a moral act. Hence the appetites, desires, and propensities of sensibility which have previously been developed, and his perception of obligation are both placed before his will, and he prefers the former to the latter. This is his first sin, and this is the first sin of every human being. But why does the child always choose wrong? Because

previous to the development of his reason, his will has constantly been under the control of his appetites and he has acquired a habit of consenting to them. On the other hand, the first affirmations of reason are necessarily feeble. He therefore chooses self-gratification in opposition to it.

10. Selfishness constitutes sin in every instance. It is easy to show that this must be so.

11. We can see what regeneration is: it is turning from selfishness to benevolence. It is the act of the will preferring the well-being of the universe to self-gratification to which it has always previously consented.

12. It is easy to see the necessity of regeneration. Who does not know that unregenerate men are universally selfish? And who does not know that selfish men thrown together could never be happy? I have often wondered what those persons mean who deny the necessity of regeneration. The truth is, it is self-evident.

13. We can see why men are commanded to regenerate themselves. If regeneration is an act of the will, nothing can be more rational than this requirement. It is of necessity their own act.

14. Notice why the Spirit of God is needed in regeneration: Men have been so habituated to gratify themselves, and their attention is so absorbed with this, that the Spirit of God is needed to develop their reason and to throw the light of heaven upon its eye that it may see at once the nature and beauty of religion in contrast with the nature and deformity of sin. This is conviction. Then the sinner needs to be charmed away from his selfishness by correct understanding of the character of God and the love of Christ. This is the Spirit's office to effect.

15. Finally, we can see what is meant by the Apostle when he speaks so often of being led by the flesh or by the Spirit. An individual is led by the flesh when his will is in subjection to the sensibility. This is the carnal mind. On the other hand, an individual is led by the Spirit when his will is in subjection to the law of his reason, which is developed and applied by the Spirit of God.

And now, beloved, where are you? Are you led by the flesh or by the Spirit? Are you selfish or are you benevolent? What would you say if you were called to appear before God tonight? Could you say, I know I am led by the Spirit of God and therefore am a child of God? Oh, beloved, search yourselves lest you be deceived!

6

HABITUAL HOLINESS, THE TEST OF CHRISTIAN CHARACTER*

1 John 3:9

"Whosoever is born of God doth not commit sin; for his seed remaineth in him: and he cannot sin, because he is born of God."

In this discourse I shall inquire:

    I. *What sin is not.*
   II. *What sin is.*
  III. *What to be born of God is not.*
  IV. *What it is.*
   V. *What the seed which remains in Christians is not.*
  VI. *What this seed is.*
 VII. *What is not intended by the assertion that whoever is born of God does not and cannot commit sin.*
VIII. *What is intended by this assertion.*
  IX. *How a Christian may be distinguished from a sinner.*

I. *What sin is not.*
1. Sin is not a part of the soul or body.
2. It is nothing infused into either soul or body. Some talk as

Ibid., No. 4, February 15, 1843.

if the whole being—soul and body—were saturated with sin, but this is absurd.

3. Sin is neither a taint of corruption in, nor a lapsed state of, the constitution. The Bible does not make it so, and reason certainly affirms it to be something entirely different from this.

4. It is nothing which is or can be transmitted from parents to children by natural generation. This would contradict the Bible definition of sin, and the supposition is in itself a ridiculous absurdity.

5. Nor does sin consist in any weakness, debility, or inability, either natural or moral, to obey God. The Bible nowhere makes it consist in this, and certainly common sense does not.

6. Nor does it consist in any appetite, passion, or mere feeling. These we have already seen, in a former lecture, are constitutional, involuntary, and in themselves wholly destitute of all moral character.

7. Nor does sin consist in any degree of excitement of these propensities in appropriate circumstances; for in the appropriate circumstances, they are inevitably excited.

8. Nor does sin consist in any state or act of the intelligence; for it also is obliged to act, and we can only be responsible for its operations just as far as we can regulate it by willing.

9. Nor does sin consist in any outward actions; for these are necessitated by the supreme end chosen, and in themselves are wholly destitute of all moral character.

II. *What sin is.*

1. As I said in a former lecture, the primary faculties of the mind are intelligence, sensibility, and free will. This we know from consciousness. The intelligence is that power which thinks, affirms, reasons, and reflects. The sensibility is the power of feeling which includes all appetites, desires, passions, or emotions whatever. The free will is the power which wills.

2. The will is always *influenced* by motives originating either in the intelligence or the sensibility. The will always chooses some object or acts in reference to some motive; we know by consciousness that these motives are either duties perceived by the intelligence or the awakened susceptibilities of the sensibility, which always invites the mind to seek the gratification of its

appetites and passions for their own sake. I do not mean that the action of the intelligence and the sensibility are so isolated from each other that either of them acts in perfect independence of the other; for we know that every thought and affirmation of the intelligence is accompanied by some feeling of the sensibility, and on the other hand, that every feeling awakens in the intelligence, affirmations, thoughts, and reasonings to a greater or lesser extent. But what I mean is that some motives originate in and are addressed to the will by the intelligence, and some on the other hand originate in the sensibility, and as such, influence the will.

The distinction of which I am speaking is just what everyone means, when speaking of the difference between being led by propensity or passion, and reason. The intelligence and sensibility mutually influence each other, but one or the other takes the lead. In other words, the mind, which is a unity, in thinking *feels,* and in feeling, *thinks.* When the intelligence reveals and imposes obligation, it is always echoed by the sensibility; and on the contrary, when some appetite or desire is excited in the sensibility, the intelligence is awakened into thought respecting it. In the one case, the sensibility follows in the wake of the intelligence, and in the other, the intelligence in the wake of the sensibility; but in all cases the action both of the sense and intelligence is indirectly under the control of the will, which by its sovereign power always determines which shall be dominant.

3. The mind affirms itself to be under obligation to obey the law of the reason just as I suppose the mind of God imposes obligation on Him. The holiness of God consists in His obeying the law revealed and imposed on Him by His own infinite and eternal reason, and so the holiness of all moral beings must consist in their voluntary conformity to whatever their own reason affirms to be obligatory. *Holiness, then, is that state of the will or heart which consists in the voluntary consecration of the whole being to God.*

4. Sin is the exact opposite of this and consists in the consecration, by the will or heart, of the whole being to the gratification of self. This is selfishness, which we have already endeavored to show is the substance of all the sin in the universe. Whatever, in the action of the will or heart, is not conformed to the law of love, as perceived by the reason, is sin—whether it be omission

of duty or the commission of that which is positively prohibited. *Entire conformity of heart and life, therefore, to all known truth is holiness, and nothing short of this is or can be.* If people deny this, it is because they do not know what they say and have not the idea of holiness before their mind at all. The law of God is one—a unity, and to talk of being partly conformed to it and partly not is to overlook the very nature both of the law and of conformity to it. The law of God requires perfect conformity of life and heart to all the truth perceived, and *this is moral perfection in any being*—the only sense in which any being can be morally perfect in any world. Suppose there is a moral pigmy whose standard of truth is No. 1. Now if he fully conforms to that, he does his whole duty. So you may increase the scale to 2, 5, 10, 20, and moral perfection will still consist in conformity to the light possessed. Suppose you ascend the scale to ten thousand or a million, it is still the same until you arrive at God himself, and this is just what constitutes the moral perfection of God. All the truths in the universe are known to Him with absolute certainty, and He conforms to all He knows. Since His knowledge cannot increase, His holiness cannot either, while that of all finite beings does and will to all eternity. Angels encounter moral situations of which they are totally ignorant, and to which they are not morally conformed, but their state of will is such that as fast as they learn them they conform to them. Hence, their holiness is constantly increasing; and so it must be from the lowest to the highest degree of moral capacity. Everything, then, short of living up to the light we have, is sin, and every moral act is either right or wrong.

III. *What to be born of God is not.*

1. Regeneration does not consist in the creation of any new faculties. We have faculties enough, more than we use well, and we need no more.

2. Nor does it consist in a constitutional change. A constitutional change would be far enough from a moral change, and it would be hard to tell what good it would do.

3. Nor does regeneration consist in implanting, or infusing any piece, parcel, or physical principle of holiness into the soul. What can be meant by a principle of holiness when such lan-

guage is used to designate something aside from holiness itself?

4. Nor does it consist in a change of the constitutional appetites and propensities. These have no moral character in themselves and need no change. They only need to be rightly regulated.

5. Nor does regeneration consist in the introduction or implantation of a new taste. There could be no virtue in regeneration if it consisted in any of these things, and they all are mistakes overlooking the nature of virtue.

IV. *What to be born of God is.*

1. To be born of God is to have a new heart.

2. We have seen that the old or wicked heart is the same as the carnal mind, and that the carnal mind or wicked heart consists in the devotion of the will to self-gratification. Self-gratification is the ultimate end chosen. One chooses self above God.

3. To be born again, or born of God, is to make a radical change in the ultimate intention or choice of an end. It is called being born again because it is a change of the whole moral character and course of life. Christ says, "Except ye be converted and become as little children, ye shall not enter into the kingdom of heaven" (Matt. 18:3). The phraseology is figurative and emphatic, because when a moral being has changed his ultimate intention, he must of necessity live an entirely new life, the reverse of what it was before.

4. It is called being born of God, or from above, because sinners are influenced to make this voluntary change by the Word and Spirit of God. I say *voluntary* change, because everyone is perfectly conscious that he was voluntary in it, and because it must of necessity be voluntary if it has any moral character in it. I might add, that unless regeneration is voluntary, backsliding from it would be naturally impossible, and obedience a necessary outcome, which are as false in fact as they are absurd in theory.

V. *What the seed which remains in Christians is not.*

1. It is not a physical germ, root, sprout or taste inserted into the soul. If so, then falling from grace is naturally impossible, and perseverance naturally the necessary outcome. This theory

robs religion of all virtue whatever.

2. The seed is neither love nor any other holy exercise. In other words, it is not religion at all. Religion is voluntary conformity to the law of God, and to say that this remains in the Christian could have no meaning. The truth is, the Apostle, in the text, is asserting why this voluntary conformity is continued. It then cannot be the seed.

3. It does not consist in any new principle implanted in the soul.

VI. *What this seed is.*

1. It is the Word of Truth which regenerated him—that is, in view of which he changed his ultimate intention or heart. Truth is frequently called seed in the Bible: "Being born again, not of corruptible seed, but of incorruptible, by the word of God, which liveth and abideth for ever" (1 Pet. 1:23). "Of his own will begat he us with the word of truth, that we should be a kind of first-fruits of his creatures" (James 1:18).

2. The Word of Truth is called the seed of God, because it is introduced and made known to the mind by the Holy Ghost. Hence, we are said to be "begotten of God." It is His truth that quickens the mind into right voluntary action. Now everyone knows, by his own consciousness, that this is the way in which he was born again. Listen to a young convert tell his experience. He begins to tell of some truth which arrested his attention and convicted him—how he thought of one thing after another, that he perceived this and that and the other thing to be true as he never did before, and that finally he made up his mind, in view of what he thus saw was true, to repent. Now, what is he doing? Why, he is giving the history of his regeneration, and giving it in detail. But does he know the history of his regeneration? As well as he knows anything else under heaven. To be sure he did not see the Spirit, nor did he perceive that it was the Spirit, because the Spirit directs to Christ, but he is conscious that he did see the truth as he never saw it before. And he is conscious that he was perfectly voluntary under its influence.

3. This seed, which has once broken the power of selfishness, remains in him, that is, in his memory, so that he can sin only by letting it slip. "Let that therefore abide in you, which ye have

heard from the beginning. If that which ye have heard from the beginning shall remain in you, ye also shall continue in the Son and in the Father" (1 John 2:24). Also, "If ye abide in me, and my words abide in you, ye shall ask what ye will, and it shall be done unto you" (John 15:7). This truth, as I said before, is not a piece of something which God puts into you, nor is it religion nor love, but it is that which once subdued your will and will not cease to influence you unless you let it slip.

VII. *What is not intended by the assertion that whoever is born of God does not and cannot commit sin.*

1. To be born of God cannot mean that a holy being has no power to commit sin. Adam was a holy being and he sinned, as did also the "angels which kept not their first estate." If there were a lack of natural power to sin, there would be no virtue in obedience. This position would contradict innumerable facts. Perhaps very few have ever been born of God who have not afterward been guilty of sin. This is a matter of consciousness. Most of the histories of good men recorded in the Bible show that they did fall into sin, and the Bible everywhere assumes that there is danger of this. If the Bible assumed otherwise, it would destroy free agency and the possibility of being sinful or holy.

2. It would also thus make John contradict himself, for he was writing to regenerate persons, but he continually assumes that they could sin and were in danger of sinning. Nor can it mean that one who is born of God never does in any instance sin under the force of temptation. This would contradict all the rest of the Bible.

VIII. *What is intended by this assertion.*

1. It is intended that since the truth of the gospel has once broken the power of passion and appetite in a man and gained the consent of his will, and since it remains in him—that is, in his memory—he will not, as a matter of fact, consent to indulge himself in any form of sin.

2. *Cannot* is here used in its popular sense, as it generally is in the Bible. Such language must neither be strained nor cut to the quick. It is used just as it is now used in popular conversation. Suppose I say I cannot take twenty-five dollars for my

watch. What do I mean? Not that I have no power to take it, but that I am unwilling to take it. If I say I cannot throw this table across the room, the nature of the case shows that I use cannot to indicate a natural impossibility, but in the former case I use it merely in the sense of a strong unwillingness. It is in this sense that it is used in the text, just as it is used every day in every store on Broadway.

3. It is intended, then, that *with all Christians, holiness is the rule and sin the exception.* If there be sin at all, that sin is only occasional as opposed to habitual, and it is so infrequent, that, in the strong language of John, it may be truly said, they do not sin. If sin is not so rare as to be merely occasional instead of habitual, the text is absolutely false. For example, suppose I should say a man is not a drunkard. I should not be understood to say he had never been drunk in his life, but I should certainly be understood to say that at most his fits of intoxication were extremely rare. John, as a writer, expresses himself very strongly, and I might read many passages from his writings showing that he does not intend such terms in an absolute sense, but to state that in Christians, their aversion to sin and their purpose of obedience are so strong and fixed that it may be said in strong language that they cannot sin.

> And every man that hath this hope in him purifieth himself, even as he is pure. Whosoever committeth sin transgresseth also the law: for sin is the transgression of the law. And ye know that he was manifested to take away our sins; and in him is no sin. Whosoever abideth in him sinneth not: whosoever sinneth hath not seen him, neither known him. Little children, let no man deceive you: he that doeth righteousness is righteous, even as he is righteous. He that committeth sin is of the devil; for the devil sinneth from the beginning. For this purpose the Son of God was manifested, that he might destroy the works of the devil. Whosoever is born of God doth not commit sin; for his seed remaineth in him: and he cannot commit sin, because he is born of God. (1 John 3:3-9)

4. It must be intended that Christians only sin by being diverted from the consideration of the truth by the force of temptation. This is the least that this and similar passages can mean. It is not intended to assert what *ought* to be true of Christians but what is so as a matter of fact. He is drawing the very portrait of a

Christian and hanging it up for all the church in all ages to view.

IX. *How a Christian may be distinguished from a sinner.*

1. They cannot be distinguished by profession of faith. For doubtless many sinners make profession, and some Christians do not.

2. Nor can they be distinguished by their observance of the forms of religion, their creeds or opinions, their church standing, nor by the emotions or feelings which they manifest. Emotions are as natural to the impenitent as to Christians and are no distinguishing test.

3. The Christian, however, is *benevolent,* while the sinner is *selfish.* These are their ultimate states of mind, and will manifest themselves in both by a natural necessity.

4. The Christian is influenced by reason and the sinner by mere feeling. If you wish to influence a sinner, you must appeal to his feelings, for nothing else will move him. He has not learned to yield his will to the dominion of truth. But the Christian has devoted himself to truth, and is always influenced by it. He knows that the feelings effervesce, boil or freeze, just as circumstances vary; while truth is forever the same. Said a brother to me not long ago, "I am distressed about my wife. She is very full of feeling and can be affected by appeals which are calculated to awaken it, but I cannot influence her by truth." I replied that this was truly a dark sign and I now say that I should have no hope for my wife, or anyone else, who cannot be influenced to duty *by the simple truth,* unaided by appeals to the sensibility.

5. The Christian obeys all known truth, on all subjects, while sinners conform to truth only on those subjects that are enforced by public opinion. Truth is the Christian's law, and he conforms to it fully, whether in opposition or conformity to public opinion. But notice! A sinner will conform to some truths *outwardly*, but not to all. And he will not conform from his heart. Public sentiment is a god which most people obey and worship.

6. Christians adhere to principle in the face of all opposition, while sinners give way before it. Let opposition rise ever so high, you will see the true Christian stand like a rock and breast the dashing wave—*he will not shrink or quail.* Not so with the sinner. He will conform to truth while all is smooth, but when the

tide begins to rise, you see him yield to its force and ride along with it wherever it goes. "By and by he is offended."

7. It can never be said of a true Christian, "Sin has dominion over him." But some form of sin has dominion over sinners universally. Sometimes it assumes one type and sometimes another, but sin is their master.

8. Christians obey the spirit and letter of the moral law, but sinners obey *only the letter*, if they do that.

9. When a Christian sees the truth on any subject, he will obey it; a sinner will see and acknowledge it, and continue on in his sins. His appetites, not his conscience, are his master.

REMARKS

1. Every real Christian lives habitually without sin. Nothing is more common than to find large classes of those who profess religion who acknowledge that they are living in sin. You ask them, "Do you not know this is wrong?" "Yes," they say, "but no person is expected to live without sin in this world. We must sin some." Since the Bible is true, such persons are deceived and on the way to hell. If that is religion, what is Christianity? "But," you will say, "I know what you say of this text cannot be the meaning, for it is not my experience." Poor soul! This excuse will do you no good, for God's Word is true—whatever your experience—and in the day of eternity, where will you be if you rely on this? Now, do you cry out and say, "Why this is awful, for if it be true, what will become of the great mass of Christians?" Let me tell you, all true Christians will be saved, but hypocrites God will judge. Said a woman to a minister not long ago, "Do you confess your sins?" Confess your sins! What did she mean by that? Why, she meant to inquire whether every time he prayed he confessed, not that he had been a sinner in times past, but that he was now actually sinning against God! She, with many other professors, actually seemed to think Christians should sin a little all the time in order to keep them humble and to have something to confess. Indeed!

2. It is a dangerous error to inculcate that Christians sin daily and hourly. It sets the door wide open for false hopes and fills the church with the victims of delusion.

3. It is equally dangerous to say that their most holy duties are sinful—that sin is mixed with all we do. What! Then John should have said, "Whosoever is born of God commits sin daily and hourly: however, the seed of God remaineth in him, for sin is mixed with all he does!" It is a self-evident fact that whatever is holy is not sinful. Holiness is conformity to all perceived obligation, it is an act of the will, and must be a unity. If, then, holiness be a unity, a compliance with all perceived obligation, sin is not and cannot be mixed in it. Christ says, "Ye cannot serve God and mammon" (Matt. 6:24). And James says, "For whosoever shall keep the whole law, and yet offend in one point, he is guilty of all" (James 2:10). A person, therefore, knowing obligation to rest on him and not fulfilling it is living in sin and is not a Christian. It is in vain to appeal to experience which is contrary to the Bible.

4. All who live in the omission of duty or commission of what is contrary to known truth are living in habitual sin and are not Christians.

5. How infinitely different is the doctrine of this discourse from the common view and what is generally inculcated. A celebrated minister in giving the definition of a Christian said, *"He has a little grace and a great deal of devil."* Now where did such a sentiment as that come from? From the Bible? No! From a ruinous accommodation of the Bible to a false standard. And yet so current is such a sentiment that if you deny it, they look astonished and say, "Why, I guess you are a perfectionist!" Now read the language of the Confession of Faith of the Presbyterian Church right alongside what John says. The Confession of Faith says: "No mere man since the Fall is able, either of himself, or by any grace received in this life, perfectly to keep the commandments of God, but doth daily break them in thought, word, and in deed."* And with this almost all the standards of the church agree. It is the common sentiment of the church. Now I would ask how this harmonizes with what John says in the text and in many other places in this epistle! Let me say he is *not* here speaking of some Christians who have made rare attainments,

---

*Finney refers to Question 149 in *The Westminster Standards, The Larger Catechism* and to Question 82 in *The Shorter Catechism* (Philadelphia: Great Commission Publications, n.d.).

but of the common attainment. Now, which is right? By which will you be tried at the judgment? By the Bible or the common standards? You know very well which.

6. When any, therefore, live in the habitual omission of known duty, or habitual commission of what they know to be contrary to truth, we are bound to say they are not Christians. This is not a want of charity, but a love of the truth. Suppose an infidel should meet you with the Bible in his hand and, pointing out what it describes a Christian to be, should ask you, "Do you believe the Bible speaks the truth?" And suppose he should then point to those Christians who live daily and hourly in the omission of known duty, in violation of perceived obligation, and should ask you if you believe they are Christians, what would you say? What would you feel bound to say to maintain the honor of the Bible? The answer is plain. The truth is, the common view on this subject is a flat denial of the Bible, a ruinous accommodation to the experience of carnal people who profess religion.

7. Beloved, if this is so, it behooves us to ask ourselves whether our experience harmonizes with the Bible or the popular standard. Not whether we think we were converted some time ago, not what feelings we may have had—but are we at present conformed to all the truth we know. Does the seed remain in us? The test is for *habitual perfection of moral character*. He who has it is a Christian. He who has it not is not a Christian. Now, where are you? Where would you be tonight if summoned to the judgment? Could you lay your hand on your heart and say, "Lord, you know all things, you know I love you. You know my life is a life of conformity to all your known will"?

7

CHRISTIAN WARFARE*

Galatians 5:16, 17

"This I say then, Walk in the Spirit, and ye shall not fulfil the lust of the flesh.

"For the flesh lusteth against the Spirit, and the Spirit against the flesh: and these are contrary the one to the other; so that ye cannot do the things that ye would."

This passage has been greatly misunderstood, or else the Apostle has contradicted himself. Leaving out of view verse 16, and assuming the design of verse 17 is to assign the grounds of the assertion in verse 16, many of the expounders of the Scriptures have understood verse 17 to declare that in consequence of the flesh lusting against the Spirit, and the Spirit against the flesh, persons who really wish to be holy cannot. So it has all along been generally understood. I repeat, if this interpretation be true, the Apostle contradicts himself. Verse 16 positively asserts that those who walk in the Spirit shall not fulfill the lusts of the flesh. This interpretation of verse 17 makes him say that in consequence of the opposition between the flesh and the Spirit, those who walk in the Spirit, after all, cannot but fulfill the lusts of the flesh. But this interpretation entirely overlooks the fact that verse 17 is designed to establish the assertion made in verse 16. In

---

*Ibid., No. 5, March 1, 1843.

verse 16, the Apostle says, "Walk in the Spirit, and ye shall not fulfil the lust of the flesh." Why? "Because," he says, "the flesh lusteth against the Spirit, and the Spirit against the flesh, and these are contrary the one to the other"; that is, they are opposites. What then? Why the obvious inference, "that ye [those who walk in the Spirit] cannot do the things that ye would," in case you were not walking in the Spirit. In other words, you who are walking in the Spirit cannot fulfill the lusts of the flesh. The simple principle is you cannot walk after the Spirit and fulfill the lusts of the flesh at the same time, because it is impossible to perform two opposites at once.

In further remarking on this text, I intend to show:

    I. *What Christian warfare does not consist in.*
   II. *What Christian warfare does consist in.*
  III. *The difference between careless and convicted sinners.*
  IV. *The difference between saints and convicted but unconverted people, who profess to have faith.*
   V. *That a warfare would have existed had man never sinned.*
  VI. *Several causes that have aggravated this warfare.*
 VII. *How this warfare may be modified and abated.*
VIII. *That warfare will, under a more or less modified form, continue while we are in the body.*

I. *What Christian warfare does not consist in.*

1. It does not consist in a conflict between the will or heart, and the conscience; for the Christian has a new heart, and the new heart and the conscience are at one. The new birth consists in the will's rejection of self-gratification as the supreme end, and adoption of the law of the reason. Therefore, regeneration harmonizes the will and the conscience, for the conscience is nothing else but the reason in a given function.

2. It does not consist in a war with inward sin but with temptation. Some persons talk about fighting with their inbred sin. But what do they mean by such language? I have no objection to persons using such language if they will only say what they mean, but the truth is, to talk of a Christian's fighting with inbred sin is to talk stark nonsense. *What is sin? Sin is an act of*

the will. It is choosing self-gratification in preference to the will of God. This, and nothing else, is sin. To talk therefore of fighting *inbred* sin is to talk of the will fighting itself. It is a choice warring upon itself; nothing can be more absurd. We may fight with temptation but not with sin in ourselves.

II. *What Christian warfare does consist in.*

1. It consists in a conflict between the will and the sensibility. By the sensibility, as I have repeatedly said, is intended that primary faculty of the mind to which all feelings, desires, and passions belong. The desires and passions of the sensibility are generally called propensities. The Christian warfare is a warfare kept up between the will and these. For example, the appetite for food seeks its own gratification, and so do all the other propensities of the mind. Since gratification is the only end at which the sensibility aims, obviously, it is blind to everything else. It knows nothing of measure or degree. To give the will to the gratification of these, therefore, is to subject it to a lawless power, and wholly to set aside the law of God as revealed in the reason. This is sin; it is giving the will to seek gratification for its own sake. This is the whole business of sinners. But in regeneration, the will rejects the gratification of these for its own sake, as an end, and gives itself to the end demanded by the reason—universal well-being. It takes ground over lesser ends. But these propensities still exist and must be resisted. That the sensibility and its susceptibilities still need a curb after regeneration is a matter of universal experience with Christians, and is directly asserted in the Bible. In the text, the Apostle says, addressing Christians, "Walk in the Spirit, and ye shall not fulfil the lust of the flesh." The term *flesh* in the Apostle's time, represented what we now mean by the sensibility. The reason I use the term "sensibility" rather than the term "flesh" is I think it today expresses the intended idea more definitely. When a previously accurate term has, in the wear of time, become less exact, it is our duty to adopt modern language representing the same idea. To express the idea of the text, I would say, "Walk in the Spirit, and ye shall not fulfill the propensities of the sensibility."

2. The Christian warfare is a war between the will and Satan. It is his great object to keep the will in subjection to the propensi-

ties of the sensibility. Hence, he directs all his efforts to arouse these propensities, and through them to enslave the will.

3. This warfare is a warfare between the heart and the world. The world presents ten thousand allurements on every hand, adapted to arouse the propensities and to lead the will to gratify them. Against these allurements, therefore, a war must be maintained.

4. It is a warfare against constitutional temperament. Many temptations originate in peculiar temperaments, such as the sanguine and impetuous temperament, or the nervous temperament. Few have failed to observe the influence of temptation arising from this source.

5. It is a warfare with habit. When habits have been formed, everyone knows the difficulty of overcoming them. Why is this? Because habit naturally originates temptation, and this temptation is great in proportion to the strength of the habit.

6. It is a warfare with a polluted imagination. Many persons have kept their imagination upon such objects and brooded over them so long that it almost spontaneously creates the most polluting pictures and presents to the will the most seductive conceptions. Who does not know this? A warfare must be steadily maintained against all these creations of a polluted imagination.

7. It is a warfare with temptations arising from the law of association. By the law of association, I mean that capacity of the mind by which one thought suggests another, and that again another, until a whole series has passed before the mind. Now where the associations are corrupt, they present powerful temptations to the will, and warfare with these must be maintained.

8. It is a warfare for the control of the attention and thoughts. Many things in a world like this, within and without, catch the attention and carry off the thoughts and through them arouse clamorous temptations. Everyone is aware, to a greater or lesser extent, of the effort required in certain circumstances and relations to restrain and keep under control the thoughts and attention. All these temptations, in the last analysis, arise in the sensibility; and Satan, the world, constitutional temperament, polluted imagination, the law of association, and vagrant thoughts are but different forms in which the susceptibilities of the sensibility are peculiarly aroused and inflamed.

III. *The difference between careless and convicted sinners.*

1. The careless sinner has no warfare between his will and his sensibility at all. He is not convicted of the evils of self-gratification, and does not see where his propensities are leading him. Hence, he is led along without even attempting resistance. The convicted sinner, on the other hand, sees the evil of sin—that the reign of his propensities is a ruinous despotism from which he must have deliverance. Hence, he attempts to resist their demands, but is continually overcome. All his efforts are unsuccessful, and his resolutions are blown away as chaff before the wind.

2. The careless sinner does not know what temptation is. While floating upon the current, he is unconscious of its strength, and because he moves with it, even imagines that he does not move at all. But the convicted sinner has learned its nature. He has become aware that he is floating on the stream of death, and of the necessity of escaping from its current. He therefore attempts to stem it, but finds it all in vain. He finds that when he would do good, evil is present with him.

3. Careless sinners make no effort to improve, and consequently do not know what resistance they would meet with if they should. They are like a man who has been bound in his sleep, who even when he awakes remains ignorant of what has been done and consequently makes no attempt to break his bonds. But the convicted sinner does make strenuous efforts. He sees himself standing on a slippery place from which he must immediately escape or perish. He is on an inclined plane, moving rapidly toward the edge, from which he must plunge to the depths of hell. He therefore makes mighty resolutions of reformation, but without success. He slides downward with accelerated speed, finding that the commandment which was ordained to life is unto death, for sin taking occasion by it deceives and slays him.

4. Both are slaves, but the careless sinner is not aware of his bondage. He knows not to what tyrant he is subject; but a convicted sinner does. He sees that he is a captive sold under sin. He is alarmed, and exerts himself to escape from his bondage. He arises to flee, but is overtaken by his master and dragged back to his service.

Such are prominent differences between the careless and convicted sinners. Romans 7 is an illustration of the warfare of a convicted sinner.*

IV. *The difference between saints and convicted but unconverted people, who profess to have faith.*

1. Both have constitutional appetites, passions, and propensities, which are liable to be excited in the presence of those objects to which they correspond. Hence, both are liable to temptation from these sources. These appetites and propensities have in themselves no moral character in either case. Since they are wholly involuntary, how could they be sinful? A man would be called deranged if he called the appetite for food sinful. But it can be so as much as any other appetite, desire, or propensity. *Sin,* therefore, neither in the true nor deceived professor of faith, consists in these; but *sin is consenting to indulgence under forbidden circumstances.*

2. Both see the necessity of resisting their excited appetites and propensities, and both make resistance of some sort. But the Christian's resistance is effectual. He holds them in subjection. This is the uniform representation of the Bible. The text says, "Walk in the Spirit, and ye shall not fulfil the lust of the flesh." So in Rom. 6:14 it is said, "For sin shall not have dominion over you; for ye are not under the law, but under grace."** On the other hand, the efforts of the unconverted professor of faith or backslider are ineffectual, and their temptations continually overcome them. In Romans 7, the Apostle is speaking of exactly this state. He presents a case to show the ineffectual struggles of a mind attempting to overcome sin by resolutions without love, and therefore is consistently overcome. Nothing can be more certain than that the Apostle here intended to show that the law could not sanctify the mind. He is clearly speaking throughout the chapter of the relation of the law to the selfish mind. When he says *I,* he merely supposes it to be his own case as an illustration, just as any other speaker or writer often does. We say *I,* not intending to describe our present actual state, but to set the case before the mind of those we address. The representation undeni-

---

*See especially both *Principles of Liberty* and *Principles of Victory* for a thorough study of Romans 7 and 8. Both are published by Bethany House Publishers.

**See especially, "Sanctification Under Grace," in *Principles of Liberty,* pp. 55-63, on this verse of scripture.

ably is that he is continually overcome of temptation, which in chapter 8, and in numerous other places in the Bible, is denied to be true of a real Christian. The truth is, this chapter is an exact history of the experience of every mind laboring under conviction, and I may add, it is the exact opposite of a gospel experience.

3. The heart of the unconverted professor of faith or backslider is with the temptation. This is the real difficulty with him, and his conscience only distresses and leads him to wish and resolve, in opposition to the real choice of his heart. Now, while his heart remains devoted to self-gratification, of course all the resolutions and efforts which he makes in opposition to it must be without love, and therefore legal. They are wrung out of him by the action of his conscience arousing his fears, and since his heart remains unchanged, and since the heart or ultimate intention always governs the conduct, his resolutions always fail of course. It is impossible that any resolution or effort should stand and be effectual against the supreme preference of the will. But the Christian's heart, on the contrary, is with his conscience, and therefore his resistance is effectual. Since he really chooses what his reason demands, temptation is in direct opposition to his supreme choice; and if he yields to it, it must be by a radical change of his ultimate intention. He is therefore able to put down temptation, and to keep it under his feet.

4. The convicted professor of faith resolves and tries in the absence of love, and of course he fails and is overcome. But the Christian does not make resolutions. He has energetically tried them and found that they avail nothing. Perhaps there never was a sinner converted, nor a backslider restored, until he had tried his resolutions and legal efforts so thoroughly as to be compelled to give them up, absolutely despairing of ever escaping by them. But when he has used up all his own stock and finds himself totally bankrupt, then he will come to Christ for capital—he goes *directly* to Him as the only deliverer. This leads him away from himself, renders him benevolent, and makes him free. While, therefore, the legalist depends on watchfulness, prayer, and resolutions to keep him from falling under temptation, the Christian knows better and depends wholly on the strength of Christ.

5. The unconverted professor of faith or backslider calls upon

Christ, and thinks he depends upon Him, but in fact, he really does not know what dependence is, while the true Christian actually depends on Christ. It is remarkable that those who have no faith call themselves in their prayers "poor creatures," make promises, tell Christ they will trust Him, and yet after all do not overcome. But the true Christian knows he once made this mistake, and now makes it no more. He now knows what it is to depend on Christ by faith and by love to serve Him. He is sustained by the love of God shed abroad in his heart by the Holy Spirit.

V. *A warfare would have existed had man never sinned.*

1. Warfare is inevitable because of the existence of constitutional appetites and susceptibilities. They did exist before the Fall, otherwise our first parents could not have fallen. In Eve, for example, these appetites could be excited to temptation by their appropriate objects; otherwise, objects of temptation might as well be presented to a table. These excited susceptibilities had no moral character in themselves, they were excited in her, in her purity, and if she had resisted them she would not have sinned. So susceptibilities would have existed in all the race if we never had fallen, and in the presence of their appropriate objects would have invited the will to seek their gratification.

Susceptibilities are an inherent part of the constitution, and all moral beings, doubtless, find it necessary to curb them in conformity to the demands of their higher nature. Satan and all his angels actually fell under the temptation presented to them by the susceptibilities; and, as I showed in my last lecture, every child, in beginning to act morally, does the same.

2. Temptation, in some form, may, and doubtless will, exist forever. As long as moral beings have constitutions, this must be so in all worlds. As we have already said, Satan and all his angels and our first parents were actually tempted in their holy state. And we know Jesus Christ was, and had a mighty warfare—to such a degree as to have no appetite for food, and to seek the wilderness in His distress, just as you and I have often, under similar circumstances, gone into the woods or some other seclusion to be alone. What Christian has not often felt so? They are beset so tremendously, and such a struggle develops that they can have no peace day or night, and often seek a place where they can vent their prayers or groans alone.

Thus was Christ tempted, and thus, in His warfare, did He fly from the face of man and seek the solitude of the wilderness, where He might contest the point even unto death. He seems to have been assaulted in all the weakest points of human nature. And having fasted until He was famished, He was besieged through His appetite for food, and in every other way the devil could invent, until he saw it was all in vain and left Him. The Apostle says, "He was in all points tempted like as we are, yet without sin" (Heb. 4:15). It is in vain, then, to think that temptation is peculiar to a fallen state. If men had understood this, they never would have fallen into the ridiculous blunder of calling their constitutional susceptibilities indwelling sin. They would have taught men to control and regulate, rather than call the nature God has given them sinful.

VI. *Several causes that have aggravated this warfare.*

1. The sensibility originally responded with equal integrity to all the perceptions of the mind, whether of sense or reason. It was equally susceptible to all its objects. We all know that when we look at certain objects, corresponding feelings begin to glow in the sensibility. For example, if we look at a beautiful object, the corresponding feeling will naturally be awakened. Now all the susceptibilities of the constitution were naturally equally linked to their objects and excited with equal ease by the perception of those objects. The sensibility responded with equal readiness to an acknowledgment of duty, as to an object of sensual desire. It was not clamorous in anything, but duly and sweetly balanced.

2. But it is capable of sudden and monstrous developments in any given direction. Suppose, for example, a mother loses her child. There is a sudden *crash*, and in a moment her little blooming baby lies before her face, pale in death. What effect will this have? Why, always afterward the sight of a dead child will produce a greater effect on her sensibility than it ever did before. She indeed *used* to be affected—even to tears; but now such a sight seems to absorb her whole sensibility. She stands convulsed whenever she looks upon it, and sobs a shower of scalding tears. Now, why is this? Because development of her sensibility in that direction overbalances everything else. She sits thinking and weeping and goes sighing about the house, renewing her grief at the sight of every object connected with her darling. So it is with

the susceptibility to fear. A man is thrown from a horse, or rides a wagon with a runaway horse; he is peculiarly fearful in similar circumnstances the rest of his life. Perhaps his house is enveloped in flames when he wakes in the night, and he escapes with great difficulty. This event may bring his sensibility into such a relation to fires that all his life after, whenever the fire bells ring, he is thrown into a tempest of agitation, hardly able to control himself. It is said of a young man who escaped from Lake Erie, which was burned there, that he could not even hear it named without becoming visibly distracted. I am now speaking of facts which everyone knows respecting monstrous developments of the sensibility, and these facts incontestably prove that the balance of the sensibility may be destroyed. Whenever such a development occurs, it seems to put out the eyes of the sensibility on other subjects so that such people don't feel as much respecting those subjects as formerly. The mother, in the case supposed, will never feel toward multitudes of other things as she formerly did, and so it is in every case, in exact proportion to the strength of this absorbing peculiarity of feeling.

3. In most cases, the sensibility is greatly developed in respect to objects of sense, and very slightly in respect to truths revealed by the reason. In the presence of objects of sense, everyone knows how readily the feelings respond to such; this needs no illustration. On the other hand, it is equally known that the reason itself is but slightly developed, and the sensibility which was originally designed to wake up and respond with instant readiness to reason's voice is hardly disturbed by its loudest utterance. Now, why is this? Because the monstrous development of the sensibility respecting objects of sense has turned its eyes away from the reason and its demands. It has given all its love to sensual objects; this has greatly aggravated the power of temptation arising from such objects.

4. In some, one appetite or passion is more largely developed, and in others, some other; hence, one has a passion for one thing, and another, for another. One, for example, has a passion for money, for company, for novel reading, or for gaming. He cares little for traveling, or intemperance, or licentiousness. But almost everyone has some ruling object of gratification to which his sensibility peculiarly responds, and the stronger this passion, or the

more monstrous development becomes, the more certain it is mightily to influence the will, and of course to be an aggravated temptation.

5. The imagination of some is greatly polluted. They have allowed themselves to read such books, to converse on such subjects, and to dwell on, or perhaps mingle in, such scenes as have filled their associations with the most fiery combustibles, and the least incident kindles the sensibility, through these, into a flame, and temptation is thus greatly aggravated.

6. A diseased nervous system is often a source of great temptation. Perhaps there is scarcely anyone whose nervous system is not, in some degree, diseased, but in some it is particularly so. Since the mind develops itself through the nervous system, and an intimate connection exists between them, it often happens that the nerves become the source of the fiercest temptations. Cases have come under my observation most strikingly illustrating this point.

7. Another source of aggravated temptation is that the will has not subjected the thoughts, appetites, desires, and passions to its control. Instead of controlling, it has consented to them in almost all their demands, except where they conflict with each other, so that the mind was compelled to choose between them. It is vastly important that the will early acquire control of all the susceptibilities, and it may be taught to do this as readily as anything else that will accomplishes. Many do not seem to see this.

Now, how is it that the will of a human being gets possession of any of his own powers and susceptibilities? The process is easily seen. See the child—at first he hardly knows how to move any of his muscles, and only after numerous efforts can he control his little hands. Next he attempts to walk, but he doesn't know how, and must learn how to control his voluntary muscles. But by many efforts he finally succeeds in getting them under voluntary control. So with the use of his tongue. All the various uses and movements of the tongue are actually learned, and to control it by the will is as much an art as the movements of an organist's fingers. Thus, a continual effort is going on in the child to get himself under his own control, and he succeeds respecting his physical powers, but does not get the control of his mental susceptibilities. Why is this? Because there is a defect in his training and not because there is naturally an insuperable difficulty in the one case and not in the other. We know he can, to some extent, acquire control of his mental powers. What is the object of sending the child to school? To discipline his mind.

One of the great difficulties with people whose minds are undisciplined is that they have not mastered themselves, but in time they will acquire enough self-control to concentrate attention for hours on the driest mathematical problems. But having never attempted or acquired the art of controlling the various propensities of the sensibility the full-grown man finds himself as incapable of regulating them as the infant is of controlling his muscles. He has not learned the art; hence, in their turbulent outbreaks they are continual temptations.

8. As I have already intimated, if the reason is very slightly developed, the sensibility with all its monstrous developments will have full swing. By the *reason* I mean that power of the mind by which it reveals and imposes the law of benevolence upon itself, and also the application of this law as fast as new applications are discovered. Where moral applications are not sought, nor the attention given to the affirmations of the reason, of course, it must remain in very slight development.

I wish to call attention to a subject everybody sees, but which is peculiarly delicate. It is said that females generally are influenced by feelings, but not by reason. A certain gentleman said of his wife, "If I wish to carry her will, I never can do it by *reasoning* with her, but must always appeal to her feelings." Why is this? Not because they have not reason, nor because it cannot be developed in them to operate as powerfully as in the other sex, but because, for ages, their whole training has been directly calculated to develop their sensibility until, as it is said, they are a bundle of nerves, and their reason is left to remain uncultivated and undeveloped.

The same is true of men. Were their reason developed as it should be, you might rattle off a string of self-evident propositions as fast as an auctioneer would knock off articles under the hammer, and they would without difficulty immediately perceive their truth. But as things are, they don't perceive them. Why? Because, while the development of their sensibility has been monstrous, their rational development has been almost wholly neglected; and now, instead of influencing them by simply appealing to their reason, you find such labor all in vain unless you can also powerfully arouse their sensibility in favor of the object you are emphasizing.

9. Another thing which has aggravated this warfare is the manner in which parents train their children. In most cases, their training is exactly adapted to monstrously develop certain appetites and passions. Instead of parents, and others who have the care of children, watching over them and keeping them from circumstances and conduct calculated to arouse their sensibility unduly, they give them up to just about as much excitement as possible until the sensibility becomes so outrageous in its demands as to carry the will in favor of whatever it demands.

10. These and other things which I might mention show how fearfully Christian warfare is aggravated. The warfare with temptation begins when a person becomes a Christian. I may add to the above specifications the fact that parents have caused diseases in their children, which continually operate to tempt their will to sin.

VII. *How this warfare may be modified and abated.*

1. By restoring health. If health is restored, of course all the temptation arising from disease will disappear.

2. By the development of the reason. As the reason wakes up, the sensibility also begins to be developed in the same direction. This is the very way in which persons become awakened and convicted. And after conversion, in proportion as the reason lays hurdles in the way of the sensual propensities, their strength and tendency are broken and subdued.

3. This warfare may be especially abated and modified by a great development of the sensibility produced by a revelation of the love of Christ. Often when the character of God in Christ is apprehended in its true light, it leaves no room for anything else. The reason stands on tiptoe, gazing steadfastly with its intuitive eye, and the sensibility turns its whole surface right out to receive the full impress of such a glorious vision.

I remember the case of a very ungodly man, who seemed to take delight in manifesting the highest contempt for religion. His wife was openly religious, but he opposed and forbade her attending meetings at a time of revival in the church. He went so far, and things came to such a point, that he could no longer find material and opportunity with which to ridicule religion. Finally, one day he thought he would go to the evening meeting to see if he could not find something there to make sport about, especially since he had heard many things about the meeting that seemed to him to promise such a result. Just before meeting time, his wife went to her closet and poured out her heart to God, and prayed Him to open the way for her to go to the meeting. As she came out she met her husband; he asked her if she wanted to go to the meeting that night. Astonished, and rejoicing, she was soon ready and they were off. While the minister was preaching, the man's attention was arrested, and about the middle of the sermon, he groaned and fell down in his seat. He was in such agony, it seemed as if he would die, and the sermon was halted. He exclaimed over and over, "Oh, Jesus, how I have abused Thee! Oh, Jesus, how I have abused Thee!"—until at last his agitation passed, leaving him in a state of perfect submission. There was a case, where by the manifestation of His character, God as it were almost immediately revolutionized a man. He said it was a view of the character of God in Christ which produced the same effect. By degrees his convictions rapidly arose until he could endure it no longer; and when he bowed his will, it seemed as though God said to all the propensities which formerly ruled him, "Peace, be still," and he has been a flaming light ever since. His tongue seems to be tuned with the praises of God. I have known him long, and he seems always the same. His warfare was greatly abated by that apprehension of the character of God in Christ. I know the effect of this by my own experience. When I was converted, for some time I did not know that I had any appetite left; all my susceptibilities seemed so perfectly absorbed in the things of the gospel. And in all this there is nothing strange. It is perfectly natural and just what might be expected.*

4. There is one particular truth which, when the Spirit has revealed it to the mind, seems forever after to exert a powerful influence on the sensibility, and that is the relation of the death of

---

*See especially, *"The Kingdom of God in Consciousness"* in *Principles of Liberty,* pp. 183-194, on Romans 14:17, "The kingdom of God is not meat and drink, but righteousness, and peace, and joy in the Holy Ghost."

Christ to our sins. People often talk about the Atonement without seeming to understand its real meaning, especially its relation to their own sins. But let them see that *their* sins caused His
death, and where's the mind that can contemplate the fact unmoved? I have known that single thought to excite all the nerves
and as it were, set the sensibility on fire so as to bring a strong
man almost to the point of a stroke.

VIII. *This warfare will, under a more or less modified form,
continue while we are in the body.*
Some have supposed that when persons are entirely sanctified, all the passions, desires and appetites of the sensibility will
invariably impel the will in the same direction the reason does.
However, such persons do not know what they say, for all these
propensities seek their objects for their own sake and are blind to
everything else. They always and necessarily urge the will to seek
their respective objects for the sake of gratification. This is temptation and creates a warfare. The appetite for food, for example,
seeks food for its own sake, and so does the desire for knowledge.
It is nonsense, then, to say that they will not solicit the will to
gratify them under improper circumstances. But when the mind
is entirely sanctified, instead of the various propensities creating
such a fiery and turbulent warfare when excited, the will will
have them under control, so that all their actions will be bland
and tranquilized.
The most that will or can be done is to harmonize them, and
it is by no means desirable that they should be annihilated. Suppose, for example, the desire for knowledge were annihilated.
What a calamity that would be! Or, the desire for food! The truth
is, all the constitutional desires should remain. They were all
given for useful purposes, and all call for their appropriate objects—for food, for knowledge, etc., and are thus constantly feeling after those things which are essential to our very existence,
and that of our race. Besides, to regulate them is a good exercise
for the will, and it is difficult to see how a mind could be virtuous
at all if all the susceptibilities of its sensibility were destroyed;
and if any of them were removed, it would doubtless be a great
evil—otherwise God was not benevolent in our creation and did
not make us in the best way.

REMARKS

1. The common notion of warring with inward sin is nonsensical and impossible. Those who use such language confound temptation with sin. They call their natural appetites and propensities *sinful*, and when resisting these, they say they are resisting indwelling sin. Multitudes, doubtless, mistake the actions of the conscience, its warnings and reproofs, for the resistance of the heart to temptation. The truth is, the Christian warfare consists in a struggle between the will and temptation from without and within, and in nothing else.

2. The warfare of one who is deceived in his profession of faith is between his heart and his reason or conscience. His heart is devoted to self-gratification, and the reason constantly disapproves of and denounces the service as wrong, and thus a continual struggle is kept up within between his heart and his reason and this he calls the Christian warfare. If that is so, every sinner has the Christian warfare, and doubtless the devil also.

3. The Christian overcomes in his warfare. This is a habitual fact as stated in Rom. 6:14, "For sin shall not have dominion over you: for ye are not under the law, but under grace." Also see Rom. 8:1-4. See also the text and context, besides numerous other passages directly asserting the same thing.

4. What a ruinous mistake it is to suppose Romans 7 to be Christian experience. I do not hesitate to say that it has been the occasion of the destruction of more souls than almost any other mistake in the world. It is fundamentally to mistake the very nature of true religion.

5. The warfare of the true Christian greatly strengthens his virtue. When he is greatly tried and obliged to gather up all his energy to maintain his integrity, when he wrestles with some fiery trial until he is in perspiration, as it is sometimes necessary for him to do, it must be that when he comes out from such a scene as this, his virtue is greatly strengthened and improved.

6. We can see, from this subject, why sinners often doubt the reality of temptation, and when they hear Christians talking of their temptations, they think that Christians must be worse than they, for they do not experience such. But the reason they are not conscious of temptations is that they have not attempted to regu-

late their propensities by the law of God. A man floating on a current is not conscious of its strength until he turns around and attempts to stem it. The same principle applies to those professing religion who entertain the same doubts. Talk about temptation! Why, they say, I am not tempted like that. Indeed! Perhaps they have never done anything else but yield to it.

7. See why the Apostle said so much about the opposition of the flesh and Spirit? He represents them as hostile, throughout his epistles, especially in Romans 6, 7 and 8.

8. Many struggle for a while in their own strength, and, through continued failures, become discouraged and give up. The temptations of their appetites and propensities are too strong for them, while they have not learned by faith to derive strength from Christ.

9. Many despair of ever becoming sanctified, because they suppose their constitutional propensities are, in themselves, sinful. They say it is in vain to talk of entire sanctification in this life, and well they may say so, if their constitutional appetites and propensities are sinful, for we know of no promise that our nature shall be revolutionized in this life or the next.

10. Others suffer distress and despair because they cannot control their thoughts when their will is weary. The will is that power of the mind which originates all control which the mind may exert over itself. But it becomes weary, or perhaps it would be more correct to say, that the brain, through which it acts, grows weary and wants rest. In sleep, the will is suspended, and hence in dreams the thoughts run lawless and without direction. It is a matter of experience with students who study hard for a long time, that they find it extremely difficult, after long and severe concentration, to keep their attention and thoughts on their studies. Why? Because their will is wearied and needs rest.

So it is with Christians who undertake to pray when exhausted. Their thoughts fly everywhere. They try to restrain their wanderings; they struggle, and, for a moment seem to get control, and then they lose it again. They try it over and over again, but with no better success, until they nearly despair. Now, what is the matter? They need rest, and ought to take it rather than attempt to force their wearied will into action. Let your will rest. God will have mercy and not sacrifice. What's the use, when a man has walked sixty miles in a day, and his will can hardly force his exhausted muscles into further action, of his attempting to use them further, and blaming himself because he cannot? Suppose a man should never go to sleep for fear he should dream and his thoughts ramble heedless of his will! Why call such things sin? Don't be confused forever and mix up sin and holiness, light and darkness, heaven and hell, so that people cannot tell which is which.

11. Some bring forward the fact that this warfare is represented as continuing, using this fact as an argument against the doctrine of sanctification. They think a soul must get beyond warfare in order to be sanctified. What! Then Adam was not sanctified before he sinned, nor Satan; nor was Jesus Christ while on earth, for it is a simple matter of fact that He had temptation. What would you think of the argument that Jesus Christ had a warfare and therefore was not wholly sanctified? And yet it would be just as good as this.

12. However sharp the conflict, if the soul prevails there is no sin. What trials Jesus Christ had! But He prevailed. "He was tempted in all points like as we are, yet without sin" (Heb. 4:15). So, if temptation should rush like a tornado upon any of you, if you will only hold on and fight it out, you have not sinned. No, the sharper the conflict, the greater the virtue of resistance.

13. The saints are no doubt preparing in this world for some high stations of usefulness, where they *may* be exposed to strong temptations. I infer this from the fact that they are placed here in circumstances exactly calculated to ripen and fit them for such a destiny. God never acts without design, and He surely has some design in this.

14. The sanctified are sometimes in heaviness through manifold temptations, if need be. Now don't infer, if you see them so, that they are not holy. Christ had His sorrows and knew what it was to resist temptation even to blood; the servant should not expect to fare better than his Lord. The truth is these trials are useful—they are but for a moment, but they prepare us for a far more exceeding and eternal weight of glory. Sorrows endure for the night, but joy comes in the morning. Under the pressure of the temptation the soul is in agony and cries out, "Help, oh, Lord, help," and He comes and scatters the insulting foe, and the

soul takes off like a rocket, giving glory to God.

15. Many have supposed for a time that their enemies were dead, but were mistaken. The fact is they are never dead in such a sense that we do not need to watch in order to overcome temptation. But let us never overlook the distinction between temptation and sin, and ever keep in mind that the *Christian warfare is not with sin, but temptation.* Never forget that Christ alone can give us the victory. Oh, for the Spirit of Christ to baptize the ministers and the churches!

8

PUTTING ON CHRIST*

Romans 13:14

"But put ye on the Lord Jesus Christ, and make not provision for the flesh, to fulfil the lusts thereof."

It is my purpose to show:

I. *What is intended by this command.*
II. *What is implied in obeying this command.*
III. *Some of the essential conditions of obedience to this command.*
IV. *Obligation to obey this command is universal.*
V. *Obedience to the requirements of this text is indispensable to salvation.*
VI. *Some of the consequences of obeying these requirements.*
VII. *Consequences of disobeying these requirements.*

I. *What is intended by this command.*

I observe that the idea is taken from the drama—"To put on a person" is to assume his character and peculiarities, as an actor does on the stage. This commandment, therefore, exhorts the imitation of Christ, as actors imitate those whom they represent.

---

*Ibid., No. 6, March 15, 1843.

II. *What is implied in obeying this command.*

1. It implies the putting away of selfishness. Christ was not selfish. Selfishness is the preference of self-gratification to the will of God and to the good of the universe; Christ never did this. The Apostle adds, "and make not provision for the flesh, to fulfil the lusts thereof." Here, he contrasts "putting on Christ" and "making provision for the flesh," which is the same as selfishness. Paul was more philosophical than any of the other sacred writers, and employs the language—"works of the flesh," "following after the flesh," "carnal mind," etc.—to designate the nature of sin. But the whole Bible condemns self-seeking as wrong and inconsistent with the true service of God, or imitation of Christ.

2. This command implies living for the same end for which Christ lived. What was His end? Not the gratification of self, but the well-being of the universe, and whoever puts Him on must adopt the same end.

3. It implies the same singleness of eye. Christ's eye was not double, but exclusively directed to one end—the glory of God.

4. It implies such a sympathy with Him as to beget an imitation of Him. A profound sympathy is necessary to, and naturally begets, imitation.

III. *Some of the essential conditions of obedience to this command.*

1. The first thing essential is a deep and intense study of His character until the great principle of His action is clearly perceived—the real idea of the *end* for which He lived clearly developed. Persons attempting to imitate others must give the closest attention. This is essential to the success of a dramatic actor, or any other artist. Who, when looking at a picture by West, and observing all its delicate shadings, has not been struck with the deep attention which the artist must have given to his subject?* One shade is stronger and another weaker, exactly exhibiting the position and form of each limb and the various expressions of countenance and attitude appropriate to the circumstances of

---

*Probably the American painter Benjamin West (1738-1820), who was history painter to King George III.

the person represented. Now, in order to express these things, by colorings and on the canvas, the artist must have studied most intensely. So it is with a good actor. He does not merely commit and rehearse his piece as a schoolboy does on the stage. He does not stand and spout it off in recitation style, but seeks to represent his character in dress, habit, spirit, style, manner, and everything; in this consists the perfection of the dramatic art. Now the Apostle commands us thus to put on Christ—to imitate Him—to give intense thought to get at the true idea of His character, and to commit the mind fully to the same end to which He was devoted. To enjoy a piece of poetry, you must put yourself into the same state of mind in which the author was when he wrote it. Then as you read it, your tone and manner will naturally represent him. This is the difficulty with so many in reading hymns. They read as though they did not at all apprehend the sentiment, and without emotion. The reason is, either they have not the spirit of devotion, or they have not at all given attention to the sentiment of the hymn. But to represent Christ we *must* catch His Spirit and make His grand end and aim ours. Then we shall act as He would under like circumstances.

2. Another essential is, you must fully believe that through grace you can put Him on. While you don't believe you can, of course you cannot. No one can intend to do what he believes he cannot do. It is absurd to suppose the contrary. No one intends to fly. Why? Because everyone knows he cannot. We may *wish* to fly, while we do not believe we can, but to *intend* it is impossible. So unless you believe you can put on Christ, it is utterly impossible that you should intend to do it, and this is the great reason why so many never actually put Him on.

3. You must, therefore, not only fully believe that you can, but you must actually intend to put on Christ—to make Him your whole example. Unless it is intended it will not be done; it will never be done by accident.

4. You must be fully prepared to make any sacrifice—you must count the cost and make up your mind to meet the expense necessary to the accomplishment of this end. You must make any sacrifice of friends, property, or credit which stand in the way. The Lord Jesus Christ teaches this and warns persons not to make themselves ridiculous by beginning to build without being

able to finish. The truth is, unless persons have decided to sacrifice whatever hinders their fully putting on Christ, they have not grasped the very first principle of religion.

5. You must realize the importance of doing this. Suppose a dramatic author should write an admirable drama, adapted powerfully to awaken the attention and arouse the passions of viewers of the performance, but the actors so poorly prepare themselves, and so poorly act it that they totally misrepresent him. It is easy to see how they would injure the credit both of the author and drama. So persons who do not fully put on the Lord Jesus Christ, while they profess to be His followers, are doing Him and His cause the greatest injury of which they are capable. They should then realize the infinite importance of fully representing Him.

6. Another condition of putting on Christ is that you should keep up a constant intercourse with Him. You must commune with Him in prayer without ceasing. Who does not know that an actor needs to drink into and commune with the spirit of the author profoundly, if he would truly represent him. He must get the state of mind of the man who wrote it; in short he must "*put on*" the writer. If he does not, he will misrepresent him. So there must be constant communion with the Spirit of Christ in order to put Him on and act just as He would.

7. You must not rest while there is any unrepented, unconfessed sin between your soul and Him. You must keep a clear channel. I will explain what I mean. You have seen two friends who have been agreed for a long time and have sweet fellowship together, but by and by a little difference creeps in between them—a little mist begins to obscure the channel. Now, when they meet, you will begin to see it in the eye and countenance—there is a little flutter in their manner—and unless it is immediately removed, it will increase until, finally, they will turn their backs on each other. So it is with a husband and wife. How careful they should be to keep a clear channel of mental communication. Suppose a husband has grieved his wife. Now, if he is a man of sensibility, he cannot be at ease. He goes to pray, remembers the wound which he has inflicted and can pray no further. He rises from his knees and goes and confesses to his wife the injury he has done her. The obstruction is now removed from the channel, and he is happy. So with the Christian. If he has grieved

Christ and injured His tender feelings, he can have no further communion with Him until he has repented and confessed his faults, and the tender breathings of mutual love are restored.

8. You must discontinue all self-dependence. As long as you depend on yourself, you will see no need of putting on Christ.

9. You must avail yourself of His exceeding great and precious promises. You must realize the purpose of the promises; and that they were given for you personally. The Apostle Peter says, "Whereby are given unto us exceeding great and precious promises: that by these ye might be partakers of the divine nature, having escaped the corruption that is in the world through lust" (2 Pet. 1:4). The design of the promises, then, is to beget in us a universal likeness to the Lord Jesus Christ. Now, a promise is good for nothing unless it be fulfilled. Ten thousand promises of such a character would be of no more use than a book of checks given to a poor man by Mr. Astor*, which he carries and never uses.

IV. *Obligation to obey this command is universal.*

1. By this it is not intended that all are to do exactly the same things which Christ did, for no one is, in all respects, in the same circumstances. As circumstances vary, outward duties differ. Christ practiced celibacy; in the circumstances in which He was placed, this was His duty. But it never could be the duty of mankind, generally, to imitate Him in this particular, and in many other things.

2. But it is intended that all are bound to do as He did, insofar as their circumstances are the same, that they are to do what they suppose He would do if He were in their circumstances. Suppose, for example, He were a father, a merchant, a mechanic, a lawyer, or a citizen. In early life He was a carpenter, and labored with His father at his trade. Let a carpenter ask these questions: "What sort of a carpenter was Jesus Christ? How honest was He? How did He do His work? How did He associate and converse with His fellow workmen?" Just that which you suppose

---

*John Jacob Astor (1763-1848) emigrated to America in 1783, and amassed the greatest fortune of anyone in America up to his time. He was also mentioned by Finney in *Principles of Prayer*, p. 32.

Him to be, you are to be. Suppose the Lord Jesus Christ were a merchant, upon what principles would He conduct His business? Or, if He were a physician, how would He practice? Would He avoid visiting the poor, and seek to practice only among the rich?

3. You are to consider how He would act in your circumstances, and do as you think He would. How important for a minister of the Gospel to inquire what kind of pastor Christ would be if He were in his circumstances. And so with every other man for the same reason. If Christ were a physician, what would He do? Would He reject the poor and cater to the rich? Would He say, when a poor man came soliciting His aid, "I shall not get much money for this; therefore, I do not care whether I attend to it or not"? Now, beloved brethren who are physicians, are you as you think Christ would be, taking into account the difference of circumstances? You may thus take any other occupation, even the lowest; for none that is honest is too low to forbid the supposition of His being in similar circumstances. In order to illustrate this Jesus washed His disciples' feet. In the East they wore sandals, which exposed their feet to the hot sands, and it was customary for the lowest servant of the house to wait at the door with water to wash the feet of visitors. The Savior did this to inculcate lowliness of heart and to show the spirit with which all should perform the duties of life. Whatever may be your condition, whatever you suppose Christ would be in your place, you ought to be. And it is an important question for each one to ask, "Would Christ pursue my calling if placed in my circumstances, and would He pursue it *as I do?*"

4. To put on Christ is a universal duty, evident from the following facts: it is just, right; all can do it by His grace; universal reason demands it; it is essential to the good of the universe; both sinners and saints are commanded to do it.

V. *Obedience to the requirements of this text is indispensable to salvation.*

1. The verse does not say a person must have done this his whole life to be saved.

2. But, as far as their knowledge extends, they are to put Him on and live devoted to the same end.

(1) Because everything short of this is sin.

(2) Nothing short of intending to be, or do, what He would be, or do—with our light and in our circumstances—can be acceptable to God. "Ye cannot serve God and mammon" (Matt. 6:24). What does this mean? It does not mean that you cannot serve God at one time, and mammon at another. It does mean that you must be entirely devoted either to one or the other, and cannot serve both at the same time.

(3) Benevolence is a unit and will manifest itself alike in all instances so far as their circumstances are similar.

(4) Christ was no more than virtuous, and you must be no less or you cannot be saved. I have often been astonished that people talk as if Christ did something more than His duty, and performed works beyond obligation as if such a thing were possible. Duty is what benevolence requires. Now, if Christ should do more than benevolence requires, it could not be benevolence, nor duty, and consequently, not virtue. I would ask, "Was God in making the atonement any more benevolent than He ought to be?" If so, He was not virtuous in it. The truth is, people are in the dark on this subject. No being in the universe can perform works beyond his obligation; for everyone is required to do his whole duty. Christ was perfectly benevolent, and this was His duty. And so must *you* be if you put Him on.

(5) You must be like Him or you never can be with Him.

VI. *Some of the consequences of obeying these requirements.*
Here I wish to be exceedingly candid and keep nothing back. I have often marked how much the Lord Jesus Christ differed from many who set themselves up as reformers. He would often press His hearers until almost all of them would forsake Him. Once, all but His twelve disciples left Him, and He turned to them and said, "Will ye also go away?" (John 6:67), implying that He would rather lose them than to withhold the truth. And we must not preach a false Christ, or our disciples will have the appearance of heaven and the nature of the world.

1. The first consequence is much opposition. You can expect no better usage than Christ received. "It is enough for the disciple that he be as his master" (Matt. 10:25).

2. You may expect great trials. This is the inheritance of all who will live godly in Christ Jesus. Look at Paul. While he was a

Pharisee, he went on smoothly. The gales of popular favor swelled his sails. But when he became the preacher of the cross, ah! then he knew what it was to go against wind and tide.

3. Men will accuse you of having a bad spirit. They have always brought this charge against the true followers of Christ, especially against Christ himself. He said so much about their teachers, creeds, and traditions, and rebuked them so plainly, that they finally tried and executed Him as a blasphemer.

4. You will need great meekness, and at the same time great decision of character. Without both of these qualities, you cannot endure the shock of a world arrayed against you.

5. You will subject yourself to much misunderstanding. Many wonder why Christians are so misunderstood. But it is not at all amazing. Who was ever more misunderstood than Jesus Christ? The simple fact is, a selfish mind *does not* understand the principle upon which a true Christian acts.

6. If you are misunderstood, you will of course be misrepresented. This you must expect.

7. It will subject you to the loss of many friends. They will think you are ultra-religious, carrying matters too far. And every new step you take, you will see an additional falling off. They will walk no more with you. But all the consequences are not evil.

8. You will, for example, inherit His peace of mind; this is worth more than all the world can give. You will sleep just as sweetly, eat with just as much relish, and enjoy the tranquil hours just as much as if you had all the world's favor. Persons often wonder whether such are unhappy. I answer, "No. They are the only persons who know what true happiness is."

9. His joy will be fulfilled in you. This is His promise, and His true followers fellowship with Him in all the joys He had.

10. You will share His glory in being the representative of the true God. "And the glory which thou gavest me, I have given them; that they may be one, even as we are one; I in them, and thou in me, that they may be made perfect in one; and that the world may know that thou hast sent me, and hast loved them, as thou hast loved me" (John 17:22, 23). Christ was sent to reveal the true character of God. He took the law, which lay on tables of stone, and acted it out, thus showing mankind just what God is. Without such a manifestation as was thus made of His true char-

acter, men would have always remained in ignorance. What is God? A glorious, infinite, and invisible Spirit, lying back in the bosom of eternity, where no eye can reach. What finite mind could comprehend Him? He must reveal himself; and to this end He concentrated His glory in Christ and sent Him among mankind. Everyone, then, who puts on the Lord Jesus Christ will share with Him this glory of making known to the world the true character of God.

11. You will be able to say with Paul, "For to me to live is Christ" (Phil. 1:21). The Apostle seems to have had this idea in mind, that Christ lived His life over again in him. So it will be with you. Christ renews His life in His true followers.

12. You will be able to say from your own consciousness, as John says, "Truly our fellowship is with the Father, and with his Son Jesus Christ" (see 1 John 1:1-4).

13. You will be happy in the highest degree of which you are capable in this life. And you will be no less useful than you are happy.

VII. *Consequences of disobeying these requirements.*

1. If you profess religion, you will be a hypocrite, and people will know it. There are, perhaps, some who are successful in keeping on the mask. But most betray themselves sooner or later and are known in their true character.

2. You will render peace of mind impossible.

3. You will render yourself justly despicable. All love to see men live up to their profession and naturally cry out against hypocrisy.

4. You will ruin your own soul and do the most you can to ruin others.

5. You will bring upon yourself the endless execration of all beings in the universe, both good and bad.

REMARKS

1. Those who inconsistently profess religion sometimes gain the hollow applause of the unthinking and ungodly.

2. But they never gain the *solid* respect of any class for any considerable time. Instead of this, they really lose it. For as soon as their true character appears, mankind cannot but condemn

and abhor it. Their inward lack of confidence in such people is often exhibited in a trying hour. A fact I heard from a Methodist minister made a deep impression on my mind. A wealthy man in the South, who had sat under the preaching of a worldly minister, was sick and about to die. His friends asked him if they should send for his minister. He said, "No, I do not want him now; we have been together at the horse race." They all urged him to send for somebody and mentioned several. But he rejected them all. At last he told them to call in Tom, one of his black men, because, he said, "I have often heard him pray alone." Tom came, laid his little hat at the door and inquired what his master wanted. The dying man said, "Tom, do you pray?" "Yes, master, in my weak way." "Can you pray for your dying master?" "I'll try," he repeated. "Come here, then, and pray for me." Tom drew near and poured out his soul to God for the dying man. Ah! the master knew, in his inmost soul, that his minister could not pray. Poor Tom was the man to pray.

3. The lives of many who profess religion are a most terrible burlesque on Christianity. Satan, it would seem, has pushed these into the church to disgrace it. Persons who have a strong sense of the ridiculous are often tempted to laugh at the absurd notions of religion which some manifest. They never seem to think of asking how Christ would do. I have sometimes seen servants in families where they were called to family worship come in cowering and get behind the door, altogether away from the family circle. I wonder if they think it will be so in heaven. In some families I know it is not their wish but the choice of the servant, and of course they are not to blame. Since I have been here I have seen persons take up their hats and leave the house when they see black people sitting among the whites. I wonder if such people would do so in heaven. Is not this the direct opposite of the spirit of Christ? How would Christ treat the poor slaves and the black people if He were in this country?

4. Recognize the importance of always bearing in mind the person whom you have undertaken to represent and the part you are expected to act. All can see that a minister in the pulpit and everywhere should bear this in mind—and so he should—but no more, really, than any other Christian should in his vocation.

5. It behooves us to inquire whether we have so represented

Christ as to give those around us the true idea of religion. Suppose a minister should never ask himself what idea of religion his people get from him. It is easy to see that he would be able to convey a very definite idea of it to his people. So everyone who professes faith should do. And now, beloved, do you live so as to make the impression that religion is disinterested benevolence? Who would get that idea from you? A man recently said, "If religion is benevolence, I know of but one man in our church who seems to be religious." How many do you know in this city? Nothing else is religion. Do you live so? Do *I*? If not, what will become of our souls?

6. Those who do not put on Christ are the worst kind of heretics. There is no heresy as bad as a false profession.

7. Those who are inconsistent in their profession are the greatest curse to the world.

8. Those who profess faith but who have not put on Christ should confess to those around them and instantly reform. Confess to your wife, your children, your church, your neighbors. Will you do it?

9. Sinners are altogether without excuse, and are as much bound to put on Christ as those who profess faith.

10. Unless every one of us, in his calling, fully intends to put on Christ, and keep Him on, we are on the way to hell. If you are not what you think Christ would be in your calling, you are not a Christian. How different is this from the common religion. All we see is pride, and starch, and fashion, and death. Oh, brethren, let us put on the Lord Jesus Christ, and "make no provision for the flesh to fulfil the lust thereof."

9

THE WAY TO BE HOLY*

Romans 10:4

"For Christ is the end of the law for righteousness to everyone that believeth."

In this discussion I am to show:

I. *What is not intended by the assertion that Christ is the end of the law for righteousness.*
II. *What is intended by this assertion.*
III. *How Christ becomes the end of the law for righteousness.*

I. *What is not intended by the assertion that Christ is the end of the law for righteousness.*

1. It does not mean that He abolishes the law in respect to believers. I am aware that some antinomians in the church affirm this, but it cannot be true for the following reasons.

(1) *The moral law is not founded in the arbitrary will of God,* for if it were He would have no rule of conduct, nothing with which to compare His own actions. But every moral agent must

---

Ibid., No. 7, March 29, 1843. This chapter is also found in *Principles of Liberty,* pp. 139-146. It is included here because it is an integral part of Finney's 13-part series "Holiness of Christians in the Present Life."

have some rule by which to act. Character implies moral obligation, and moral obligation implies moral law. Again, unless the law is obligatory on Him, benevolence in Him is not a virtue, for virtue must be compliance with obligation. Nor should we have any standard with which to compare His actions, and by which to judge them, so that we could know whether He is holy or unholy. Moreover, if He is capable of benevolence, it is impossible that He should not be under a moral obligation to be so; and if so, the law cannot, of course, be founded in His arbitrary will. Furthermore, He could, if the law were founded in His arbitrary will, by willing it, make benevolence vice and malevolence virtue, right wrong and wrong right. But this is absurd and impossible.

(2) *The moral law is founded in God's self-existent nature.* He never made His own nature, and consequently, never made the law. It must therefore be obligatory upon Him by virtue of His own nature which imposes it. It is as genuinely obligatory on Him as on us.

(3) He requires benevolence of us, because it is naturally obligatory on us. He made us in His own image—that is, with a nature like His own. Therefore, He could not discharge us from obligation to keep the law if He wanted, because our own reason would still reveal and impose it on us. We should perceive its obligation.

(4) If He could and should abolish the moral law, then we could have no moral character. We could neither be sinful nor holy any more than beasts can. Christ cannot be the end of the law in the sense that He abolishes it.

2. It is not intended that He abolishes the penalty with respect to believers so that they can sin without actual condemnation. Some have this view of justification: that at the first act of faith God sets aside the penalty, and it can never afterwards attach to the individual no matter what he does. But this cannot be, for:

(1) If the penalty is set aside, then the law is repealed, for law consists of precept and penalty.

(2) If the penalty were set aside, then Christians when they sinned would not need pardon; and they could not without folly and even wickedness pray for forgiveness. It would be nothing

else but sheer unbelief in their own doctrine. But every Christian knows that when he sins he is condemned, and he must be pardoned or be damned. Christ, therefore, is not the end of the law in this sense.

3. Nor is He the end of the law merely for justification, for He does not obtain for them a legal justification. Legal justification is the act of pronouncing one just in the estimation of law. This Christ cannot do in respect to any transgressor. Gospel justification is pardon and acceptance. But it never was the end or object of the law to pardon sinners. In this sense, then, it is impossible that Christ should be the end of the law, for *the law never aimed at pardoning transgressors.* The word righteousness sometimes means justification, but it cannot mean that here because Christ never aimed at legal justification, nor did the law aim at pardon. He cannot, of course, be the end of the law in this sense.

4. Nor is He the end of the law in the sense of procuring a pardon for those that believe, for this was never the end *proposed by the law.* The law knows nothing of pardon.

5. Nor is it intended that He imputes His own righteousness or obedience to them. Some suppose that Christ was under no obligation to obey the law himself, and that He can, therefore, impute His obedience to believers. But,

(1) The *law never aimed at imputation.* This was no part of its object. *Did the law require Christ's righteousness or personal holiness to be imputed?*

(2) The doctrine of imputed righteousness is founded on the absurd assumption that Christ owed no obedience to the law. But how can this be? Was He under no obligation to be benevolent? If not, then His benevolence was not virtue. He certainly was just as much bound to love God with all His heart, and soul, and strength, and mind, and His neighbor as himself, as you are. How holy should God be? As holy as He can be. That is, He should be perfectly benevolent as the Bible says He is.

(3) This doctrine assumes that Christ's works were works beyond obligation. Is this what the Apostle means when he says, "For such an high priest became us, who is holy, harmless, undefiled, separate from sinners"? (Heb. 7:26).

(4) This doctrine is a mere dogma of popery—born, bred, and supported amid its darkness and superstitions. The sufferings

and death of Christ were for us and constitute the atonement. His obedience was necessary to His making an atonement, *as a condition,* since none but a holy being could make it. Holiness is benevolence, and Christ must of necessity have been benevolent in order to make the atonement, which is a work of benevolence.

(5) The doctrine of imputed righteousness represents God as requiring:

(a) That Christ should render a perfect obedience for us.

(b) That He should die just as if no such obedience had been rendered.

(c) That despite the debt being paid twice by our substitute, we must repent as though it were unpaid.

(d) Then that we must be forgiven.

(e) And after all this, that we must ourselves obey, or be personally holy.

(f) And finally, that we must count it all grace.

What a jumble of nonsense this is! Is this the gospel of the blessed God? Impossible!

(6) The doctrine of imputation utterly sets aside the true idea of the gospel. The true idea of pardon does not enter into it. It is rather a fivefold satisfaction of justice. We are not restored to the favor of God according to this doctrine by a free pardon, but by imputed righteousness. It is not at all amazing that thinking men, when they hear such slang as this, say, "Oh, nonsense! If that is the gospel, we can have nothing to do with it."

(7) Imputation is not, and never was, the end or object of the law. The end which it seeks is righteousness or true obedience.

II. *What is intended by the assertion that Christ is the end of the law for righteousness.*

The text affirms that He is the end of the law *for righteousness.* Righteousness is obedience to the law. He is, then, the end of the law for obedience. He secures the very end aimed at by the law; that is, He makes Christians holy. As it is said, "There is therefore now no condemnation to them which are in Christ Jesus, who walk not after the flesh, but after the Spirit. For the law of the spirit of life in Christ Jesus hath made me free from the law of sin and death. For what the law could not do in that it was weak through the flesh, God sending his own Son in the likeness of sinful flesh, and for sin, condemned sin in the flesh, that the righteousness of the law might be fulfilled in us, who walk not after the flesh, but after the Spirit." What have we here? Why, an express assertion of the Apostle that Christ by His atonement and indwelling Spirit had secured in Christians the very obedience which the law required.

III. *How Christ becomes the end of the law for righteousness or obedience.*

1. Confidence or faith is essential to all heartfelt obedience to *any* law. An *outward* conformity to its requirements may be secured by fear.

2. Christ, then, must secure love or true righteousness by inspiring confidence in the character and government of God. God had been slandered by Satan, and the world believed the slander. Satan represented to our first parents that God was insincere in forbidding them to eat of the tree of knowledge, and that the result of their eating of it would be just the reverse of what God had threatened. He said, "God doth know that in the day ye eat thereof, then your eyes shall be opened, and ye shall be as God, knowing good and evil!" This was a most enticing temptation! "And when the woman saw that the tree was good for food, and that it was pleasant to the eyes, and a tree to be desired to make one wise, she took of the fruit thereof, and did eat." Now the thing to be done is to remove this prejudice which has existed in all ages. How shall it be effected?

3. Christ came to reveal the true God and the true character of His government for this express purpose. He came not only to teach, but, by His example, to give an illustration of what the law meant, and to impress the human mind with the idea that God is love. He knew very well that confidence was the thing needed, and that He had to reveal the character of God so as to beget confidence. He must hold it out in strong contrast, in a life of love before them. There was a greater necessity for this, because many of the dispensations of God toward mankind appeared severe. He had poured out the waters of the flood upon the old world and destroyed it. He had frowned upon the cities of the plain and sent them down to hell. In many other instances, He had been obliged to resort to such measures as were calculated, in the circum-

stances, to beget dread and slavish fear, rather than to inspire confidence and love. It was, therefore, necessary to adopt measures of a different nature adapted to beget faith.

4. The nature of faith renders obedience certain, so far as it is implicit. A wife, for example, is always perfectly under the influence of her husband, insofar as she has confidence in him. Suppose he is a businessman; if she has confidence in his business talents, she does not concern herself at all in his business transactions. So, if they are going on a journey and she knows him to be careful and attentive to his affairs, then she will not fret. She will never ask whether he has taken care of their baggage and whether he has procured tickets and accommodations. She expects all this, as a matter of course, and is happy in her reliance on him. But suppose she had no confidence in his character. If he is a man of business, and she lacks confidence in his judgment, then she will be all the time in distress for fear he will take some step which will ruin their affairs. If they are going on a journey, then she will, perhaps, fear that he will start off without his wallet, or forget some of his baggage, or that he will lose them on the way. It is easy to see that, so far as this lack of confidence extends, its tendency is to diminish her affection; and if it extends to his whole character, then she cannot love him. I might illustrate this in a thousand ways. If you call in a physician, and you have confidence in him, then you will take any medicine he may prescribe. I remember a case with which perhaps some of you are familiar. A certain king was sick, and he sent for a physician. The physician examined his symptoms and found his disease a dangerous one requiring a particular treatment. He told the king he would go home and prepare a certain medicine which would make him very sick while in its operation, but would remove the disease. While the physician was gone, the king received a letter warning him against the physician as though he designed to poison him. When the physician returned and presented him the medicine, he immediately swallowed it, and then handed his physician the letter which he had received. That was faith; it placed him entirely under the control of his physician. It is easy, therefore, to see that if Christ could only restore faith among men, then He would, of course, secure obedience.

5. Faith in God's character is the foundation of faith in His

promises. Many people seem to go the wrong way to faith. They try to exercise faith in the promises along with faith in His general character. But Christ takes the *opposite course,* revealing the true character of God as the foundation of faith in His promises.

6. He baptizes them by His Spirit and actually works in them to will and to do. How wonderfully Christ seems to work to get the control of believers. Unless He can get into their confidence He cannot do this, but as soon as He can inspire faith He has them under His control. We see the same law among men. See a human pair, by securing mutual confidence, wind imperishable cords around each other's hearts. Then, for one to know the will of the other is to do it. They do not need to be bound down nor driven by the force of penalties. This is the way of the seducer who can "smile and smile and be a villain still." He lays his foundation deep in the confidence of his victim until he may laugh at all that her parents may say and do against him. He gains such domination so as to control the will more absolutely than if he could wield it by his hand. Such is the natural result of getting *into* the confidence of another. They will and do at our bidding. Thus Christ gains the heart and works in us to will and do of His good pleasure.

7. The way to be holy, then, is to believe. "Then said they unto him, What shall we do, that we might work the works of God? Jesus answered and said unto them, This is the work of God, that ye believe on him whom he hath sent" (John 6:28, 29). "That they may receive forgiveness of sins, and inheritance among them which are sanctified by faith that is in me" (Acts 26:18).

This only would I learn of you, Received ye the Spirit by the works of the law or by the hearing of faith? Are ye so foolish? having begun in the Spirit, are ye now made perfect by the flesh? Have ye suffered so many things in vain? if it be yet in vain. He therefore that ministereth to you the Spirit, and worketh miracles among you, doeth he it by the works of the law, or by the hearing of faith? Even as Abraham believed God, and it was accounted to him for righteousness. Know ye therefore that they which are of faith, the same are the children of Abraham. And the scripture, foreseeing that God would justify the heathen through faith, preached before the gospel unto Abraham, saying,

In thee shall all nations be blessed. So then they which be of faith are blessed with faithful Abraham. For as many as are of the works of the law are under the curse: for it is written, Cursed is every one that continueth not in all things which are written in the book of the law to do them. But that no man is justified by the law in the sight of God, it is evident: for, The just shall live by faith. And the law is not of faith: but, the man that doeth them shall live in them. Christ hath redeemed us from the curse of the law, being made a curse for us: for it is written, Cursed is every one that hangeth on a tree: that the blessing of Abraham might come on the Gentiles through Jesus Christ: that we shall receive the promise of the Spirit through faith. (Gal. 3:2-14)

What shall we say then? That the Gentiles, which followed not after righteousness, have attained to righteousness, even the righteousness which is of faith. But Israel, which followed after the law of righteousness, hath not attained to the law of righteousness. Wherefore? Because they sought it not by faith, but as it were by the works of the law. For they stumbled at that stumblingstone; as it is written, Behold, I lay in Zion a stumblingstone and rock of offence: and whosoever believeth on him shall not be ashamed. (Rom. 9:30-33)

In Christ, then, the believer is complete; that is, He is all we need. His offices and relations meet all our necessities, and by faith we receive their redeeming influences.

REMARKS

1. From this subject, we may see why the gospel lays so much stress on faith. It is the only way of salvation.

2. This method of saving men is perfectly philosophical. And, as we have seen, Christ thus works himself into the very heart of believers.

3. It is the only possible way, in the very nature of the case, to secure love. God might command and back up the command with threatenings, but this would only fill the selfish mind with terror, leaving its selfishness unbroken, and even grasping at its objects amid the roar of its thunders. In the very *nature* of mind, then, to secure obedience, He must secure confidence. Why, look at Eve! The moment she doubted, she fell. And so would all heaven fall if they should lose confidence in God. Yes, they would *fall*! They would no more retain their obedience than the planets

would retain their places if the power of gravitation were broken. Everyone knows that if the power of attraction were destroyed, suns, stars, and planets would run lawless through the universe, and desolation would drive her plowshare through creation. So, break the power of confidence in heaven, and every angel there would fall like Lucifer and universal anarchy prevail.

4. What I have said does not represent virtue or holiness as consisting in mere emotions of complacency or in loving God merely for His favors; but the exhibition of His character in Christ begets in us real benevolence. It shows us what benevolence is and stimulates us to exercise it. Nearly all preachers and writers of the present day confuse religion with mere complacency in God for His favors. Both gratitude and complacency may, and often do, exist in the impenitent mind. It must, therefore, be a fundamental mistake to confound these with true religion.

5. Christ, by exhibiting His benevolence, begets His own image in them that believe; that is, they are naturally led to yield themselves up to the transforming tendency of this view of His character. This, the law could never secure in a selfish mind.

6. I said the doctrine of imputed righteousness is another gospel or no gospel at all. And here I would ask, "Is not this quite another way of salvation?" According to this way, instead of imputing righteousness to them, God makes them righteous.

7. The gospel is not an evasion of the law. It comes in as an auxiliary to accomplish what the law aims at, but cannot effect, because it is "weak through the flesh."

8. We see who are true believers—those who love God supremely and their neighbor as themselves. Unless your faith begets obedience, it is not the faith of the gospel.

9. We can see the sustaining power of faith. This is not well considered by many. If the head of a family secures its confidence, he controls it easily; if not, there is a perpetual tendency to resist him. The same principle operates in state governments. They are firm insofar and no further than they are based upon the confidence of their subjects. So it is in the business world. Everything is prosperous as long as confidence is secured. When confidence goes, the tide immediately turns the other way. Why are so many houses in this country, which were once supposed to

be perfectly stable, tumbling down around the heads of merchants? Because confidence is destroyed. Restore that, and immediately things will assume a different aspect. Every merchant in New York will feel the impulse, and ships from abroad will come freighted down with merchandise. This principle is equally efficient and necessary in the divine government. This, the devil well understood. Hence his first effort was directed to its overthrow. But ministers too often put it in the background, and hence the reason of so much failure in the work of reforming the world. Christ, on the other hand, always put it foremost, and His declaration, "He that believeth shall be saved," is the unalterable law of His government.

10. Unbelievers cannot be saved since their lack of confidence necessarily keeps the soul from obedience from the heart.

11. Do you ask, "How can I believe?" I turn to you, and ask, "How can you help believing?" Christ has died for you to win your confidence. He stands at your door offering blessings and assuring you of His good will. And you can't believe! What! And the Son of God at the door! But perhaps you stand back and say, "Christians can believe, but how can I, a poor, guilty wretch?" And why not you? Come, let your anchor down upon the character of God, and then if the winds blow, let them blow. If the ocean tosses itself, and yawns till it lays bare its very floor, you are secure, for God rules the winds and the waves. But I hear someone say, "I am such a backslider." Yes, and you are likely to be. Unless you believe, you will continue to go right away from God. Come, instantly, and believe. Come, all you sinners; come now, who profess faith and He will write His law in your hearts; it will no longer be to you a law on tables of stone. Can't you believe it? Yes. Oh, yes. Then let us come around the throne of grace and receive Christ as the end of the law for righteousness.

10

WHAT ATTAINMENTS CHRISTIANS MAY REASONABLY EXPECT TO MAKE IN THIS LIFE*

1 Thessalonians 5:23, 24

"And the very God of peace sanctify you wholly; and I pray God your whole spirit and soul and body be preserved blameless unto the coming of our Lord Jesus Christ. Faithful is he that calleth you, who also will do it."

In this lecture I shall consider:

    I. *What sanctification is.*
   II. *What is not implied in it.*
  III. *What is implied in it.*
  IV. *What is intended by the sanctification of body, soul, and spirit.*
   V. *What is not implied in the sanctification of body, soul, and spirit.*
  VI. *What is implied in it.*
 VII. *What attainments Christians cannot expect in this life.*
VIII. *What attainments they may reasonably expect to make in this life.*

Ibid., No. 8, April 12, 1843.

I. *What sanctification is.*

1. To sanctify is to make holy, to set apart, to consecrate. Both the Old and the New Testaments use the word in this sense. For God to sanctify us is for Him to secure in us the consecration of ourselves to Him. To sanctify ourselves is to consecrate ourselves wholly to Him.

2. Sanctification, then, is holiness, purity, or benevolence. Benevolence, as we have seen in former lectures, is good willing, and is the ultimate intention of the mind; in other words, it is obedience to the requirements of the law of God; it is what the Bible means by love, which it declares to be the fulfilling of the law.

II. *What is not implied in it.*

1. It does not imply any change in the constitution.

2. It does not imply any change in the temper, disposition, or state of the mind that would render sin impossible. To suppose this is absurd. The angels who did not keep their first estate were certainly sanctified, but they sinned, and so did Adam.

3. Nor is it implied in sanctification that we are not liable to sin.

4. Nor that it is certain that we shall not sin, immediately and surely, unless supported by the Spirit of God. There is no evidence that even the saints in heaven would continue their obedience if the Holy Spirit were withdrawn.

5. Nor is it implied that a sanctified soul has no further warfare with temptation. I showed in my lecture on the Christian warfare that this would have existed if man had never fallen, and will exist, in some form, forever.

6. Sanctification does not imply that there is no further growth in grace. The Lord Jesus Christ, all admit, was sanctified, but He grew in grace. And so shall we, as fast as our knowledge increases, not only in this, but in the future world.*

7. Nor does it imply freedom from errors in judgment or opin-

---

*Charles Finney believed he was filled with the Holy Spirit, justified, and sanctified when he was converted. All of his life he grew in grace, and had deeper spiritual experiences. As his knowledge increased, and as his capacity to have these experiences was enlarged, he could be of greater service to Christ and His Kingdom.

ion. I don't know how it could be shown, either from the Bible or from the nature of the case, that this is implied in sanctification, even of the saints in heaven.

8. Nor does it imply a uniform state of the emotions. Christ's emotions were not always the same. He had His sorrows and His joys, and, from the very nature of the sensibility, the feelings must vary as the circumstances do.

9. Nor does sanctification imply a constant and great excitement. The idea that a great excitement of the emotions is essential to sanctification has arisen out of a radical mistake respecting the nature of religion. It has been supposed that the love required by the law of God consists in the highest possible state of the emotions. Now, if this is so, or if emotion constitutes any part of religion, then Christ was often in sin, for He did not exhibit any more excitement than other men. Those who maintain this sentiment, then, overlook the fact that religion consists in benevolence, and that emotion is no part of it.

10. Sanctification does not imply the same degree or strength of love which we might have exercised had we never sinned. There is not a saint in heaven who does this, and the law requires no such thing. It only requires us to exercise all the strength we have.

11. It does not require a constant tension or strain of the mind.

12. Nor does sanctification imply a state of mind of which we cannot be certain by consciousness. It would be strange legislation indeed which should require such a mysterious, intangible state of mind as that. The truth is, it is naturally impossible that such a state should be required by an intelligible law. Indeed, how could one repent, or know it if he did, under such a requirement, or perform any other duty?

III. *What is implied in it.*

1. Sanctification does imply present obedience to the law of God, that is, benevolence. Benevolence consists in regarding and treating every known interest according to its relative value, and, as I have shown in a former lecture, it is a unit—a simple choice—a choosing good for its own sake.

2. We have also seen that bodily actions are connected with,

and controlled by, the will—so that willing necessitates corresponding outward actions. Sanctification, therefore, implies outward obedience—a correct life.

3. We have also seen that emotions, desires, and thoughts are connected with and controlled by the will indirectly. Sanctification, therefore, implies thoughts, desires, and feelings corresponding to the state of the will so far as they can be regulated by it. Some have less control over their attention, and consequently over their thoughts and emotions, than others; but whatever is possible to anyone, he can do by willing, and nothing beyond this is obligatory.

4. Sanctification implies an honest intention to promote the glory of God and the highest good of being, to the full extent of our ability. Such an intention necessarily embraces the following elements:

(1) It is disinterested. It chooses universal well-being for its own sake.

(2) It is impartial respecting all interests, whether of friends or foes, rich or poor, bond or free, in exact accordance with their perceived value.

(3) It has no expiration date.

(4) It is supremely to God, because His happiness is the supreme good.

(5) It is equal to men. If you drop either of these latter elements, it is no longer virtue.

5. We have seen that intention, or the choice of an end, necessitates the adoption of corresponding means; therefore, sanctification implies the choice of appropriate means to the universal good of being.

6. It implies charitable judgments—these are the natural results of benevolence. "[Charity] thinketh no evil" (1 Cor. 13:5). When you see a person making severe and harsh judgments, you at least have reason to fear he is not sanctified.

7. It implies peace of mind. "Peace I leave with you," says Christ (John 14:27).

8. Joy in God comes with sanctification.*

9. Sanctification implies absence of condemnation, "There is

---

*See chapter 16, "Joy in God." page 219.

therefore now no condemnation to them which are in Christ Jesus" (Rom. 8:1).

10. Implicit faith is implied in sanctification. The sanctified soul really believes, so far as he understands, the truth of God.

11. Sanctification brings delight in all the ordinances and duties of religion, so far as they are understood.

12. A sanctified person has a compassionate temper. Whenever it is seen that persons do not have this spirit, you may know they are not sanctified.

13. Sanctification implies the absence of all selfishness. Selfishness, in any degree, is inconsistent with sanctification.

14. Implicit and universal reliance on Christ for support and aid come with sanctification. You cannot remain obedient any longer than you remember where your strength is.

15. Sanctification requires holding all we are and have entirely at the divine disposal. Sanctification must include all these as fully as the illumination of the individual requires.*

IV. *What is intended by the sanctification of body, soul and spirit.*

1. By the language, "body, soul, and spirit," we are able to understand the whole being, and the thing intended is the perfect subjection of all the appetites and propensities to the entire control of the will of God. Some of these appetites and propensities originate in the body, and some in the mind; but all must be controlled in reference to the highest good of being.

2. The harmonious development of the sensibility so that it shall respond to all perceived truths and relations is intended in this language. In my sermon on the Christian warfare, I spoke of the monstrous development of the sensibility, of the influence it has upon the will in the direction in which it is developed. I there remarked that a perfect balancing of all its susceptibilities would greatly abate the force of temptation. Everyone knows how forci-

---

*It should be noted that sanctification is not so much an experience that one has in the past, but *a benevolent relationship* to God and the universe in their proper relation. As knowledge increases, and as reliance on the Spirit of Christ increases with our knowledge, our benevolent relationship to our Creator will deepen—"morning by morning new mercies I see."

bly the appetites and passions wake up and clamor for indulgence. Although neither holiness nor sin belong to these, in themselves, yet it would be vastly favorable to virtue if they were all
brought into harmonious subjection to the law of the reason.
Here let me say that no physical influence is exerted on the mind
or body by the Spirit to change the sensibility. The mother whose
sensibility is so developed by the loss of her child is not brought
into such a state by any physical influence; nor is such an influence *needed* to secure such effects. Let sinners see the love of
Christ in its real relation to themselves, and it is directly adapted
to enkindle their emotions. It is the Spirit's office to take the
things of Christ, to show them, and thus secure this result. This
He actually effects in Christians. To be sanctified, then, is to
have not only the will consecrated to God, but also the sensibility
brought into harmonious action under the control of the will.

V. *What is not implied in the sanctification of body, soul and
spirit.*

1. It is not implied that the constitutional appetites, passions, and propensities are extinct. They certainly were not in
the Lord Jesus Christ, and whoever supposes this necessary in order to achieve sanctification has not well considered the matter.
Without their continued existence, we should be incapable of any
moral action whatever.

2. Nor that their nature is so changed that they all exclusively impel the will to obey the law of the reason. It belongs to their
very nature for each to seek its appropriate object, for its own
sake. For example, the appetite for food seeks food, not for the
glory of God, but for its own sake. So it is with every appetite and
desire of the soul. Each is blind to everything but its own object,
and seeks that for its own sake. To say, then, that they must be so
changed as to impel the mind only in the right direction is to say
that their very nature must be changed. Each of them, naturally,
impels the will to seek its object for its own sake. It is the province of reason to give direction to their blindness, and of the will
to gratify them in strict subjection to the law which reason prescribes.

3. Sanctification does not imply that the appetites are so far
suppressed or annihilated as to be in no degree a temptation.

They were not so in Eve, for she fell under the temptation presented by her appetite for food. And we need not expect ever to get into any such state.

VI. *What is implied in it.*

1. That these propensities are all harmoniously developed according to the light enjoyed.

2. That they become easily controlled by the will, as in the person of Christ.

VII. *What attainments Christians cannot expect in this life.*

1. They cannot expect to get above what Christ was. It is enough for the servant to be as his Master.

2. Of course they cannot reasonably expect to get beyond a state of warfare. Christ had a warfare, not with sin, not with conscience, for it would be nonsense to call this Christian warfare, but with temptation, and no one will deny that He was entirely sanctified. And here I wish to notice a very singular fact. Those who deny this doctrine say that if Christians were perfect, they would have no further warfare. But where do they get that idea? Not from the Bible, for there is not a single passage in it, that I know of, which teaches any such thing.

3. They cannot expect to get beyond the necessity and capacity of growth in grace; I mean growth in degree, not in kind. We shall doubtless grow in grace through all eternity. The Bible says that Christ grew in favor with God; He grew in grace, and so will every Christian.

4. They cannot expect to get beyond this possibility or liability of sinning. This would be to get beyond the possibility of obedience and to cease from being a moral agent.

5. Nor may they expect to get so far as not to need the means of grace. They must, of necessity, need the assistance of the Spirit, of the ordinances of prayer, and of the Sabbath. To deny this is downright nonsense. While human nature remains what it is, it must need the means of grace as much as it needs food, light, or anything else which is indispensable to well-being. God never makes minds holy by physical force, but by means; therefore, means will always be necessary. Did not Christ himself use them?

VIII. *What attainments they may reasonably expect to make in this life.*

1. God does not, and cannot, reasonably require impossibilities of moral agents.

2. It is reasonable, then, to think that we can do whatever He requires of us, and to expect to do it. Our ability to comply with His requirements is implied as strongly as possible in the command itself. If not, it can have no binding force upon us.

3. God cannot lie. It is, therefore, reasonable to expect to receive any measure of grace which He has expressly promised. Not to expect such grace is to distrust God.

4. God has commanded us to obey His law; and we must intend to obey it or we are not Christians. But we cannot intend to obey it unless we consider it possible; this is naturally impossible. I appeal to every hearer. Can you really intend to render obedience from the heart to what you regard as impossible? We cannot intend to obey unless we believe it possible to obey the spirit of the law. We may, therefore, reasonably expect to keep the law.

5. The first verse in this text is the prayer of an inspired Apostle for the sanctification in this life of the whole body, soul, and spirit of Christians. He prays that they may be preserved in this state, blameless, until the coming of the Lord Jesus Christ. Now, if this is an inspired prayer, it reveals the will of God on this subject. It is admitted that it includes all that I have said— that is, sanctification in the higher sense. Notice that he adds, "Faithful is he that calleth you, who also will do it." It is reasonable, then, to expect its fulfillment.

6. But some object to this. Although they may say it is true that this and kindred promises do really pledge sufficient grace to secure this result, yet, since they are conditioned upon faith, it is unreasonable for us to expect to avail ourselves of them unless others have done so before us. And in confirmation you are pointed to the great and good men who have lived in different periods of the church, and told that they did not attain it. I waive, for the present, the answer to this objection.

REMARKS

1. This must be an important question. I have been astonished beyond all measure that this doctrine has been called a

fancy. What! Is the fundamental doctrine of the degree of holiness attainable in this life to be called a fancy? If so, then it is the fancy of the universe; and God and every angel is intensely interested in securing its success.

2. We must hold up some standard. If you tell a sinner to repent, you hold up before him the standard to which he ought to conform. And even if he should deny that any others had actually repented, you would still insist upon it, that it is his duty, whether others had or not, and also, that if he did not repent, he could not be saved.

3. Christians must aim at some standard, but they cannot aim at any state which they deem impossible; they might as well aim to fly. How essential, then, that we should ascertain what the true standard is and hold it up before them.

We have seen that sin consists in choosing self-gratification as the supreme end, and that *holiness,* on the contrary, *consists in supremely choosing the glory of God and the good of His universe.* We have also seen that they cannot coexist in the same mind—that while the will or heart is right, nothing can, for the time being, be morally wrong. On the other hand, while the heart is wrong, all is wrong; that is, it is totally depraved. The only question, then, is: can we reasonably expect to remain in that state? I said this expectation was supposed to be unreasonable unless others could be pointed out as examples. But if no one has ever availed himself of these promises, it by no means follows that no one ever will; on the contrary, the progressive state of the world, and the progressive nature of religion, warrant and demand the belief that future generations will make indefinitely higher attainments than the past. The golden age has not gone by; those who think so have not well considered the matter. If anyone will compare the time of the Apostles with the present time, and take in all the characteristics of both, he will see that on the whole, the human family has made great progress. There is a radical error in the custom of looking back instead of forward for the golden age; and the common notion that the world is decrepit is exactly the reverse of truth. Every successive era is marked by a decided advance in science, art, philosophy and civilization; this is in exact accordance with the whole tenor of prophecy, which warrants and demands the expectation of vastly higher attainments in the future than have ever yet been made.

The temperance reformation shows that it is now common for drunkards to make attainments which were once regarded as almost impossible. Who has not witnessed the Washingtonian, almost working miracles pulling the drunkard out of the gutter. And shall we extinguish hope respecting the church, and make it an exception to the progress of the world?

4. One of the greatest obstacles in the way of both physical and moral improvements is the existence of false opinions and expectations in regard to the degree of elevation to which God desires to bring mankind in this world. I have examined Mr. Miller's theory, and am persuaded that what he expects to come after the judgment will come before it.* Read chapter 65 of Isaiah. The prophet there speaks of advancement in the creation of new heavens and a new earth. The reason men have so little idea of the thing intended in such predictions is that they have such meager views of the grace of God. If the world is to be converted to the present standard, it is true that such predictions cannot represent its state. What is the church dreaming about if they cannot see the necessity of a higher standard? The man who cannot see that is as poor a philosopher as he is a Christian. Why, brethren, what would it avail if the whole world were converted to the standard of the current religion?

5. Suppose this promise had been read to those to whom it was given; how could they have believed it on the theory that they were not to expect higher attainments in the future than they then witnessed? Why, they would have said, the world never will be converted because it never has been. And what would you reply to that? Suppose the same objection were made now, and it were said, it was not done in the days of the Apostles, nor at any time since, and are we to expect to accomplish what never has been done? Suppose, further, ministers were engaged in pointing back to prove that the world can never be converted. Why, they would say, "The church never has converted the world, and therefore it never will. You must be getting proud if you think we shall do more than good men before us have done." And then, suppose they should go back and hunt up all the fanaticism,

---

*Willam Miller (1782-1849) was founder of Adventism. He predicted Christ's Second Coming in the year 1843.

enthusiasm, and extravagancies of the Crusades, and other attempts to propagate the Christian religion. And instead of pointing out these evils as a warning to the church, as they ought to do, they were doing it to prevent any attempts to convert the world now. What would be thought of all this? It would justly be regarded as ridiculous; yet this is exactly the course adopted respecting the doctrine of sanctification. The fact that the promises have not been taken seriously accounts for the fact that they have not been more generally realized in the experience of Christians.

6. To deny the reasonableness of this expectation is to lay a stumbling block before the church. Suppose you should exhort sinners to repent and then tell them they could not, neither in their own strength, nor by any grace received. What else would that be than a stumbling block, over which if they believed you, they would stumble into hell? So to tell Christians that they ought to be sanctified and that it is attainable, and yet that no one can attain it in this life is the very way to prevent them from attaining it. If they believe such instruction, it will as certainly prevent their spiritual progress as a general outcry against missions would prevent the conversion of the world.*

7. But if this expectation is unreasonable, what is reasonable? What may we expect? How much higher can we rise? Who can tell? Who will point to some definite standard?

8. People doubt this view of sanctification because of:

(1) A false philosophy of depravity and holiness. When men make sin consist in emotions instead of selfishness, they overlook the very nature of virtue, and are deluded as a matter of course.

(2) Unbelief. Our opinions on such questions must depend on our faith and the state of our hearts.

(3) Radically defective Christian experience, or rather, having had none but a legal experience.

(4) Overlooking the fullness of the gospel provision.

(5) Confusing it with Antinomian Perfectionism.

(6) False views with respect to what constitutes entire sancti-

---

*Charles Finney's spiritual progress, from the time of his conversion, can be found in *Answers to Prayer*, a book keyed for study with *Principles of Prayer*. Both are published by Bethany House Publishers.

fication. Many say the Bible represents the Christian warfare as continuing until death, and that this warfare consists in fighting with sin. Where do they learn this? Not in the Bible. The Bible does indeed represent the Christian warfare as continuing until death, but it never represents it as consisting in fighting with sin. What is sin? Sin is a heart, or will, or choice, contrary to the will of God. To fight with sin, then, would be to fight with our own present choice or voluntary state of mind—a choice warring on or against itself. This is absurd. The Christian warfare consists in warring with temptation, not with sin. Some say that Christians are commanded to grow in grace, and if they once arrive at perfection, progress is at an end. They thus set up a man of straw, and then fight it.

9. This is a serious question to all Christians. I cannot tell how I feel when I hear professors of religion say they cannot give time for its examination. A professor of religion said to me not long ago, "I cannot take time to examine this subject," and yet he had the strangest misunderstandings about it. It is enough to make one weep tears of blood—to see the darkness which prevails, and yet the apathy and unwillingness to inquire. Beloved, let us know the truth that it may make us free. Let us give ourselves up to the teachings of the Spirit that we may be "sanctified wholly, and preserved blameless unto the coming of our Lord Jesus Christ."

11

NECESSITY AND NATURE OF DIVINE TEACHING*

Philippians 2:12, 13

"Wherefore, my beloved, as ye have always obeyed, not as in my presence only, but now much more in my absence, work out your own salvation with fear and trembling. For it is God which worketh in you both to will and to do of his good pleasure."

In this lecture, I shall discuss:

    I. *The necessity of a divine influence in regeneration and sanctification.*
    II. *The kind of influence needed.*
    III. *The employment of this kind of influence.*
    IV. *The consistency and cooperation of divine and human agency in the work.*

I. *The necessity of a divine influence in regeneration and sanctification.*

1. A selfish mind will, as a matter of fact, never recover of itself to holiness. This will appear evident from the nature of selfishness. Selfishness consists in committing the will to self-gratifi-

---

Ibid., No. 13, June 21, 1843. Also cited: Hebrews 13:20, 21; John 16:13, 14; John 14:26.

cation, or the indulgence of the constitutional propensities.

2. Selfishness is the supreme *choice* of the mind. It is choosing self-gratification over and above all other and higher interests. It is making self-gratification the *ultimate end*—the thing around which the mind makes every other thing revolve, and which is therefore chosen for its own sake.

3. I have shown in a former lecture that *choice* necessitates outward actions—including the attention, and through it the thoughts, emotions, and desires. The choice of an *end* necessitates the use of *means* for its accomplishment, and gives direction to the action of all the mental powers. As choice directs the intelligence, it obviously largely decides the motives addressed to the mind through *it*. As desire and feeling are greatly dependent upon the intelligence, and as that is directed by choice, it follows that choice, to a very great extent, decides the motives that shall address the mind through the sensibility. Thus, all the actions and states of mind are necessarily controlled by choice. Hence, while a given choice exists, it naturally shuts the mind to a great degree from the influence of all objects inconsistent with itself, and gives the attention to all those things which accord with it. A man, for instance, who gives himself to making money will naturally so direct his attention to things connected with that object, he will be very little influenced by anything else.

4. Choice is necessarily an act of the will, and is, therefore, free. But the freedom of the will consists in the power *not* to choose, without motives, but to choose in view of any given motive—to choose or refuse any object presented to it. But no mind can choose an object which it does not perceive. Hence, whatever prevents perception, prevents choice—whatever prevents perception of motive or object of choice renders it impossible for the mind to choose that object.

5. If a choice diverts the mind from one class of objects or motives to another, and the mind, though entirely free, fails to perceive objects from which it is thus diverted, it does not possess within itself the means that will ever secure its choosing in accordance with them. I do not mean to say that an existing choice, whether selfish or holy, *absolutely* prevents the mind from perceiving any motives to a choice contrary to itself; for, as I showed in my lecture on the Christian warfare, our sensibility will al-

ways lay us open to temptation, however holy we may become. But a holy choice naturally shuts out, as far as possible, motives hostile to itself and keeps its attention upon the opposite class. On the other hand, a selfish choice cannot utterly hush the voice of reason and shut out all motives of holiness, but it naturally does so as far as it can. As a matter of fact, we find selfish minds so much open to motives of selfishness, and so diverted from all others, that selfish motives have the entire influence over them. Unless, therefore, some agency outside itself is employed to engage the attention, and to cause the mind to apprehend and consider another class of motives than those to which it has committed itself, the case is hopeless. While the mind is thus taken up and engrossed, it will not perceive objects of a different character so as to come under their influence, but will be drifted along to the depths of hell. All its choices will be between different forms of selfishness. It has committed itself to the stream, and despite the spontaneous rebukes of reason, it will float onward. Persons may even hear daily the best instruction and the most solemn warnings and yet so divert their attention from it as to feel its power little, if any. Thus Judas was always thinking of money, so that even the preaching of Christ did him no good. So also, multitudes of persons have so employed themselves in selfish pursuits that although they hear, every Sabbath, the most pungent and solemn truths, they do not seem to be in the least degree affected by them. They even sit in the house of God plotting schemes of selfish enterprise, and thus, by the action of laws of their own minds, rush on to certain destruction unless arrested by some foreign influence.

6. Another point to be considered is that spiritual truths are not addressed to us through the senses, and since sensual objects are constantly appealing to the propensities, and calling off the attention, a spiritual influence is constantly needed to keep up the attention to the great truths of religion. It is therefore certain that even converted persons need a constant divine influence to keep them from relapsing—to hold up to their view constantly the motives to holiness.

II. *The kind of influence needed.*
1. It needs to be spiritual in opposition to material. It needs a

spirit to gain access to the mind and draw it off from the material objects around us.

2. The influence necessary is moral as opposed to physical. It must be something which can influence one to choose. The will is not like a steel spring which can be bent by force; it must be influenced by motives. Physical power cannot move will; it moves freely.

3. It must be an enlightening influence so as to supplant and put away the darkness of the mind. Not only does the sinner move in an envelope of darkness which must be driven away, but there needs to be a constant blaze of light poured upon the Christian to detect his deficiencies and lead him forward. When a Christian has backslidden and become selfish, what but the light of heaven can remove his darkness and delusion?

4. This influence needs to be sufficiently wise and powerful to arrest and keep the attention. It is evident that an influence is needed, not merely to *argue* and *gain the assent* of the mind, but so to convince as to gain and keep the attention. Nothing is more common than for persons to assent to arguments without really perceiving their true force. An influence is therefore needed that can actually *show the truth* to the mind, quicken the conscience, and develop the sensibility in its favor. Where any truth is presented to the mind, it gives increased power to the truth if a corresponding feeling can be aroused. An agency is therefore needed that knows perfectly the laws and whole history of our minds, and just how to approach them in order to make them feel—and to possess them of the true knowledge of God. Who has not been struck with the difficulty of making sinners understand the true nature of religion? Even those who profess religion stumble at the true character of God. I was astonished at this, on hearing of certain objections made to my sermon about putting on Christ. You recall I said in my sermon that we ought, in all circumstances, and in every calling, to inquire what Christ would do if He were in our place—even if He were a physician, a mechanic, or a street-sweeper. "What!" say certain ones, "compare Jesus Christ to a street-sweeper or a washerwoman! It is blasphemous! I can't go to hear him again." Now, do let me ask, what do such persons know about religion? Why, if they had seen Him washing His disciple's feet, they would at once have declared He could not be the Christ! What! Suppose any necessary

and honest labor below Christ! I wonder if they think it was below Him to be a carpenter. Some infidels maintain that it is altogether below God to take any notice of this world. They think it
would lower His dignity to concern himself about it.* Shame! We
clearly see that those who profess religion do not know the nature
of true religion. If they did, they would never indulge their foolish
prejudices against black people or on a thousand other points on
which they should be as honest and solemn as they would be at
the judgment. They need an agency to teach them the truth
about God and His service.

This agent must be able to reveal to the mind such truths as
are calculated to inspire confidence and love. Otherwise all his
testimony will only confirm their selfishness, and leave them still
"carnal, sold under sin." He must also possess immeasurable patience. Men often lose their patience, even parents with their own
children. What patience then is necessary in order to influence
men to obey the will of God! Moreover, He must also be omni-
present and characterized by vast benevolence. Just think what
benevolence is required! Atonement is made, but sinners do not
heed it; and here something additional must be done to remove
the blindness and overcome the obstinance of man—to lead him
to accept its offers and obey its precepts.

III. *The employment of this kind of influence.*
1. The Holy Spirit strives with every generation and with
every individual altogether voluntarily. He receives no pay for it.
Oh, how great must be His benevolence! His influence has all the
characteristics above specified. It is spiritual, as described in
John 16:7, 8: "Nevertheless I tell you the truth; it is expedient for
you that I go away: for if I go not away, the Comforter will not
come unto you; but if I depart, I will send him unto you. And
when he is come, he will reprove the world of sin, and of righteousness, and of judgment."

This influence is moral, as opposed to physical. He works in
us *to will and to do,* by motives, by truth. James 1:18, "Of his
own will begat he us, with the word of truth, that we should be a

---

*Precisely the position of Plato and Aristotle; hence, the joy Greek thinkers
must have found at Paul's preaching of our compassionate God through Jesus
Christ!

kind of first fruits of his creatures." 1 Pet. 1:23, "Being born again, not of corruptible seed, but of incorruptible, by the word of God, which liveth and abideth forever." John 17:17, "Sanctify them through thy truth: thy word is truth." All these passages not only assert that the Spirit exerts an influence, but plainly teach that it is moral in kind. The atonement of Christ furnishes the motives by which to effect the work, both of converting sinners and sanctifying saints. If it should occur to you that there were persons converted before the atonement was made, I answer that it was through that class of truths which the Atonement presents. They were foreshadowed in the Jewish ritual and revealed in prophecy. It certainly was not by merely legal influences. Law only drives a sinner to despair. What! A selfish sinner brought to love by the threatenings of the law? Impossible! Conscious of his selfishness and guilt, he looks up and sees God clothed in terrors and frowns, with the red thunderbolt in His hand to dash him to hell. Has this a tendency to induce in him a disinterested submission to and love for God? No, directly the contrary. It condenses his selfishness into fiercer opposition. But how different the manifestation of love in the Atonement! It is, as Paul says in Rom. 12:20, "Therefore if thine enemy hunger, feed him; if he thirst, give him drink; for in so doing, thou shalt heap coals of fire on his head." If you meet your enemy, you may scold and threaten to shoot him; while you upbraid him, he may blush; while you threaten, he may tremble; but he will not love. We know by our consciousness the influence of such a course. But if we manifest benevolence toward him, we heap coals of fire on his head. We change him into a friend. So, when the sinner sees God all love instead of frowns, with what a magic power it wilts him! While he sees only the signs of wrath, he stands as unbending as a marble pillar, and if he weeps, his tears are the tears of a rock. But as the Spirit shows him the things of Christ, he is instantly embraced—his stubborn knees bow, his heart breaks, and he lies flat, subdued at the foot of the cross. Such is the work of the Spirit.

IV. *The consistency and cooperation of divine and human agency in the work.*

1. We are conscious of being active in every step of the work. The Spirit does not first convert men, and they then become ac-

tive. We are conscious that we are perfectly active all along, every step of the way—just as much in business or anything else in the world.

2. The Spirit is employed not to suspend or set aside our own voluntary agency, but to secure the right direction and use of it. He could not make us holy and save us without our own agency, for *holiness consists in right voluntary action.* To talk of being made holy passively is to talk stark nonsense. The thing is impossible.

3. We need the Holy Spirit to free us from the snare of the devil. Otherwise, we confine ourselves to the influence of selfish motives, despite our freedom and responsibility. The Spirit works in us *to will* and *to do*, of course, since willing necessitates doing. He addresses himself to the work of influencing the will, because that is just the place to begin. All the actions we perform which are good are truly ours, but, the agent who persuades us to them is the Holy Spirit. He wisely charms our wills into conformity to the will of God.

REMARKS

1. In all this work, we are conscious only of the influence of truth as the Spirit presents not himself to our view, but the truth. We are conscious of *perceiving*, and *acting*, and *feeling* in view of the truth, but of nothing else.

2. See the error of those who are expecting and waiting for a physical change and a physical sanctification. A great multitude of impenitent persons are waiting to be passively converted, and those who profess religion encourage them in it. They are also waiting to be sanctified in a similar way. Although this notion has been prevalent and its sway in the church extensive, I do not hesitate to say that there is nothing more absurd and unsupported by the Bible. It is a superstitious notion—as though the divine influence were like an electric shock, or some such influence. It is to overlook the very nature of religion and of the Spirit's influences, and has ruined thousands, and, I may say, millions of souls.

3. Whenever we find our attention drawn to the consideration of spiritual things, we may know that the Spirit is at work with

us, and we should conduct ourselves accordingly. If a sinner knows that the Spirit strives with him, the way is easy. Does truth seem to have a stronger influence than formerly? Do solemn influences come in upon the mind from abroad? It must be the work of the Spirit. Walk softly lest you grieve Him away.

4. The truths of the Bible never influence us *inwardly* unless they are revealed to us individually and driven home to us by the Spirit. I have feared a great many overlook this. They read the Bible as they would a catechism or lesson, and often wholly overlook its real import. They must have the Spirit to make it plain to them. They never seem to have a passage brought home to them by the Spirit. But to read the Bible this way does them no good, but infinite hurt—the mind hardens under it, and this is the reason so many read it without finding its spirit. The truth is, it is not enough that it has been revealed to Isaiah and Paul—it was never meant to be a rule of life as a mere outward thing; you might as well have it on tables of stone; it is a mere savor of death unto death unless it is so revealed to you as to be spirit and life. You must be taught what its meaning is by the Spirit of God. What Christian does not know this is true in his own consciousness?

You have sometimes read a hundred passages, and they seemed to do you no good. No, it seemed as though you could find nothing to suit you in a whole volume of promises. But eventually God makes one come home to you like electric fire. It sets you all in a glow and becomes food for many days. It serves also as a key to many other deep things of God. We observe the same thing in the biographies of distinguished Christians. How often we hear them talk about the Spirit giving them the meaning of a passage. They had read it before a hundred times, and it seemed to possess no special meaning—they had only an outside view of it. But suddenly they saw in it a profoundness of meaning they had never conceived; it is as light from heaven.

5. We have power to resist the Spirit. The will has the command of the attention, and if, when the Spirit presents truth, the will averts the attention and continues to do so, the Spirit might present it forever and it would do no good. Hence we are commanded not "to resist"—not "to grieve" the Holy Spirit, and to "work out [our] salvation with fear and trembling, for it is God

which worketh in [us] both to will and to do of his good pleasure"
(Phil. 2:12, 13).

6. Objects of sense, habits, the world, the flesh and Satan
render divine influence constantly indispensable.

7. See the vast patience, painstaking, compassion, perseverance and love of the Holy Spirit. I shall never forget the impression made on me by the thought that entered my mind once
when reflecting on the work of the Spirit. I asked myself how long
it had been since I was converted, and what the Spirit had done
for me during all that time. I could testify that during all that
time, through all my provocations, He had faithfully continued
to strive, to lead and guide me until that moment, in His work of
love. Oh, how could I ever grieve Him again!

8. How greatly our ingratitude must grieve Him. I have been
afraid Christians do not think enough of their indebtedness to
the Spirit. They often seem to regard the Savior with great consideration, the Father with less, and the Spirit with none at all,
or but little; whereas all the persons of the Trinity are equally interested and engaged for our salvation, and have equal claims to
our gratitude. The Father gave the Son, the Son made the Atonement, and the Spirit secures our acceptance of it.

9. See what Rom. 5:6 means: "For when we were yet without
strength, in due time Christ died for the ungodly." Without the
Atonement, the Holy Spirit could not sanctify us for lack of motives adapted to slay our selfishness. But the Atonement gives
Him that power over us.

10. God is often employed in influencing the decisions of our
will when we are not at all aware of it. How often men find themselves having arrived at thoughts and made up decisions for
which they cannot account to save their lives. This is often the
case with even impenitent sinners. Perhaps some of you can remember instances of decisions which saved your life. I can remember such instances in my own history. It would be extremely
interesting to gather up facts on this point. We would doubtless
find many wonderful things coming to light respecting the inter-
vention of the Spirit.

11. The Spirit is always in His people, but often His inward,
gentle teachings and whisperings are drowned in the dim of outward objects. He loves to lead the mind in His own straight way

by gently breathing His influences upon the soul. But oftentimes the mind is in such great excitement and bustle that it cannot hear Him speaking in his own inward sanctuary.

12. The mind is often diverted from His teachings by the teachings of those who are not under His influence. I have often heard people say that they had a sweet time in their closet on the Sabbath morn, but after attending the service, had found it all dissipated. The teachings they heard there conflicted with those of the Spirit of God, and they grieved Him by giving it their attention.

13. Excitement, measures, and talk often quench His influences. When persons give themselves up to much talk, there is little inward communion; and when there is so much to promote religion by outward means, the mind grows poor and lean and takes up with the deception and show of outward religion.

14. See the importance of having the inward ear open, and of understanding that the senses are not to be confused with the outward organs of sense. The ear is not a sense but the organ of the sense of hearing. It is no more to be confused with the sense than is the trumpet you hold to the ear. So the eye, the bodily organ of sense, is no more the sense itself than are your spectacles. The glasses do not see, nor does the eye, but the sense of sight sees through them. Hence, you can keep your senses awake and active while you dispense with the outward organs. Why do you shut your eyes when you pray? To prevent your attention from being diverted from God. In like manner you can close your outward ear so that you may hear God speak. Did it never seem to you as if you actually heard Him speak—sometimes speaking a Bible passage? I recall a time, a number of years ago, when the Lord showed me His glory. His presence appeared so vividly that I never suspected, at the time, that I did not see His glory with bodily eyes. Soon after I was converted, I would go before, or at the break of day, to get brethren up to pray (and I may say that was the first morning prayer meeting I had ever heard of). One morning I could not get them up; I felt distressed, and in my agony was going away to pray. All at once the glory of God blazed around me, and it seemed as if all nature praised the Lord, and none but men looked down and were mute. I wondered that they could not see. It seemed to have been some such view that Paul

had when he could not tell whether he was in the body or out of it. When persons experience this, it seems more than a figure of speech to talk of seeing God; but if you want to see Him, you must let the inward senses be awake to the influence of the Spirit.*

15. See how the soul is sanctified by the Spirit and by belief of the truth. When the Spirit presents the truth, you must believe it. Sanctification is, and must be, by faith.

16. See the importance of understanding the necessity of divine influence? The reason is that the mind has so wrapped itself within selfish influences that the Spirit alone can break the spell that binds it. Its greatness is evident by the same reason.

17. The necessity for the Spirit's influence is our sin; and hence, His influence never ought to be brought up as an excuse for our obedience or disobedience.

18. All the holiness on earth is induced by the Spirit.

19. If you grieve away the Spirit you are lost. Nothing else in the universe can save you.

20. See what it is to be led by the Spirit? It is to yield to His influences.

21. How amazingly careless many persons are in disregarding the influences of the Spirit. Until you are more careful how you talk and act, you will never know what it is to be taught of the Spirit. There is a man who would not grieve his wife for any consideration, but will daily grieve the blessed Spirit. The Spirit stands far from such a man, knowing it will do no good to mediate. Poor man! If He continues to grieve the Spirit, he will soon do it once too often and never be forgiven.

---

*See the accounts in *Answers to Prayer*, chapters 2-6.

12

FULLNESS THERE IS IN CHRIST*

Colossians 2:9, 10

"For in him dwelleth all the fulness of the Godhead bodily. And ye are complete in him, which is the head of all principality and power."

The connection in which this text stands shows that the Apostle is laboring to establish the distinction between an outward legal religion, and religion by faith in Christ. For this purpose, he warns them in verse 8 to "beware lest any man spoil you through philosophy and vain deceit, after the tradition of men, after the rudiments of the world, and not after Christ." And in verses 20-23, by an earnest and solemn appeal, he strives to tear them away from "subjection to ordinances . . . after the commandments and doctrines of men." Indeed, the main purpose of the whole epistle was to secure the Colossians in the religion of faith, and cut them off from legalism.

In the present discussion it is my design to show:

    I. *What is not intended by the declaration that Christians are complete in Christ.*

    II. *What is intended.*

    III. *Some things which are demanded by our nature, cir-*

Ibid., No. 14, July 5, 1843.

cumstances, and character in order to complete well-being.

IV. *The conditions on which this completeness may be realized in our own experience.*

I. *What is not intended by the declaration that Christians are complete in Christ.*

1. When it is said we are complete in Him, it is not intended that we are complete in the sense of an imputed righteousness. You will recall I labored to show that the doctrine of imputation is an absurd and a dangerous dogma. It is not necessary here to dwell on that point again. It is enough to say that God could no more perform works beyond obligation than any other moral being, and that therefore there could be no righteousness to impute. Moreover, a transfer of moral character is naturally impossible.

2. It is not intended that all Christians have, as a matter of fact, so received Christ as to realize this completeness in their own character and experience; nor is it asserted in the text that anybody ever did or ever will.

II. *What is intended.*

It is intended that in Him all the demands of our being are met—that a full provision is made and set forth by God to meet all our wants, to make us all that God desires we should be.

III. *Some things which are demanded by our nature, circumstances, and character in order to complete well-being.*

The question is, "What do men really need—what must the Savior have in order to be the Savior we need?"

1. Our nature and circumstances expose us to innumerable trials and temptations. I have dwelled primarily in these lectures on the trials arising from our peculiar nature in the circumstances in which we are placed. None are exempt from them. Even in the garden of Eden, man's nature and circumstances occasioned trial. This, on the whole, is not to be regretted. Such trials are to our advantage if we use the help afforded us in meeting them. They "worketh for us a far more exceeding and eternal weight of glory" (1 Cor. 4:17). But as a matter of fact, the circumstances are such, and men have so abused their nature, that the

trials which they endure are extremely great, and the help which they need must be both adapted and adequate to meet all their wants in this respect.

2. Our frailties and infirmities are great, in consequence of our long abuse of ourselves. All the appetites and passions are greatly aggravated in their demands—the nervous system rasped up to the highest pitch, the habits inveterate. Each successive generation is placed under some additional weakness, until like the reed, man is liable to be swayed by every breeze, or carried adrift on the ocean of life like a vessel torn from its moorings and driven by a tempest. Hence, we need strength for our frailty, and grace sufficient for our infirmity.

3. Our ignorance is very great, and since men are influenced by motives, they can be influenced toward God and holiness only in proportion as they are enlightened. The motives to sin are bold and obtrusive and seen by the ignorant, but the reverse is true of motives to holiness. Hence, men must have a Savior able to enlighten and charm them away from the influence of things seen and temporal, and bring them under the influence of things unseen and eternal.

The longer I live, the more I am astonished at the ignorance of men in reference to religious truths. Even Christians scarcely know their ABC's. Very few of them are able to give any good reason for the doctrines of their faith. Hence, the great mass readily receive dogmas published by the press and promulgated from the pulpit, which, to thinking minds, are palpably at war with human reason. Take, for example, the doctrine of imputed righteousness. Is it not astonishing that it was not at once seen that there can be no work which is beyond obligation and of course no righteousness to be imputed? What more could God do than benevolence demanded of Him? The Atonement and all His other works are virtuous only because they are carrying out the law of benevolence. Jesus Christ was bound to be benevolent as much as any other being, and of course His righteousness could no more be imputed than that of any other holy moral agent—no more than Gabriel's.

Now, how does it happen, how can it be that men should believe such an absurd dogma as this unless from sheer ignorance? Why, the whole gospel is another gospel if this doctrine be true. It was Christ's object to save men from their sins, and not to throw over their filthy, ulcerated backs a robe of imputed righteousness. I call it ignorance to hold such a dogma, because an intelligent being understanding it, and the objections to it, can't believe it. And this is but a specimen of many other things equally gross which are sanctified in the creeds and common faith of the mass of the church. It is full of superstition, errors, and ignorance or a thousand subjects. The Reformation cast off many, but many were left, some of which time has outgrown, and others it has not. We only get right by getting an insight into the gospel.

It is truth coming in that thrusts error out, and we therefore need somebody to deliver us, to teach us the very ABC's of religion. We want some patient instructor who will be willing to teach us over and over even the same things. "What's that?" "A." "What's that?" "B." Now go back to *A* again, and ask, "What's that?" "I don't know," says the pupil. "Well," says the kindhearted teacher, "that's A," and thus, again and again, until he remembers it. Thus Christians need to be instructed by some kind agent who will not tear their souls and sternly frown them away, but who will soothe them into love, and then gently remove their errors, and engraft the word of truth.

4. We have a subtle adversary of great power and malignity. It has become unpopular to say much about the devil; people have become so incredulous respecting his existence. This state of things is doubtless the result of his dark agency, since, if men doubt his existence, they will the more readily become his prey. But the Bible holds other language. It requires men to pass the time of their sojourning here with fear—"to be sober, be vigilant; because our adversary the devil, as a roaring lion, walketh about, seeking whom he may devour" (1 Pet. 5:8). It represents him as possessing great subtlety, and being ready to take ten thousand advantages, even turning himself into an angel of light to delude and destroy souls. And what man is able to resist him—to detect all the villanies and subtleties of a mind as old and malevolent as his? I have often felt that the devil would just as certainly have my soul, in spite of all my endeavors against him, if Christ did not save me as I existed.

Who has not found that sometimes the devil has made a lie appear so much like truth that we would be ready to take an oath it was truth. No doubt, ten thousand times persons have thought the Lord was leading them, when in fact, it was the devil who had involved them in a web of lies and deceptions and was hurrying them on to the precipice of ruin. A man who does not know these things will never make much effort to get away from him. From him? From thousands of them—all leagued to destroy. Who can protect us? Our Christian journey lies all the way through an enemy's country, with throngs of devils prowling about on all sides, and if the Lord does not deliver us, the devil will have all of us.

5. Our education, habits, and prejudices all give him a decided advantage over us. He has been weaving his web of villanies and lies for thousands of years, and with all his profound experience, great mental capacity, and legions of comrades, he is able to weave his devilish plots into everything. You cannot have a benevolent society but what he must have a hand in it—even if you are starting a Bible society, his counsel and agency must have a place. He has a corner at every missionary meeting and carefully watches its workings. Anyone who will look narrowly into those projects which are supposed to be the most benevolent can hardly fail to see that the devil has a hand in them, and is exercising his diabolical craft to pervert them to evil.

If I had time to take up the habits, opinions, etc., of society generally, I could show snares and pitfalls and ambushes arranged with wonderful subtlety and adaptation, and awfully effective for the ruin of mankind. These are not less manifest in family and even individual relations, and at all peculiar crises of life, taking advantage of habits, education and susceptibilities to work out the endless overthrow of men.

Again, I ask, how can we escape him? Who can deliver us? We need one wiser and mightier than he to defeat him and to effect our escape.

6. We need a propitiation for our sins who will render it consistent for God to pardon us. What is the reason that the governor of this state felt a difficulty in pardoning a well-known criminal? Because he feared the influence it would have to loosen the bands of society. It was not done with an unwillingness to gratify him nor a desire to gratify any malevolent feelings; it was done to prevent the strengthening of the bands of wickedness. So it is in the government of God. Pardon must be extended to sinners only on

grounds that will not impair but uphold the influence of the government. Something must be done to propitiate, as the gospel calls it—there must be an atonement, or sin could not be forgiven without the greatest danger to the public interests, and God could not be just in exercising pardon. There must then be a Savior who could make an atonement and thus meet this necessity.

7. We need an influence that can break our hearts and bring us to repentance—not only to atone for, but to reclaim us. That is a very slim gospel, which merely pardons men and then leaves them to achieve their own victories over the world, the flesh and the devil. It would never save any man. We need a gospel which will come to us where we are, break up the deep foundations of our selfishness, and transform us to love.

8. Not only do we need thus to be initiated into the spirit of the gospel, but we need to be kept all along the way to glory. We need a Savior who will watch over us until He gets us within the sacred enclosure. Should He forsake us, even at heaven's golden gate, we should turn away and go back to hell. We must be placed safely within to be secure.

9. But in order thus to keep us, He must possess such surpassing loveliness, and radiate such charms, as to draw away the soul from all other fascinations and lovers. He must be able, as it were, to make us sick of love, so that we would follow Him through any trials and all seductive influences, unattracted by any of them from our steadfast devotion to His love. We need somebody to *draw* us. If God should flash His livid lightnings and hurl His blazing thunderbolts upon us, and if He should roll up into our faces the lurid fires of perdition, it might amaze and horrify us, but it would do us no good—it would not *draw* us to Him—it would not call out our love. When Elijah passed by Elisha, he cast his mantle upon him, and forthwith, Elisha left the oxen and all and went after Elijah. I have often thought it seemed to charm him. So also, Christ, as He passes by a soul, seems, shall I say, so to captivate it that it would seem as if He could lead it even through hell. I do not know but He could. If circumstances demand the sacrifice, it would kiss His cross and say, "Drive your nails and crucify me. I willingly endure it for Christ's sake, who loved me and gave himself for me." Oh, we do not want a legal Savior, but one "in [whom] dwelleth all the fulness of the

Godhead bodily," in whom we are complete, whose beauties can ravish and enchain our hearts. What is a Unitarian Savior good for? Pooh! We do not need such, but we need one who can so captivate us that if a thousand racks* and gallows stood in the way, they would not deter us from following Him wherever He would go.

10. In short, we need a Savior able and willing to *save* us, not only in eternity but here in this world. We need Him daily, and unless we have such a one, we must constantly wallow in the gutters of iniquity and its consequent misery. We need our every want met and our souls made complete in all the will of God—to be filled with His fullness.

IV. *The conditions on which this completeness may be realized in our own experience.*

1. One condition is a realization of our necessities. The Lord Jesus Christ said to one of the churches of Asia, "Because thou sayest, I am rich, and increased with goods, and have need of nothing; and knowest not that thou art wretched and miserable, and poor, and blind, and naked: I counsel thee to buy of me gold tried in the fire, that thou mayest be rich; and white raiment that thou mayest be clothed, and that the shame of thy nakedness do not appear; and anoint thine eyes with eyesalve, that thou mayest see" (Rev. 3:17, 18). One grand defect in the way of people is that they are so full in themselves and so increased in goods in their own estimation that they fail wholly to discover that they are in need of Christ in all things—that their necessities are as vast as the wants of their whole being. They must realize this.

2. Another condition is, we must realize that in Him we have all we need. Now, people often admit this in words but not in fact. They often think there is something so peculiar in their case, in their habits, education, relations, or trials, that Christ cannot save *them*. They seem to think Christ can save everybody else but them. But they must understand that they are complete in Him whatever their relations, trials, habits and circumstances. They must realize this.

---

*An instrument of torture that stretches the body.

3. Another condition is the renunciation of self-dependence in all respects. A man must not depend on his learning, his own philosophical insight, or anything else, or he will never depend on Christ. He must become a fool that he may be wise. Just as far as he thinks he can get along without Christ, he will get along without Him, but it will be away from God. When an individual has so much self-dependence, he really has not faith in the existence of God, nor in His attributes. Self-dependence is allied to infidelity. "Every good and every perfect gift is from above, and cometh down from the Father of lights" (James 1:17). If God withheld from us that for which we are dependent on Him, nothing but certain destruction would ensue. This dependence runs through all moral as well as natural life, and it must be felt and acknowledged.

4. You must despair of finding help anywhere else. While a man runs to anybody and everybody and puts more confidence in men than in God, he may go to the best man on earth, to an apostle, or an angel, and it will avail him nothing. He might as well go to a child, as far as any efficient help is concerned. I have told sinners sometimes, "I won't pray for you, nor have anything to do with you, if you are going to depend on me and put me in the place of the Savior. Away with you to Christ if you want help." Some of the last years that I labored as an evangelist, the church depended on me so much that it cost me more effort to get them to look to God than to perform the requisite labor to convert sinners, and it is so now. I was afraid to come here on this account, and feel now, brethren, that you have depended on me more than you have any right to. God abhors a particular type of trusting in an arm of flesh. Many will flee to books, to anything, and sometimes even to the Bible, putting it in the place of God and cleaving to such vain help until God compels them to look to himself alone.

5. You must cease to rest in *means* of any kind, I do not mean that we must cease to use means as means, but they are not to be put in the place of God, or substituted for a Savior. I wish I could impress on you how much those who profess religion, all men, trust means more than God, and put them in the place of Christ. You must cease from this entirely if you wish for completeness in Him.

6. You must give up your cowardly unbelief and dare to trust Christ wholly. Do you know that unbelief is a form of cowardice? I try sometimes to make people see that they *dare not* trust Him, and to show them that they must have more courage or they never can be complete in Christ. Lean bravely on Him if you would be filled with His love.

7. You must give up your love of reputation with men. When you really come to Christ, you will see what Christ meant when He said, "If they have called the master of the house Beelzebub, how much more shall they call them of his household?" (Matt. 10:25)."[They will] cast out your name as evil" (Luke 6:22). You must bear all this. Be content to hear them misrepresent you, impute evil motives, look contemptuously, slight your company, stare at you, to see if the dilation of the pupil of your eye does not indicate insanity. Expect this as certainly as you give yourselves up to be led by Him in all things. Do not worry about them. They need your pity more than your frown. They, poor souls, do not know what they do.

8. You must forsake all that you have. You must spare no passion, have no sinister end, but give up all, be crucified unto the world. I know this is a great step to take, but you must do it or die. You must thus reckon yourselves to be dead indeed unto sin in order to reckon yourself alive unto God, through Jesus Christ our Lord.

9. You must confide in Him for all you want and believe that you are *complete* in Him, not partly so. No matter what new want you discover, or into what new circumstances you come, believe that Christ has sufficient grace for every emergency, however great—otherwise He is not a full Savior to you.

REMARKS

1. See why Christians are so imperfect. It is because they don't realize their want, and do not take Him as a complete Savior.

2. They will remain imperfect while they know so little of Jesus. I was conversing with one of the principal men in the state on sanctification. He agreed with me in theory as to its attainability, and then said that as a matter of fact, nobody would real-

ize it in this world. I replied, if you knew what you ought to know about Jesus Christ, you would as soon cut off your right hand as say that. A lack of knowledge of Jesus leaves men in sin and makes them weak against it. I have often thought of the sons of Sceva the Jew, who attempted to cast out devils "in the name of Jesus, whom Paul preached," and when they had commanded an evil spirit to come out, he replied, "Jesus I know, and Paul I know, but who are ye? And the man in whom the evil spirit was leaped on them, and overcame them, and prevailed against them, so that they fled out of that house naked and wounded" (Acts 19:15, 16). They did not know Christ, and consequently experienced only defeat. Suppose they had told their experience afterwards, to prove that nobody ever did or could cast out devils? Ah! It is one thing to hear and read about Christ, and quite another to trust Him, know Him, and become complete in Him.

3. While they place so much reliance on human teaching and so little on divine teaching, they are likely to remain imperfect. Let them stand in that relation in which God has placed them, and both human and divine teaching profit the soul; but when men hear the minister or one another and depend on what he says more than on what God says by His Word and Spirit, it is fatal to a growth in divine things. As many as are led by the Spirit of God, they are the sons of God.

4. While men rest in the letter and overlook the spirit of the gospel, they will of course remain imperfect.

5. The same will be true as long as they put their works in the place of Christ, or their watchings, their resolutions, and legal efforts.

6. Also, while their guides and leaders are blind, and while the shepherds frighten away the sheep from their pastures, they will not know Christ as Savior.

7. Many who profess religion don't know Christ because, as it were, they have only been converted and baptized unto Moses. Others have received John's baptism unto repentance; and still others know Christ only as an atoning Savior. They began in the Spirit and are now trying to become perfect by the flesh.

8. Wherever there is an imperfection in Christian character, there must be ignorance or unbelief, for the text is a *promise* that covers the whole field of our necessities. It is remarkable how the

Bible abounds with promises both general and specific. Some cover our whole necessity; others point to specific wants. The specific promises seem to be given to satisfy our ignorance and infirmities so that our general confidence should stand in hours of trial; and yet to some minds, a general declaration implying a promise like that in the text, affords greater strength than any specific promise.

9. How few realize that if they are not complete in Him, it is because of unbelief. The truth is, it is because they have never known the exercise and power of faith.

10. Doubts respecting the doctrine of entire sanctification are unbelief, for it is impossible that anyone should doubt this who has implicit faith in what Christ says. If sufficient grace is promised, the doubts are unbelief.

11. Many deceive themselves by saying, "I believe the promise but I don't believe I shall fulfill the condition." The truth is, believing the promise is fulfilling the condition. How many nullify the promises in this way. They say they believe that the promise *would be* fulfilled if they complied with the condition, but this they know they do not do, and have no confidence that they will. And instead of blaming themselves for it, they really turn it into a virtue calling it *self-distrust*. Its real name is unbelief.

12. If Christ is the depositary of all we need, we see why we are commanded to "come boldly unto the throne of grace, that we may obtain mercy, and find grace to help in time of need" (Heb. 4:16). But true faith is almost universally regarded as presumption, and such boldness as exercised by Jacob, Moses, and others is exclaimed to be profane. How shocking that is, when as a matter of fact, it is presumption not to come boldly. It is disobedience to a divine requisition.

13. There is no real difficulty in the fact that the promises are conditioned on faith. For faith in the promise depends upon confidence in the general character of the promiser, and to doubt the promise is to impeach the character of him who made it. Suppose a man of great wealth and veracity should make a promise with this condition—confidence in him must be evident—as indeed every promise necessarily implies. Would there be any difficulty in the condition? Not the least. As long as we had confi-

dence in his character, we would regard it as absurd to make the condition of faith a difficulty. But, if the man was known, or supposed to be unable or unwilling, or that his general character was bad, then truly the condition would be a stumbling block. And to believe implicitly would be absurd and impossible.

14. It is impossible that unbelief should fail to make the soul wretched, or that faith should not bring it deep repose.

15. What a foundation we have for universal repose in Christ. He is a Savior who exactly and perfectly meets our case and necessities as they are. "In him dwells all the fulness of the Godhead bodily." Oh, how important that we should know Him—that our acquaintance with Him should be full! We need a more thorough acquaintance with Christ than with anybody else. There is such a thing as knowing more of Jesus, as having a more intimate acquaintance with Him than that which exists between a husband and wife, or the dearest friends. Whoever is ignorant of that is ignorant of the very marrow and fatness of the gospel. A personal acquaintance removes our filth and makes us clean. James Brainard Taylor exclaimed: *"I am clean!"** Brethren, are you clean? Are you complete in Christ? Let us go to Him and receive His fullness until we are "filled with all the fulness of God."

---

*See the *Memoir of James Brainard Taylor* by John Holt Rice and Benjamin Holt Rice (New York: The American Tract Society, 1833).

13

JUSTIFICATION*

Romans 8:1

"There is therefore now no condemnation to them which are in Christ Jesus, who walk not after the flesh but after the Spirit."

In this discussion, I shall notice:

    I. *What it is to be in Christ Jesus.*
   II. *What is intended by no condemnation.*
  III. *Why there is no condemnation to them who are in Christ Jesus.*
  IV. *What is intended by not walking after the flesh, but after the Spirit.*
   V. *None except those who walk after the Spirit are in a justified state.*

I. *What it is to be in Christ Jesus.*

Four answers have been given to this question, three of which I will briefly consider, and then I will give what I suppose to be the true one.

1. The first answer is the doctrine of eternal justification by

---

*Ibid., No. 15, July 19, 1843. This chapter is also found in *Principles of Liberty,* pp. 87-96. It is included here because it is an integral part of Finney's series: "Holiness of Christians in the Present Life."

imputed righteousness. The doctrine states that a certain number were unconditionally chosen from all eternity, to whom Christ became Covenant Head, in such a sense that they are eternally justified. This gross and absurd notion is now exploded and generally rejected.

2. The second answer is that of perpetual justification by one act of faith. The doctrine states that the first act of faith brings the soul into such a relation to God that never afterwards will it be condemned or exposed to the penalty of the law, whatever sins it may commit. The simple idea is that the penalty of the law is wholly set aside in regard to Christians.

(1) Respecting this, the first remark I make is, justification is of two kinds, legal and gospel. Legal justification consists in pronouncing a moral agent innocent of all violation of the claims of the law so that he has no charge against him. Gospel justification consists in pardoning a sinner for whatever transgressions he may have committed—in arresting or setting aside the execution of the penalty which he has incurred.

(2) Legal justification is out of the question, since all the world has become guilty before God. And to maintain that a soul is perpetually justified by once believing is antinomianism, and one of the worst forms of error. It is to maintain that with respect to Christians the law of God is abrogated. The law is made up of precept and penalty; if either is detached, it ceases to be law. It matters not whether one insists that the precept be set aside, or the penalty; it is to maintain an abrogation of the law, and is a ruinous error. It is the nature of a pardon to set aside the execution of the penalty due to past violations of the law, and to restore the person to governmental favor during good behavior. It cannot do more than this without giving an indulgence to sin. If no future sins can merit their penalty, it follows that the Christian would not be in danger of hell no matter how many or how gross the sins he might commit—or even if he should die in a state of the foulest apostasy. What an abomination is such a doctrine!

(3) This doctrine cannot be true, for no being can prevent condemnation where there is sin. I said in a former lecture that the law is not founded in the arbitrary will of God, but in the nature and relations of moral beings. Whatever penalty is due to

any act of sin, is due, therefore, from the nature of the case, so that every act of sin subjects the sinner to the penalty. Pardon cannot then be prospective—sin cannot be forgiven in advance, and to maintain that it is, is to make Christ the minister of sin.

(4) Again, if Christians are not condemned when they sin, they cannot be forgiven, for forgiveness is nothing else than setting aside the penalty. And therefore, if they are not condemned, they cannot properly pray for forgiveness. In fact, it is unbelief in them to do so. What else can it be, when the sin, whatever the size, has not exposed its perpetrator at all to the penalty of God's law?

(5) This notion cannot be true, because the Bible uniformly makes perseverance in holiness, that is in *obedience*, just as much a condition of final acceptance with God as repentance or one act of faith. For my part, I must say, I don't know where the Bible makes salvation depend on one act of faith. Those who hold this dogma ought to tell us where it is taught.

(6) The Bible, to the contrary, expressly declares, "When a righteous man turneth away from his righteousness, and committeth iniquities, and dieth in them; for his iniquity that he hath done, shall he die" (Ezek. 18:26). What can be more distinct or explicit than this declaration? I know not how it has been overlooked or can be evaded.

(7) If this doctrine were true, it would follow that if Christians are not condemned for one sin, they would not be for ten thousand, and that the greatest apostates could be saved without repentance. But what kind of a gospel is that? It would overthrow the entire government of God. A pretty gospel! Strange kind of good news!

(8) Moreover, as I have said before, if the penalty is abolished with respect to believers, then the law must be. To them, its precept ceases to be anything other than simple advice which they may do as they please about adopting or obeying.

(9) Finally, every Christian's experience condemns perpetual justification. Who of them does not feel condemned when he sins? Now, he either is condemned when his conscience affirms that he is, or his conscience is at opposition to the government of God—affirming what is not true. And when under its rebukes, persons yield and go and ask pardon, they are guilty of disbelief

in their doctrine, and thus add one sin to another. The truth is, every Christian's conscience condemns the doctrine, and it obviously is evil, and only evil, and is evil continually in its whole tendency.

3. The third answer is that there will be no final condemnation. Without saying anything about the truth or falsity of that doctrine here, I remark that the text says no such thing. It says, "There is *now* no condemnation." With this Rom. 5:1 agrees. "Therefore, being justified by faith, we have peace with God, through our Lord Jesus Christ." Indeed, this is the general representation of the Bible.

4. The fourth answer which has been given is this: "To be in Christ is to have a personal, living faith in Him—it is to abide in Him by a living faith." John 15:4-7: "Abide in me, and I in you. As the branch cannot bear fruit of itself, except it abide in the vine, no more can ye, except ye abide in me. I am the vine, ye are the branches. He that abideth in me, and I in him, the same bringeth forth much fruit: for without me ye can do nothing. If a man abide not in me, he is cast forth as a branch, and is withered; and men gather them, and cast them into the fire, and they are burned. If ye abide in me, and my words abide in you, ye shall ask what ye will, and it shall be done unto you." 1 John 3:5, 6: "And ye know that he was manifested to take away our sins; and in him is no sin. Whosoever abideth in him sinneth not: whosoever sinneth hath not seen him, neither known him." 2 Cor. 5:17: "Therefore if any man be in Christ, he is a new creature: old things are passed away; behold, all things are become new." I might quote many other passages, all setting forth that there is no condemnation to those whose faith secures in them an actual conformity to the divine will. To all others, there is condemnation.

To be in Christ is to be under His influence so as not to walk after the flesh but after the Spirit—to receive constant divine influence from Him, as the branches derive nourishment from the vine. This intimate connection with Christ, and spiritual subjection to His control, are fully taught in many passages in the Bible. Gal. 2:20: "I am crucified with Christ: nevertheless I live; yet not I, but Christ liveth in me: and the life which I now live in the flesh I live by the faith of the Son of God, who loved me, and gave himself for me." And Gal. 5:16-25: "This I say then, Walk in the Spirit, and ye shall not fulfil the lust of the flesh. For the flesh lusteth against the Spirit, and the Spirit against the flesh: and these are contrary, the one to the other: so that ye cannot do the things that ye would. But if ye be led by the Spirit, ye are not under the law. Now the works of the flesh are manifest, which are these: Adultery, fornication, uncleanness, lasciviousness, idolatry, witchcraft, hatred, variance, emulations, wrath, strife, seditions, heresies, envyings, murders, drunkenness, revellings, and such like: of the which I tell you before, as I have also told you in times past, that they which do such things, shall not inherit the kingdom of God. But the fruit of the Spirit is love, joy, peace, longsuffering, gentleness, goodness, faith, meekness, temperance: against such there is no law. And they that are Christ's have crucified the flesh with the affections and lusts. If we live in the Spirit, let us also walk in the Spirit."

II. *What is intended by no condemnation.*

1. *To be condemned* is to be under sentence of law. Those who are condemned *are not only unpardoned for the past, but also for their present state of mind.* They are not justified on the ground of either law or gospel, but the whole penalty due to all their iniquity is out against them.

When it is said that there is no condemnation, it is not intended that they never were condemned, but that *their past sin is all pardoned.* They are wholly delivered from exposure to the penalty due to their sins. In addition to this, it is intended that *in their present state of mind they obey the law so that the law does not condemn their present state.* It does not mean that they will not be again condemned if they sin, but that *while they are in Christ Jesus they are free from all present condemnation.*

III. *Why there is no condemnation to them who are in Christ Jesus.*

1. Not because they are of the elect and eternally justified.

2. Not because Christ's righteousness is so imputed that we can sin without incurring exposure to the penalty of the law.

3. Not because we are perpetually justified by one act of faith. This, as we have attempted to show, is an antinomian and dangerous error.

4. Not because God accepts an imperfect obedience. There is a general opinion abroad, that somehow or other, God accepts an imperfect obedience as genuine. Now it seems to me that this is a very erroneous view of the subject. The truth is that God has no option about this matter any more than any other being; for the law exists and makes its demands wholly independently of His will and whatever it demands. The law demands whatever the nature and relations of moral beings demand and that, as moral governor, He is bound to enforce and nothing else. Now what is there in reason or the Bible to sanction the idea that God will, or can, accept an imperfect obedience? The Bible insists on our serving Him with the whole heart—on our being perfectly benevolent—and proposes no lower standard. Nor could we believe it if it did. What kind of obedience is half or imperfect obedience? No one can tell; consequently, no one can intentionally render it. The very idea is absurd.

5. But to him that is in Christ Jesus, there is *now* no condemnation because he *is* in Christ Jesus in the sense above explained. Christ does not shield him from the penalty while he continues to violate the precept, but He saves him from sin, and thus, from the penalty. The text says, "To those who walk not after the flesh, but after the Spirit." Now mark the result; let us read. In the seventh chapter, he spoke of a law in his members which brought him into captivity to sin and death—that is, under condemnation. Now he says (8:2-4): "For the law of the Spirit of life in Christ Jesus hath made me free from the law of sin and death. For what the law could not do, in that it was weak through the flesh, God sending his own Son in the likeness of sinful flesh, and for sin, condemned sin in the flesh: that the righteousness of the law might be fulfilled in us, who walk not after the flesh, but after the Spirit." Here he asserts that the reason God sent His own Son in the likeness of sinful flesh, and for sin, condemned sin in the flesh was "that the righteousness of the law might be fulfilled in us, who walk not after the flesh, but after the Spirit." Now, public justice having been satisfied by the Atonement, the heart being brought into conformity to the law, there is a good reason why they should be pardoned. The same thing is meant by "writing the law in the heart."

6. Again, there is no condemnation to him who is in Christ Jesus, because he "walks not after the flesh." This same thought

is contained in Gal. 5:16-24: "This I say then, Walk in the Spirit, and ye shall not fulfil the lust of the flesh. For the flesh lusteth against the Spirit, and the Spirit against the flesh: and these are contrary, the one to the other: so that ye cannot do the things that ye would. But if ye be led by the Spirit, ye are not under the law. Now the works of the flesh are manifest, which are these: Adultery, fornication, uncleanness, lasciviousness, idolatry, witchcraft, hatred, variance, emulations, wrath, strife, sedition, heresies, envyings, murders, drunkenness, revellings, and such like: of the which I tell you before, as I have also told you in time past, that they which do such things shall not inherit the kingdom of God. But the fruit of the Spirit is love, joy, peace, longsuffering, gentleness, goodness, faith, meekness, temperance: against such there is no law. And they that are Christ's have crucified the flesh with the affections and lusts." Here the fruit of the Spirit is just what the law requires; therefore, there can be no condemnation.

7. This assertion must either mean that when we are in Christ we do not sin, or that in Him we can sin without condemnation. Now, what does it mean? It cannot mean the last, for that would make Christ the minister of sin. No individual can sin without breaking the law, for sin is the transgression of the law. The first, then, must be the meaning and this agrees with what the Scriptures teach: "Without [holiness] no man shall see the Lord" (Heb. 12:14). The reason, then, there is no condemnation to them who *are in* Christ Jesus is that:

(1) In Christ their former sins are pardoned on the ground of His Atonement.

(2) While in Him they do not sin. He saves them from their sins, and therefore, from condemnation.

IV. *What is intended by not walking after the flesh, but after the Spirit.*

1. By the flesh is meant the appetites, desires, and propensities of the sensibility. To walk after the flesh is to indulge these—to give up the will to self-gratification. It is to be in bondage to the propensities so that they master and govern us. It is to be selfish.

2. But to walk after the Spirit is to obey the Spirit of Christ—it is to obey the law of God.

V. *None except those who walk after the Spirit are in a justi-fied state.*

1. By this I do not intend to say that they never were justi-fied. For it is true that individuals who once obeyed, and were of course justified, have fallen. This is the case with the angels, who did not keep their first estate, and with Adam and Eve. These were justified in the legal sense before they sinned. But many have also fallen into grievous iniquity, who have once been justi-fied in the gospel sense.

2. I do not mean that they are in no sense Christians. In the common acceptation of the term, it is not limited to those who are in a state of actual conformity to the will of God, but applies to all who give credible evidence of having been converted. More-over, it is true of Christians that they sustain a peculiar relation to God, and the term does not indicate that they never sin or fall into condemnation, but that they sustain a certain relation to God which others do not.

3. But I do mean that no one can commit sin without condemna-tion. When a Christian sins, he is as truly condemned as anyone else, and he is no longer justified any more than he is obedient.

4. I mean that no one is justified or pardoned until he obeys the law or repents, which is the same thing. By the way, it is im-portant that all should understand that repentance is not *sorrow* for sin, but a real turning away from all sin to God. Now when any individual sins, he must be condemned until he repents or forsakes his sin. Many people talk about *always repenting*—that the best acts we ever perform need to be repented of, etc. This is all nonsense and nothing but nonsense. I say again that religion is no such thing as this, and to represent it so is to talk loosely. "The soul that sinneth, it shall die" (Ezek. 18:20). Repentance is a hearty and entire forsaking of sin and entrance upon obedience to God.

5. I mean that when one has truly repented, he is justified, and remains so just as long as he remains obedient, and no long-er. When he falls into sin, he is as much condemned as any other sinner, because he is a sinner.

6. I also mean that justification follows and does not precede sanctification as some have vainly imagined. I here use the term

sanctification, not in the high sense of permanent sanctification, but of entire consecration to God. It is not true that persons are justified before they forsake sin. They certainly could not be thus *legally* justified, and the *gospel* proffers no pardon until after repentance or hearty submission of the will to God. I add, that *Christians are justified no longer than they are sanctified, or obedient, and that complete permanent justification depends upon complete and permanent sanctification.*

REMARKS

1. I have often thought and could not help drawing the conclusion that the great mass of those who profess religion are mere antinomians living in the habitual commission of known sin and yet expecting to be saved. And when they are pressed up to holiness of heart, they say, "I am not expected to be perfect in this life. I expect Christ to make up for my deficiencies." Such religion is no better than universalism or infidelity. What is such a person doing? Why, indulging his appetites and propensities in various ways which he knows to be contrary to the divine will! Ask him about it and he will confess it—he will confess that this is his daily practice; yet he thinks he is justified. But if the Bible is true, he is not. "Know ye not, that to whom ye yield yourselves servants to obey, his servants ye are to whom ye obey; whether of sin unto death, or of obedience unto righteousness?" (Rom. 6:16). But he can tell of an "experience." Perhaps he wrote it all down lest he should forget it, and he tells it the hundredth time, how he felt when God pardoned his sins—while he is now living in sin every day. Perhaps he never tells of an "experience" at all, but yet rests back upon "something which he felt" when he imagined he was converted. Now this is nothing but antinomianism, and how astonishing it is that so many should cry out so vehemently about antinomianism when they are nothing but antinomians themselves. What a terrible delusion this is!

2. Men are justified by faith in Christ because they are sanctified by faith in Him. They do not have righteousness imputed to them, and thus stand justified by an arbitrary fiction, while they are personally unholy. But they are made righteous by faith, and that is the reason they are justified.

3. To talk about depending on Christ to be justified by Him while indulging in any form of known sin is to insult Him. It is to charge Him with being a minister of sin. Not long ago, a lady was talking with her minister about certain women who were given over to dress in the utmost style of extravagant fashion. He said he thought the most dressy people in his church were the best Christians. They were the most humble and dependent on Christ. That was his idea about religion. *What did he mean?* Why, that such persons did not pretend to be holy, but professed to depend wholly on Christ. They acknowledged themselves sinners. And well they might! But what kind of religion is that? And how did he get such a notion? How else but by supposing that persons are not expected to be holy in this life, and that they can be justified while living in sin? I would as soon expect a pirate whose hands are red with blood to be saved as those who profess religion who indulge in any form of sin, lust, pride, worldliness, or any other iniquity: "Do we then make void the law through faith? God forbid: yea, we establish the law" (Rom. 3:31). But what a state of things must it be when a minister can utter such sentiment as that?

4. Such an idea of justification is open to the infidel objection that the gospel is a system of immunity in sin. The Unitarians have stereotyped this objection against faith. Ask them why they say so. They answer, "Because the doctrine of justification by faith is injurious to good morals." Some years ago a circuit judge said, "I cannot admit the Bible to be true. It teaches that men are saved by faith, and I therefore regard the gospel as injurious to good morals, and as involving a principle that would ruin any government on earth." Now, did he get this idea from the Bible? No, but from the false representations made of the teachings of the Bible. It teaches no such thing, but plainly asserts that a faith that does not sanctify is a dead faith.

5. There are many who *hope* they are Christians yet live so their conscience condemns them. "For if our heart condemns us, God is greater than our heart, and knoweth all things" (1 John 3:20). Now to teach that persons may be justified while their conscience condemns them contradicts this passage. If our own conscience condemns us, God does. Shall He be less just than our own nature?

6. A great multitude of those who profess religion are merely careless sinners. Now do let me ask, "If from the way many persons live` in the church, compared with the way many careless sinners live, is it not perfectly manifest that they are in no wise different? And is it censorious to say that they are mere hardened sinners? What will become of them?"

7. Many who are accounted the most pious are only convicted sinners. It is a most remarkable thing, and one which I have taken great pains to observe, that many thought to be converted in the late revivals, are only convicted sinners or mere legalists. The preaching makes them so. The claims of the law are held up and obligation enforced to comply with it. They are told to trust Christ for pardon and they attempt it. Many really do, while others stop short with mere resolution. All this class will go back, or stay in the church, almost constantly distressed by the lashings of conscience. If you hold up the law, they are distressed; and if you hold up Christ, they are distressed by the consciousness that they do not exercise faith in Him. Hold up either and they have no rest. They are really convicted sinners, and yet they think this is religion. In time of coldness they always sink back, but in times of revival they are aroused and driven to the performance of a heartless service which continually fails to appease the demands of conscience. They know of no other experience than this. They refer you to Romans 7 to prove that this is Christian experience and thus bolster up their hope. I recall when I had preached some time ago against this as Christian experience, a minister said to me, "Well, brother Finney, I can't believe that." Why? "Because that's my experience, and I believe I am a Christian." A strange reason! I suppose it was his experience! Great multitudes have it and suppose it genuine. I fear, in some instances, whole churches are made up of such, and their ministers teach them that this is genuine religion. What would the minister just referred to say? "That is Paul's experience, and mine too." And the people often derive much comfort from what the minister says is his experience. Oh, what teaching is this? It is high time there was a change of mind in the church on this subject. Whoever has no experience but that of Romans 7 is not justified at all, and were it not that great multitudes are deluded, it could not be that so many could sit down contented under this view of the subject.

8. One who walks after the Spirit has this inward testimony that he pleases God. An individual may think he does, when he does not, just as persons in a dream may think themselves awake, but when they really awake, find it all a dream. Individuals may also think they please God when they do not, but it is nevertheless true that those who please God know it. "He that believeth on the Son of God hath the witness in himself" (1 John 5:10).

9. This view of the subject does not touch that of the final perseverance of the saints. What I am attempting to show is that:

(1) True believers are justified or pardoned, and treated as righteous, on account of the Atonement of Christ.

(2) Those who truly believe are justified because they are actually righteous. The question is not whether a Christian who has fallen into sin will die in that state, but whether if he does he will be damned—whether, while in sin he is justified.

10. Those who sin do not abide in Christ. "And ye know that he was manifested to take away our sins; and in him is no sin. Whosoever abideth in him sinneth not: whosoever sinneth hath not seen him, neither known him. Little children, let no man deceive you: he that doeth righteousness is righteous, even as he is righteous. He that committeth sin is of the devil; for the devil sinneth from the beginning. For this purpose the Son of God was manifested, that he might destroy the works of the devil. Whosoever is born of God doth not commit sin; for his seed remaineth in him: and he cannot sin because he is born of God" (1 John 3:5-9). While they abide in Christ, they are not condemned, but if they overlook what abiding in Christ is, they are sure to fall into sin; then they are condemned as a matter of course. The secret of holy living, and freedom from contamination, is to abide in Christ. Paul says, "I am crucified with Christ: nevertheless I live; yet not I, but Christ liveth in me: and the life which I now live in the flesh I live by the faith of the Son of God" (Gal. 2:20). We must have such confidence in Him as to let Him have entire control in all things.

11. Sinners can see how to be saved. They must believe in the Lord Jesus Christ with all their heart. They must become holy and walk after the Spirit.

12. Convicted persons who profess religion can also see what to do. Have you felt misgivings and a load on your conscience?

Are you never able to say, "I am justified—I am accepted in the beloved"? You must come to Christ *now*, if you now experience condemnation.

13. There is neither peace nor safety except in Christ, but in Him is all fullness and all we need. In Him you may come to God as children, with the utmost confidence.

14. If you are in Christ, you have peace of mind. How sweetly the experience of a Christian answers to this. Many of you perhaps can testify to this. You had been borne down with a burden too heavy, crying out, "O wretched man that I am! who shall deliver me from the body of this death?" (Rom. 7:24). But your faith took hold of Christ, and suddenly all your burden was gone. You could no longer feel condemned. The stains of sin all wiped out by the hand of grace. You can now look calmly at your sins, and not feel them grind like an iron yoke. Are you in this state? Can you testify from your own experience that there is *now* no condemnation to them that are in Christ Jesus? If so, you can reflect upon your past sins without being ground down into the dust under the guilty burden which rolls upon you. The instant you experience a freedom from condemnation, your whole soul yearns with benevolence for others. You know what their state is. Ah, yes, you know what it is to drink up your spirit, and when you find deliverance you must of course want to teach others what is the great salvation—to strengthen those that are weak. And an individual who can sit down at ease and not find His benevolence like fire shut up in his bones—who does not even feel agonized, not for himself, but for others, cannot have yet found that there is *now* no condemnation. He may dream that he has, but if he ever awakens, he will find it but a dream. Oh, how many need to be aroused from this sleep of death!

14

UNBELIEF*

Hebrews 3:19

"So we see that they could not enter in because of unbelief."

In this discourse I shall notice:

    I. *What unbelief is not.*
    II. *What it is.*
    III. *Instances and evidences of unbelief.*
    IV. *The tendency of unbelief.*
    V. *The guilt of unbelief.*

I. *What unbelief is not.*

1. It is not a negative state of mind. It is represented in the Bible as sin; it cannot, therefore, be a mere negation.

2. Nor is it ignorance. Ignorance may be caused by unbelief, turning away the attention from the objects of faith. But ignorance itself is not unbelief. Nor is it absence of conviction. This is often an effect of unbelief.

II. *What it is.*

1. It is represented in the Bible as sin. It must, then, be a voluntary state of mind. It cannot belong either to the intelligence or the sensibility. For the action of both these powers is necessary.

---

*Ibid., No. 16, August 2, 1843.

193

2. It is the opposite of faith. Faith is represented as voluntary. It cannot, therefore, be conviction, since this belongs to the intelligence. Faith is trust or confidence in God; it is a committing of the soul to Him; as Peter says, "Commit the keeping of your soul to him" (1 Pet. 4:19).

3. Generically, faith as distinguished from everything else is confidence in God; but specifically, it is confidence in Christ, or in any fact, doctrine, promise, or threatening of the Bible. And I might add, faith is confidence in any truth whatever, historical, philosophical, or mathematical—or even in error. If it respects the promises of God, it is a confident assurance that they will be fulfilled. If it respects facts, it is confidence in the truthfulness of the fact.

Unbelief is the opposite of this. Unbelief is a withholding of confidence from what God says; it is distrust; it is a refusal to commit or give up the mind to the influence of a truth or promise; it is a rejection of evidence. For example, consider any of the facts recorded in the Bible. Unbelief is a refusal to credit their truthfulness, or to allow them that influence which they deserve. For instance, look at the manner in which the Jews treated the miracles of Christ. Christ claimed to be the Messiah, and in attestation of His claim, He performed many wonderful works. Here was evidence that He really was what He professed to be. If He had not furnished such evidence, it would not have been unbelief to reject His claim. He might have lived and died among them without their incurring any guilt by rejecting Him. But the works which He performed should have secured the confidence of every beholder and established His claim in every mind. But instead of yielding to the evidence thus presented, they steadfastly resisted Him, and ascribed His miracles to infernal agency. It would seem that their disposition to reject Him was so strong that no amount of evidence which He could place before them could overcome it. This was unbelief. We may apply the same principle to other things. Consider, for example, the subject of phrenology.* If an individual really lacks evidence of its truth, it is not unbelief to reject it. On the contrary, to receive it without

---

*The study of the structure of the skull to determine mental faculties and character traits.

such evidence would be mere credulity. But just as far as he has evidence of its truth, it is unbelief to refuse to treat it accordingly. So with the doctrines of the second advent. If an individual lacks evidence of their truth with which to answer the demands of his intelligence, it is not unbelief to reject them. But if he has such evidence, then to reject them is unbelief. We might apply the same principle to the doctrine of sanctification, or any other doctrine whatever, whether true or false.

4. But especially is it unbelief where individuals confess themselves convinced and do not act accordingly. If an individual confesses himself convinced of the truth of the doctrine of the second advent but does not commit his mind to the full influence of that doctrine, it is unbelief. If he admits the truth of the doctrine of entire sanctification but does not commit himself to it, and expect to realize it in his own case, he is guilty of unbelief. And it is unbelief, whether he admits it or not, if he has reasonable evidence of its truth and yet does not yield his whole being up to its influence.

III. *Instances and evidences of unbelief.*

1. A heathen who never heard the gospel is not an unbeliever as respects Christ, in any proper sense of the word. He knows nothing about it, and consequently withholds no confidence from it; but a man who lives *under* the gospel and is not controlled by it is an unbeliever.

2. A lack of assurance of salvation through Christ is unbelief. This must be so if the Atonement is general, and if faith consists in believing what is said respecting it. The Apostle says, "This is the record, that God hath given to us eternal life, and this life is in his Son" (1 John 5:11). Now if it be true that God has given eternal life to all, then not to possess an assurance of your own salvation through Christ is unbelief.

3. Not being duly influenced by any perceived truth is unbelief no matter what that truth is. Faith is a disposition to be influenced by it, or the committing of the mind to its influence, in exact accordance with its perceived importance.

4. The absence of a firm confidence and expectation that we will realize the truth of every promise given to us is unbelief. For example, God has promised parents to bless their children; then,

not to have the most confident assurance that He will do so is unbelief. And the same is true respecting every promise, either of justification or sanctification.

5. God has promised the salvation of all that believe; now, to doubt whether *we* shall be saved if we believe is both an evidence and an instance of unbelief. Remember, too, that the salvation promised is salvation from both sin and hell. To this, it is objected that the promise of salvation is conditional; and, says the objector, I have no right to believe that I shall be saved until I have believed in Christ; for faith is the condition of the promise, and to require me to believe that I shall be saved before I believe in Christ is to require me to believe a fact before it is true. To this, I answer:

(1) By inquiring of the objector, "What am I to believe about Christ?" Plainly, I am to believe *in* Him as the Savior; I am to believe that He tasted death for every man and that He hath given us eternal life. Two things, then, I must believe: first, that He died for all, and of course, for me; and second, that He will save me. Suppose an angel should believe that Christ died for all the world, would that be faith in Christ? Certainly not in the sense in which the Bible requires *us* to believe in Him; unless I believe He died for me, I do not believe in the proper sense. I must not only believe that He died for all, but for *me*; not only that justification is offered to all, but to *me*; and true faith is accepting eternal salvation at His hand. Some object to this teaching and say that the realization of the promise is conditioned on faith and that the condition must be fulfilled before I can believe that the promise will be realized and I shall be saved. This is a mere trick. It is to suppose a promise given, but on a condition that nullifies it. Suppose a rich father should give his son, before he departs for Europe, a promise in writing, and under oath, that he would supply all his wants, but the condition demanded of the son was that he should exercise full faith in the promise. He must believe that it would secure for him a supply of money in any of the banks of Europe, according to the tenor of the writing. Now, I want to know if this is a condition that would nullify the promise. Plainly not, since the condition is not arbitrary, but naturally essential to its fulfillment. If he does not confide in the promise and expect its fulfillment, it is naturally impossible that it should be fulfilled.

On the contrary, how plain it is that faith in the promise naturally secures its fulfillment. God has given the promise of eternal salvation to all who believe. The condition is not arbitrary, but natural, so that the fulfillment of the promise to each individual necessarily depends on his faith in it. Now, is it faith to stand back and say that Christ died for everybody else, and will save everybody else, if *they* will believe, and not believe yourself? What a strange objection! The truth is, if this objection be good, it nullifies every promise in the Bible. God has promised to convert the world, but the fulfillment of this promise is conditioned on the faith of Christians. For them to believe it is to deliver themselves up to it, and preach the gospel. Does this condition hinder faith? Is it a sly and artful means of evasion put in by the Promiser to prevent the necessity of His ever fulfilling the promise? No, but the condition is natural, and involves the expectation of the thing promised. So God has promised to bless the children of believers if they will believe—if they will give themselves up to this truth. Now to believe is to fulfill the condition, and for persons to take the ground of the objector is to trip themselves. The objection, then, cannot be good.

(2) In every case, faith expects the fulfillment of the promise, and this expectation is not founded upon the promise itself, but on the general character of the Promiser. If an individual does not believe a promise of God because he does not believe in the general character of God, he cannot believe in it at all. Without confidence in the benevolence and veracity of God, it is impossible to rely upon His promises; but confidence in these naturally secures such reliance.

(3) God has promised to justify and sanctify every believer, or everyone who *will believe* and expect this of Him. The condition is *natural*, and it is nonsense to say that we cannot expect to be justified and sanctified until *after* we have believed; for to believe *is* to expect. *Not to expect* is unbelief; for to expect in this case is implied in faith. Much has been said about appropriating faith, and I have been struck with the fact that believers in a limited Atonement have much to say about appropriating faith. But a limited Atonement and appropriating faith can't go together. If the former is true, the latter is impossible without a new revelation. For if Christ died for only a part of mankind, and has not revealed who they are, I would ask, how can anyone appropriate

Him to himself without a direct revelation that he is one of the elect? But against this class, those who believe in a general Atonement are consistent enough in holding the doctrine of appropriating faith; for to appropriate is simply to accept Christ, as presented in the gospel. If Christ died for all, then each may appropriate Him, and this is faith. Whoever does not appropriate Him, just as He is presented, rejects Him; he is an unbeliever.

(4) Finally, if this objection is true, salvation is impossible. For if I can never expect to be saved by Christ until after I have believed, I can never expect it at all; for I have said, true faith, and the expectation of salvation by Him, are identical.

IV. *The tendency of unbelief.*

1. It defeats all God's efforts to save those who exercise unbelief. As I have said, faith is the natural condition of salvation, and is a voluntary exercise. It cannot, therefore, be forced; and therefore, if an individual will not believe, he must be damned.

2. Unbelief defeats all God's efforts to sanctify us. *Sanctification is nothing else than delivering up the mind to the truth and promises of God.* To think, then, that we can be saved while we reject the promises is to overlook the very nature of sanctification.

3. Unbelief renders heart obedience impossible, for "without faith, it is impossible to please God."

4. It prevents the possibility of true peace. The unbeliever does not know what true peace is. His condition is in some respects like that of a sleeping person who has terrible dreams. He dreams he is endangered by a flood, by fire or other dreadful circumstances. Perhaps he imagines himself suffering shipwreck, and just on the point of being swallowed up in the waves. Perhaps he is struggling to escape from devouring flames, or he walks as a miserable outcast from society, troubled on every side, and finding nothing on which he can rest. His agony is indescribable, but in a moment he awakes, and behold, he is in a warm bed in his own secure dwelling. He thanks God it is a dream. How great the contrast between his present state and that in which his dreams placed him. Similarly the convicted unbeliever is tossed with agitation; he looks this way and that, but finds no rest. "[He is] like the troubled sea . . . whose waters cast up mire

and dirt. There is no peace, saith my God, to the wicked" (Isa. 57:20-21). Notice, however, what a change comes over him as soon as he believes. It is like the sun breaking out in an ocean of storms. He sees promises on every side, like the mountains round about Jerusalem. He sees provisions for all his wants; why should he be troubled anymore? "Bless the Lord, O my soul" (Ps. 103:1), he cries. What is this? Why here, instead of bondage, misery, and death, is endless life and peace; and the broad river of love, as pure as that which flows from under the throne of God, begins to pour its current through his soul.

5. Unbelief renders it impossible for Christ to keep us from sin. The Bible, however full of promises, may rot before him, and he go down to hell notwithstanding. Unbelief nullifies them all and leaves nothing to help him.

6. Unbelief delivers the soul into the hands of the world, the flesh, and the devil. No power in the universe can protect him against their influence without his own consent, because he is a free being. Withholding faith from God, and delivering himself up to their influence, he becomes the sport and play of every temptation that besets him.

V. *The guilt of unbelief.*

1. It is the willful rejection of the highest evidence God can give. Suppose you had an enemy who always suspected you of an intention to injure him, and although you had often tried to remove his suspicions, he should still hold this opinion. Suppose he should fall into great difficulties, and you should take great pains to help him. Suppose you should relieve the wants of his family, and provide for his children, but still he should suspect you had some sinister end in all this, which would eventually come out. Would you not think him vastly unreasonable and guilty in maintaining such prejudices? But suppose, finally, his house should catch fire, and he and his family were in an upper story, while it was raging in every apartment below. No one can offer help; there are no ladders and no means of escape. The floor beneath him begins to give way, and the roof is about to fall in; they stand at the windows and shriek for help. Suddenly one rushes through the flames, from one flight of stairs to another, with his hair and clothes on fire, until he reaches the trapped family. He

instantly seizes him with one strong arm and his children with the other, and carries them safely below. While he is doing this, the man swoons with terror. As soon as he opens his eyes, he finds himself in the arms of his deliverer, who, with the utmost solicitude and tenderness is fanning him and restoring him. His first exclamation is, "Your children are all safe!" He soon discovers that his benefactor is no other than the object of his former suspicions. Now suppose he should still not be convinced; what an abomination would this be! How everyone would execrate such a willful and unreasonable rejection of the highest evidence he could give of his benevolence toward him. But suppose further, he were condemned to death, and his benefactor should voluntarily step forward and die for him. What an amazing prejudice and obstinacy would be manifest if he should entertain suspicions of the sincerity of the substitute's love.

Now let me ask, what further evidence could God give of His love to mankind than He has given? Besides crowning their life with as many blessings as their circumstances render it possible to bestow, He adds the gift of His own Son to die for them. He has thus given the highest possible evidence of His good will toward them. What damning guilt, then, must their unbelief bring. Suppose the sovereign of an extensive empire is seeking to promote the highest possible good of his subjects through the administration of the most excellent laws. But one province of his empire goes into rebellion. He has power to crush it all at once. But suppose, that instead of marching an army bristling with bayonets among them, and desolating them with fire and sword, he should lay aside the robes of royalty, and in a most unassuming manner go among them and attempt to teach them the nature of his own character and laws and the importance of conformity to his will for their highest good. But suppose again, they would not believe him, but suspect him of some sinister motive. How astonishing this would be! And if, to convince them of his love, he should even die for them, who would not expect this to subdue the rebellion?

Now see the blessed God administering the law of benevolence impartially throughout His universe. Our world rebels. He comes in the person of His Son, in the humble guise of humanity. He goes about among mankind, revealing to them the character and will of God, and endeavoring to secure their confidence. And when they reject His instructions and will not believe, rather than fail to accomplish His end, He dies for them on the cross. What higher evidence could God give of His love than this? And how outrageous is the unbelief which willfully rejects it all? What more could He do? Can you think of anything more? How damning, then, must be the guilt of unbelief!

2. It is treating God in the worst possible manner. We never do our friends a worse injury than when we distrust them without a cause. Should a husband become jealous and distrustful of his wife without a cause, what greater injury could he do her? It would pierce like a dagger to her heart. Or, should a wife manifest unreasonable suspicions respecting her husband, what more could she do to render him wretched? He would say, "Have you any reasons for your suspicions?" Let me ask that husband, who is conscious of his integrity, and has tender sensibilities—let me ask that wife, who is virtuous, and values the confidence of her husband as she should, "How would you feel? How would you expostulate in the circumstances supposed?" And what would be more directly calculated to bring the blight of death upon the peace of a family than such unreasonable distrust on the part of a husband or wife? Now look at God's great family. What family ever had such cause of confidence as God's has? And what father ever had such cause of complaint? What husband was ever so distrusted by a wife as the blessed God by the church, which He bought with His own blood? See that husband! He is pouring his complaints all abroad and loading down the air with his sighs. Now, I ask again, is this lack of confidence not the worst possible kind of treatment? Men naturally feel insulted whenever their veracity and integrity are called into question. And has God no sensibility? Is it no grief to Him to be treated as a liar the world over?

3. Unbelief dishonors God in the highest degree before others. Suppose a father should send his son to a university and should give him a book of checks, assuring him that they were good to supply all his wants. But suppose the son should show that he had no confidence in it, and should be struggling to meet his expenses and to obtain his books. Would not this be to publish the worst things in the most effectual way about his father? What,

then, does unbelief publish about God? See that one who professes religion, with the Bible full of promises in his hands, going all about complaining and mourning over his spiritual poverty, when God has said He is more willing to give His Holy Spirit to them that ask it than earthly parents are to give good gifts to their children, and that His grace shall be sufficient for us. What is he doing? Why, he is representing God in the worst possible light, as guilty, not only of lying, but of lying under oath. For "God, willing more abundantly to show unto the heirs of promise the immutability of his counsel, confirmed it by an oath: that by two immutable things, in which it was impossible for God to lie, we might have a strong consolation, who have fled for refuge to lay hold upon the hope set before us" (Heb. 6:17, 18).

REMARKS

1. We have noted what to think of those who say they cannot realize that the promises will be fulfilled. Can't realize! Listen! Suppose your child should say, "Pa, you promised to give me a New Year's present, but I can't imagine that you will." You would say, "My child, do you think I lie? Have I not given you my word that I would give you a present?" What higher evidence can men have than the solemn word and oath of God? What shall make it more sure? Who shall underwrite for Him? If what He has said does not satisfy you, He can give no security. Can't realize! Horrible!

2. We have noted what to think of those who say they believe, but are not duly influenced by their faith. They profess to believe in the necessity of salvation and in the eternity of hell torments, but they don't act respecting themselves or others, as the magnitude of these truths demand. The fact is, they don't believe at all.

3. We see that no doctrine is believed any further than it influences the conduct. What is faith? It is, as we have shown, the delivering of the mind to the influence of known truth. It follows, then, that there is no faith where the conduct remains uninfluenced.

4. Heretical conduct proves heretical faith. The truth is, all heresy belongs to the heart; however holy a man's creed may be, if his conduct is wrong, he is heretical in heart.

5. We see the wickedness of admitting that the gospel proffers entire sanctification in this life, and yet not expecting it. There are those, as you know, who admit that the gospel proffers entire sanctification on condition of faith—they admit that its provisions are ample, and yet do not expect to possess it in this life. What is that but unbelief?

6. We see also the wickedness of saying that the expectation of it is unreasonable and erroneous. They say that to believe we shall actually attain entire sanctification in this life is a great and dangerous error. What is that but unbelief in its worst form?

7. Men are guilty who teach that it is an error to expect sanctification in this life, and raise the cry of heresy against those who do teach them to expect it. If it is promised, it must be sheer unbelief and dreadful guilt to doubt it.

8. The good men who formerly rejected this doctrine did not see, and admit, the fullness of the provisions. President Edwards, for example, did not admit this, and it is manifest from the account which he gives of his wife's experience, as well as from his writings generally, that he had no such idea before his mind.

9. But what shall we say of those who make this admission, and yet do not expect the blessing? They do not seem to understand that this is unbelief. They say they do not distrust God, but they distrust themselves. This is a great mistake. If faith is implicit confidence in God's promises, and if these promises cover full provisions for sanctification, then there is no room left for self-distrust; in that case, self-distrust is distrust in God. Take, for example, this promise: "And the very God of peace sanctify you wholly; and I pray God your whole spirit and soul and body be preserved blameless unto the coming of our Lord Jesus Christ. Faithful is he that calleth you, who also will do it" (1 Thess. 5:23, 24). Here is a promise covering the wants of our whole nature. Now, what is that state of mind which does not expect its realization? Is it self-distrust or distrust in God? It is downright unbelief. It is virtually saying, "Lord, you have promised to 'sanctify me wholly in soul, body, and spirit,' but I don't believe it. I don't believe you can; I have such distrust in myself."

10. There is no consistency in making the admission of full provisions, and then rejecting the expectation of being sanctified by them.

11. How can the expectation of being sanctified in this life be rejected without unbelief in view of 1 Thess. 5:23, 24? Suppose I get up and read this promise: "And the very God of peace sanctify you wholly; and I pray God your whole spirit and soul and body be preserved blameless unto the coming of our Lord Jesus Christ. Faithful is he that calleth you, who also will do it," and then turn around and say, "Now, brethren, I warn you against believing that He will sanctify you." But the promise comes thundering back: "Faithful is he that calleth you who also *will* do it." Suppose I rally again and say, "Edwards, Payson, and Brainerd were not sanctified, and why should *you* expect to be?"* What would that differ from the course adopted by most of the ministers at the present time? But here comes up the old argument, that although provisions are made, yet they are conditioned on faith, and I have no right to expect sanctification until I believe. I answer, faith and expectation are identical; if you do not expect sanctification, you do not believe God and are making Him a liar.

12. To tell men not to expect to be wholly sanctified in this life, and preserved blameless, is to warn them not to believe God.

13. You can see why you do not enter into rest. It is because you have no faith. You have not cast your anchor. You are like a vessel drifting along the majestic Niagara toward the falls. The vessel is approaching destruction but the captain will not let down its anchor, although he knows the rocks are within reach upon which it might fasten and be safe. Without faith you are like a man in a dungeon, to whom a golden chain is let down, and who is exhorted to lay hold and be drawn up, but will not.

14. It is wicked to expect to sin all our days. God has said, "Sin shall not have dominion over you: for ye are not under the law, but under grace" (Rom. 6:14). Therefore, to expect to live

---

*Jonathan Edwards (1703-1758) was most famous for his labors during the Great Awakening in America. See *The Works of the Reverend Jonathan Edwards* in 8 volumes (Worcester: Isaiah Thomas, 1808, 1809), First American Edition.

Edward Payson (1783-1827) was an American clergyman. See *Payson's Complete Works* (Boston: Hyde, Lord, and Duren, 1846).

David Brainerd (1718-1747) was a young, courageous American missionary to the Indians, whose life was popularized by the writing of Jonathan Edwards, *Works, ibid.,* Vol. III.

carrying about a load of sin until you die is abominable wickedness.

15. The church is never likely to be holy while it is exhorted to unbelief instead of faith. It is a horrible thing that much current teaching is nothing else than teaching men *not* to believe God. And lest they should expect sanctification, they are pointed back to those who profess to come short of it—to antinomian perfectionism—and to everything which may bring the doctrine into disrepute. They are warned against it, as if it were the pestilence. Oh, my soul, what is this! Is this the way the church is to be sanctified? My brethren, if you mean to be kept from sin, and antinomianism of every kind, and from every other delusion, take hold of these promises and believe. Expect them to be fulfilled and they will be. But if you doubt, you will walk in blindness. For, the prophet says, "If ye will not believe, surely ye shall not be established" (Isa. 7:9).

15

GOSPEL LIBERTY*

Galatians 5:1

"Stand fast therefore in the liberty wherewith Christ hath made us free, and be not entangled again with the yoke of bondage."

In this lecture I shall show:

    I. *What is intended by the yoke of bondage.*
    II. *What it is to be entangled with it.*
    III. *What is the liberty here spoken of.*
    IV. *How Christ makes us free.*
    V. *The danger of becoming entangled again.*
    VI. *When Christians are in bondage.*
    VII. *What is their remedy.*

I. *What is intended by the yoke of bondage.*

The Apostle had immediately under his eye the ceremonial law of the Jews. This is evident from the whole context. Judaizing teachers had come in, trying to engraft the cumbersome ob-

---

*Ibid., No. 17, August 16, 1843. This is the final lecture in the 13-lecture series: "Holiness of Christians in the Present Life." They were reported for *The Oberlin Evangelist* by Rev. S. D. Cochran. The next three sermons conclude Finney's sermons and lectures for *The Oberlin Evangelist* for 1843.

servances of the Jewish ritual upon the gospel. This so grieved the Apostle, who felt it to be such a departure from Christ, that he declared they were fallen from grace in complying with such instruction. But it was not simply because he rejected the ceremonial law, and regarded it as useless, that the Apostle thus resisted the observance of it, but because he had his eye on a principle of the greatest importance to the church. Why was the ceremonial law a yoke of bondage? Because it had no tendency to reform the heart, and thus render its own observance a matter of choice. Any precept given us contrary to the state of mind in which we are is a yoke of bondage. And this is true, whether it be a precept of the Old or New Testament. The principle is universal. You may see it in the conduct of children. Impose some requirement upon them contrary to the state of their hearts and you will never fail to see that their obedience is not cheerful but constrained—a mere servitude. Every requirement, then, and *spirit* of which we have not, is to us a yoke of bondage.

II. *What it is to be entangled with it.*

1. To see a rule of duty, and feel our obligation to comply with it, and yet have no heart to enter into the spirit of it, is certainly to be entangled with a yoke of bondage. The obligation presses on the one hand, and the heart rejects it on the other, and the condition is one of restless distraction. The law given at Mount Sinai was a galling yoke for this reason. The Apostle says, "[It] gendereth to bondage" (Gal. 4:24). Previous to a distinct perception of its claims, men may not be aware of its influence. Paul says, "For I was alive without the law once: but when the commandment came, sin revived, and I died" (Rom. 6:9). Paul, seeing what the law required as duty, yet having no heart to perform it, found it a snare. You can easily see how it was. Let anybody be practicing any injurious indulgence ignorantly, and there is no sin in it; but let light be thrown into his mind on the subject, and the true nature of the indulgence made known to him, and that moment the struggle commences. Before, he could practice it without compunction, but now his conscience is awake; his appetite still demands it, and the more clearly he sees the law the more he is entangled until his heart goes fully with the requirement.

2. To take *pains* to conform to the letter of a law, while destitute of its spirit, is to be entangled. Many persons set themselves with great punctiliousness to keep every point of the law, and yet, after all, never feel themselves any better off. Why is this? Because it is mere letter service; there is no heart in it; the more such service is rendered, the more exacting is conscience, and the further the mind is from peace.

3. To strive to satisfy the demands either of the law, the gospel, or the conscience without faith and love is to be entangled. The case supposed in chapter 7 of Romans represents an individual as setting himself to obey the moral law without its spirit, and the result was perfect failure. The same is true of persons setting themselves to obey the gospel without its spirit. They are like a man in a horrible pit of miry clay. Every effort toward obedience only seems to render them less disposed to obey, and to create greater enmity to the service. The same is true of all attempts to satisfy the demands of conscience, while the heart repels the service.*

4. To undertake and assume responsibilities to which we are not equal, that is, to undertake to do anything in our own strength, is to be entangled. Let an individual go about any duty, or assume any responsibility without the spirit of it, and in his own strength—by dint of his own resolutions, without faith—and he will find himself more entangled the further he goes, just as long as this is his condition.

5. Covenants, vows and promises where Christ is not consulted, and depended upon, only serve to entangle the soul. Sometimes persons write covenants of the most solemn and binding character, with the design to hedge themselves in so that they will not dare to sin; but it does no good, and only brings the soul under a more dire condemnation.

6. Undertaking to do or to be anything to which the spirit of Christ does not lead you, whether obligatory or not, if you undertake it without love, it will only be a snare. Thus the law "gendereth to bondage."

---

*See especially, "The Revival of Sin and the Law" and "License, Bondage, and Liberty" in *Principles of Liberty*; and "Legal Experience" and "Religion of the Law and the Gospel" in *Principles of Victory*.

III. *What is the liberty here spoken of.*

1. The word liberty is used in two senses:

(1) As opposed to necessity. In this sense, it consists in the power to choose or refuse any object of choice.

(2) As opposed to slavery. Slavery is not, as some have supposed, a state of involuntary servitude, for strictly speaking, there is no such thing. Every act the slave performs is really as voluntary as the act of any other man. His muscles would not move without will. Slavery is a state in which a man feels constrained to choose between what he regards as two evils. He selects between two alternatives, both of which he abhors. He knows he must labor or be whipped, and he prefers labor to suffering as the lesser of two evils. Slavery, then, is where a person feels himself shut up to take a course, which on the whole he does not love, but which he takes rather than to do worse. For example, a person in the marriage state without love may discharge the outward duties of that relationship during life, rather than to separate and sustain all the evils attendant on such a course. So a person may live under a government which he abhors, and yet, rather than subject himself to its frown, may meet all its requisitions. This is acting on the principle of slavery. A person might be compelled to act on the principle of slavery here in New York as absolutely as in the South and may as much abhor the service. The difference between one here and one there is that *there* he fears the lash or some other physical affliction, while *here* he fears some other evil, which is equally efficient, as he views it, to drive him to the abhorred task. Religious legalists are slaves in this sense. Their duties are not something which they love, but which *must* be attended to or a greater evil endured. Their service is not performed out of love for the required task, but as the only way to escape the rebukes of conscience or the wrath of God.

2. This liberty is that of faith and love. When persons come to love, then they delight in acts of love as a matter of course. They are so free in obeying God that they do only what they on the whole prefer to do. They would do this whether there was any command or not, as long as they could see its relation to the good of the universe.

3. In short, this liberty is benevolence. It consists not in the annihilation of obligation but in possessing the Spirit of the re-

quirement. Turn to 1 Cor. 13:4-8 and mark the characteristics of love which the Apostle there lays down.

> Charity suffereth long, and is kind; charity envieth not; charity vaunteth not itself, is not puffed up, doth not behave itself unseemly, seeketh not her own, is not easily provoked, thinketh no evil; rejoiceth not in iniquity, but rejoiceth in the truth; beareth all things, believeth all things, hopeth all things, endureth all things. Charity never faileth; but whether there be prophecies they shall fail; whether there be tongues, they shall cease; whether there be knowledge, it shall vanish away.

This description of charity, or benevolence, shows that the free man naturally acts according to the requirement. It is spontaneous with him. He acts from a *principle within* himself rather than from a *law without*. He does not act from restraint, but obedience is with him as it was with Christ. Christ did not need the sanctions of the law to induce obedience, but what the precept required was just what, above all other things, He loved to do. So it is with those who are in this liberty. They do not act under the rod.

4. They are not governed by authority, but act spontaneously from choice. They only need to know what will please God, and they do it willingly and readily. They do not neglect to do what is required of them, but they do it from love, and that is the perfection of liberty. When a man is able to choose in any direction in all circumstances, and does as his mind directs, that is the highest liberty in the universe. That is freedom in its highest sense.

IV. *How Christ makes us free.*

1. Not by abolishing the moral law.

2. Not by discharging us from any obligation to fulfill any or every duty.

3. Not by relaxing the claims of any moral precept, in either the Old or New Testament.

4. But as freedom respects the ceremonial law, He fulfilled and abolished it, so that nobody is under further obligation to obey it.

5. And as freedom respects the moral law, He makes us free by writing its prinicple and all its spirit in our hearts. And what a sweet way this is! Suppose we should thus govern our children.

What delightful families we should have. All our commands would be the very thing they choose, so that for us to intimate our will would be to see it sweetly done. When Christ begets the spirit of liberty in us, and then shows us the outward precept, the precept is just what we are predisposed to do, and of course it will be done by us cheerfully.

6. He makes us free by making the course of conduct prescribed in the whole Bible as natural and spontaneous as it is with himself; therefore, we are free in the same sense that He and all others in heaven are. God, no doubt, feels bound to be benevolent, but His will is just what His infinite reason requires, and He is, therefore, infinitely free, and so is the Lord Jesus Christ. This is just the freedom He seeks to bestow on us.

7. He accomplishes this by His indwelling Spirit. He comes to reside in us that He may beget in us the same state of mind there is in Christ, whom the Holy Spirit is to present to us.

8. He liberates us by so revealing Christ to us as to gain the implicit confidence and affection of the soul. It is not accomplished by any physical force. How do we, if we want to get the confidence of persons, exhibit to them such views of our character as to win their confidence and love. So Christ, by revealing himself in those traits of His character which He knows are adapted to win the confidence of men, brings them into the same state of mind with himself. He shows them that He is love, well knowing that this is the easiest way to make them love. There is no other way to make men benevolent. Weep yourself if you want others to weep. Suppose a father is benevolent and he wants to make his children so too. How can he do it? By using the rod? By drilling them in the catechism? No. By acting it out before them. One great reason the children of professedly religious parents are so seldom converted is because the parents so constantly command them without sufficient manifestations of benevolence. They are commanded to read the Bible, to go to Sabbath school, to do their tasks in such a way that it becomes irksome to them instead of attractive and interesting. Let parents only temper all their commands sufficiently with benevolence and it would not be so. It is thus that Christ wins the hearts of sinners and makes them free. When He came, the idea of true religion was almost lost in the world, but He acted it out in His whole life. His disciples

looked on and wondered, until finally they caught the flame. And what then? Why, they shook the world with it. And it is the exhibition of this spirit alone which can consummate the victory and liberate our race. By this means He makes us free from the yoke of bondage—from obligation to keep the ceremonial law, from the penalty of the moral law, from the spirit of bondage, from the dominion of sin and from the power of the world, the flesh, and the devil—by writing His law in our hearts. This is the glorious liberty wherewith Christ makes His people free.

V. *The danger of becoming entangled again.*

1. The least unbelief brings bondage. Let a wife lose confidence in her husband in any respect, and in that respect her obedience will be constrained and stiff. So it is in religion. If there is any lack of confidence, instead of your service being free and outgushing, it will be forced and heartless.

2. Grieving the Holy Spirit will beget bondage. Whenever He withdraws His presence from the mind, it falls right into bondage.

3. Allowing ourselves the least selfishness naturally leads into bondage. Remember, religion is benevolence. The least selfishness, then, is bondage of course.

4. Any abstraction of the mind from Christ, of course, begets bondage. No person, as a matter of fact, lives a spiritual life without Christ. We must feed on Him. We need Him as much as we do our natural food. We maintain our liberty only by thinking on Him and communing with Him continually.

5. Any attempts to coerce the mind by oaths, vows, covenants, and resolutions beget bondage. If a man has the Spirit of Christ, he does not need these, and if he has not, he can never get it in this way. I have known persons to pray all night and work themselves up to the most solemn vows and covenants which they could frame, and yet it availed nothing. There was no religion in it—not an atom. And when persons attempt to coerce themselves in this way, they universally fail.

6. Taking upon your conscience an obligation to conform to any particular forms and ceremonies not prescribed by Christ breeds bondage. It is truly astonishing to see to what an excess the Jews loaded themselves down in adhering to what they sup-

posed were the requirements of the ceremonial law. They multiplied days, traditions, tithes, and purifications almost without end. So it has been in the Church of Rome. She multiplied her vows, pilgrimages, and fasts to such an extent as could result in nothing else but a mere outside show working the destruction of souls. Even undertaking to conform with those that *are required*, in your own strength, is enough to bring any soul into terrible bondage.

7. But the multiplying of holy days, religious observances and ceremonies, cannot result in anything else but bondage. Even among Protestants, how many regard it as duty to observe Christmas. I have been afraid our Methodist brethren were becoming entangled. They seem to consider it a duty to watch out the old year, and in the new, and no matter how tired, they must be there to satisfy both custom and conscience. Even monthly concerts come to be a yoke. The truth is, we are bound to resist such things whenever they come to be regarded as binding on the conscience. Holy days in the Romish church have become so numerous that in many of the Catholic countries, if you employ a man to work, you get very little out of him.

8. Church covenants bind people especially if there is anything in them contrary to the law of reason and of love. We hear of no such thing in the Apostles' days. The truth is, I am jealous of them. One embraces one thing, and another, another; the first thing you know, you are in the harness. I have known several cases of this kind. Let no one be bound by anything but the law of love, which is the perfect law of liberty.

VI. *When Christians are in bondage.*

1. When the duties of religion are a burden, we are in bondage. While we are in liberty, duties are no burden. As an old writer says, "I sought all nature through to find something like the burden of Christ, and could find nothing until I came to the pinions of the dove, which instead of weighing down bear up the soul on high."

2. When the form is observed without the spirit and power of godliness. Many have, and keep up, the form very scrupulously when the life and spirit have gone. But their piety is like a mere lifeless corpse, or hollow shell.

3. When driven by conscience instead of being drawn by love. Oh, how many are attempting to live by mere resolutions forced up by conscience without one particle of love to Christ!

4. When they don't find their heart spontaneously doing what is required. When the waters of life do not flow spontaneously out from them—when it is not nature's promptings to pray, to give to the poor, or perform any other duty. When persons have the spirit of religion, instead of needing a command, they feel an inward going of the soul in the right direction, and the performance of duty gives them sweet enjoyment.

5. When the soul has no peace and no enjoyment in religion, it is under the yoke of bondage. True liberty is essential peace and blessedness.

VII. *What is their remedy.*

1. People will never get into liberty by any legal, heartless efforts. That is beginning exactly at the wrong end; it is beginning on the outside to work inward instead of beginning at the inside to work outward. People often become prodigiously excited, and go to doing, doing, doing under the pressure of obligation; but where is the relief? This is particularly the case in many protracted meetings and special efforts; when the meetings stop, where is their religion? I am not saying anything against such meetings. But against the manner in which the truth is too often preached and the meeting conducted. The process is suited to set the sensibility on fire with powerful excitement and leave the heart unsubdued to love. This is all wrong, and only adapted to foster mere heartless legality.

2. The only remedy for bondage is faith in Christ and application of His blood. "This is the work of God, that ye believe on him whom he hath sent" (John 6:29). Cast the whole soul upon Him to receive the spirit of obedience. I have often seen persons striving and pushing for months, but all to no avail. They were not one whit better, and it was not until they saw that it would not make them better if they should continue thus a thousand years, and until they cast themselves wholly on Christ to receive the spirit of obedience from Him, that they entered into gospel liberty. "Come unto me, all ye that labour and are heavy laden, and I will give you rest. Take my yoke upon you, and learn of me;

for I am meek and lowly in heart: and ye shall find rest unto your souls. For my yoke is easy, and my burden is light" (Matt. 11:28-30).

REMARKS

1. You may see from this subject the difference between a legal and a gospel religion. A legal religion is *works* without love, a gospel religion is *works* by love. A brother said the other day that he did not understand this distinction. Why, it is obvious as the distinction between day and night! Both the true Christian and the legalist works; but the one works with love, the other without. They both do the same things outwardly, but the one is free and the other a slave in the performance.

2. The moral law is called the perfect law of liberty, because it was ordained to life, and when obeyed in its spirit, gives life. But why do persons find it unto death? Because when the spirit is lost, the letter kills. When it is legally, that is, heartlessly obeyed, it works our overthrow instead of our deliverance.

3. See what is intended by such passages as Gal. 5:18, "But if ye be led of the Spirit, ye are not under the law"; and Rom. 6:14, "For sin shall not have dominion over you: for ye are not under the law, but under grace."* It is not intended that the law is abolished but that its spirit has become their law. They are not under it in such a sense as to need its sanctions to press them up to duty.

4. Many feel that their religion is mere slavery—a hard, uphill business. The language of their heart is, "It is hard to obey, and harder still to love." But they are ignorant of the true nature of religion. It is the easiest thing in the world to him that has it. Legalists complain about this world—that it is such a bad one, so hard to live in, and keep right. But it is not such a hard world as they think. Religion certainly does not make it any harder but altogether easier. The difficulty with those who find it such a hard world is that their hearts are bad, and if they find it a severe task to obey God, it is because they have not the spirit of obedience. If

---

*See especially, "Sanctification Under Grace" on Romans 6:14, in *Principles of Liberty*, pp. 55-64.

they have any religion, it is of the wrong kind, and they are entirely deceived. If they think all others have the same kind that they have, they are mistaken. Some persons, when they see others joyful, say those people are deceived. They don't feel so themselves, and they wonder how anybody can. And then they point to Romans 7, or to David Brainerd, who, although a good man, was so hypochondriacal that his experience would be gloomy as a matter of course. Such persons are always suspicious whenever they see any of the spirit of liberty manifested. And I am not surprised, for men are naturally suspicious of those whose experiences are beyond their own. How strange it must appear to the masses, and how it must arrest them to see persons almost dance for joy when they emerge from bondage, and yet this is not amazing. Why, see that slave, with his back all blistered in the sun, set free. Is it strange that he should leap and bound about with fullness of joy? It is thus that Christians feel, and the Bible commands them to rejoice; but legalists don't understand it, and think they are possessed of the devil. Why, I have sometimes heard persons say, "That's not *solemn*—its fanaticism." And then they turn to some gloomy slave with a dead body strapped on his back, and groaning under his burden, and say, "That's the humble one—he's none of your visionaries!"

5. Multitudes have no true idea of gospel liberty. They have made a credible profession of religion and are toiling out its duties; but what liberty means they do not know—and perhaps they are even ministers of the gospel! Of course such persons don't expect liberty. I recently heard of a revival in which the minister said to inquirers, "Don't expect to be happy in this world; I never was, nor do I expect to be, until I get to heaven. I don't know what it is to have *enjoyment* in religion." Now, there is a fundamental error in such instruction. Not happy! Had I been present where such instruction was given, I would have told that minister that he was not a converted man if that was his experience. It is thus that a legal religion is inculcated on converts by legalists. But how many persons are just here—afraid to find any other way for fear it will lead to delusion! Oh, that it might be seen that a religion which does not produce present peace and blessedness is not, of course, a religion of love. It is false.

6. Any course of instruction that presses duty without hold-

ing up Christ is like requiring labor without food and brings into bondage. It is like requiring the Israelites to make brick without straw, and those who give such instruction are obliged to whip, and scourge, and abuse the dear church of God to get the little service they do out of them. Hold up duty without Christ, and legality is inevitable. They are starved for lack of Christ. But let them see Christ and they will work, of course, as duty is appropriately enforced.

7. It is the other extreme to hold up Christ without calling to duty that begets antinomianism. To feed the church with Christ and leave her inactive is the way to produce a religious dyspepsia. But give the church the right food and enough work to do, and she will thrive. Only let us have the bread that comes down from heaven, and we shall have spiritual health, and even physical health, if we only have work enough to keep us busy.

8. If we may believe the confessions of the great mass of those who profess religion, they are in bondage. I labored for many years to convert sinners but saw them fall, under the legal instruction of ministers, into bondage. I labored and prayed for them night and day, and do now, and yet they seem to know little of liberty. They often, by their looks, seem to ask, "Is this Christianity?" "Is this the boasted religion of Christ?" "Wherein does it differ from the Jew's religion?" A man said to me once with great honesty, although in vulgar language, "The gospel is not what it is cracked up to be." His idea was that the gospel promised liberty but did not confer it. Now, how many would say just that if they would tell their hearts? They would say "The gospel is not what the Apostle said it was." Yes, poor soul, it is, but you have not got it. Taste and see. Come to the gospel feast. You have compassed that mountain long enough. Don't expect Christ to make you free while you turn your back on Him.

9. When the power of religion is gone, the form but hardens the heart, and makes men more pharisaical and hypocritical every day. What would you have a man do? Cast off his profession, stop prayer, and go back to the world? No, just love and serve in the spirit. But if you will not do this, then give up your profession; that is my advice. Do you doubt whether God would rather have you give up your profession than live in mere form and heartless obedience? "I would thou wert cold or hot. So then

because thou art lukewarm, and neither cold nor hot, I will spew thee out of my mouth" (Rev. 3:15-16). How loathsome to Him are the mockeries and slavish obedience to His holy will! The text represents Christ as actually vomiting them up. Now, I would not recommend apostasy but condemn hypocrisy and bring you to Christ.

10. None really understand this liberty but those who have experienced it, and those who have experienced it cannot find language to express it.

11. Many exclaim against antinomianism who are mere legalists, while both these characters are an abomination to God.

12. When the shepherds attempt to drive instead of lead the flock, they lay a snare before them. We cannot make people love by whipping, scolding, and driving them. God has given His law with its sanctions, but He opens His blessed heart to beget love. Dearly beloved, are any of you in bondage? Have you left your first love? Did somebody tell you that you must go down into the valley of humiliation, and did you go? Alas! What a mistake! You should have gone up to the mountain by faith. What is true humility? Will you return to your first love? And will you "commit the keeping of your souls to him in well doing, as unto a faithful Creator"? (1 Pet. 4:19). Let us all go to Christ to receive our liberty.

16

JOY IN GOD*

Habakkuk 3:17, 18

"Although the fig tree shall not blossom, neither shall fruit be in the vines; the labour of the olive shall fail, and the fields shall yield no meat; the flock shall be cut off from the fold, and there shall be no herd in the stalls: yet I will rejoice in the Lord, I will joy in the God of my salvation."

In this lecture I will show:

> I. *What is implied in the state of mind which the prophet describes.*
> II. *This state is indispensable to peace of mind and to salvation.*

I. *What is implied in the state of mind which the prophet describes.*

1. The true knowledge of God. The prophet would not have said what he did unless he had known God as He really is—a being in every way worthy of confidence and unfailing trust.

2. Perfect confidence in God, in His natural and moral attributes, His natural perfection and His moral character is also implied. Observe, he says, even though all temporal mercies are withheld and fail, he will yet rejoice in God. Though calamity of

---

*Ibid., No. 20, September 27, 1843.

the severest kind should fall upon him and all around him, yet he will confide in God fully, and with the utmost assurance. God should be to him a source of joy—deep, constant, never-failing even though He should in His just indignation do all those things.

3. Perfect sympathy with God is implied in this state of mind. His language is consistent with no other state than one of complete and universal sympathy with God in all His works and ways. Not only does the prophet have confidence in God as just and righteous, but he joyfully, and with his whole soul, enters into the spirit which God cherishes toward all objects. The prophet views the objects with the same eye, acquiesces most entirely in the glorious manifestations of God's indignation against sin, and rejoices with a full heart, even in the midst of the judgments of His hand. God is regarded as equally good in His judgments and His mercies—to be rejoiced in as much when in holy indignation He chastises a rebellious nation as when in mercy He pours blessings upon the penitent and obedient; to be adored with supreme and unspeakable love in all the wonders of His work, in His fearful visitations of merited punishment, no less than when in His grace, He causes the mountains of plenty to be opened and streams of prosperity to flow to every quarter of the land.

And this state implies more than mere submission, in the commonly understood religious use of that term. The prophet did not barely *tolerate* God's dealings in His providence; his language means not simply that he would not find fault, that he would not murmur or complain, that he would tolerate God so far as not to go into overt rebellion against Him. But what does he say? "I will rejoice in the Lord, I will joy in the God of my salvation." He goes the whole length of full and overflowing joy and ecstatic rejoicing.

God, though He delights not in the death of a sinner, but desires rather his return to life and happiness and salvation, yet renders the righteous retribution which the good of universal being demands. He does so not in the spirit of revenge and malice, but from a holy and unalterable regard to the dictates of impartial benevolence; and in all this display of God's judgment, He is everlastingly and unchangingly at peace with himself, and forever rejoices in the consummation of right and the maintenance of eternal justice in accordance with, and subservient to, the great end of universal good. In this work of His, God does, and cannot but rejoice, for His name is Love. So the righteous prophet also rejoiced in sympathy with God and in complete conformity of heart to the same great end.

4. God is regarded as the all-sufficient portion of the soul. Though all else should fail, still his joy would be overflowing, perennial. No circumstances whatever could have any power to quench the flame of love, no wind to parch the soil and dry the current of holy joy in the soul.

This state of mind is such that the soil cannot be deprived of its portion while God lives and reigns, while He holds the throne and sways the scepter of infinite love. The mind cannot be robbed of good, of happiness and joy, of an all-satisfying portion, while God endures; though all else gives way and disappears, God remains, and the soul is full.

5. The prophet implies that this state of mind includes universal and joyful acquiescence in all God's will. An intelligent mind, in being able to adopt the language of the prophet, must be, as are the blessed above, in harmony with the divine will.

II. *This state is indispensable to peace of mind and to salvation.*

1. Without this state of mind, the providence of God will continually distress and disturb. Unless you can see calamity and judgments come upon men for their sins, and behold them with joy and peace, you cannot be happy; for these things are and must be constantly taking place. Men must be able to rejoice in God, let Him do what He will. They must be able to depend on His wisdom and love, and feel assured that He can make no mistake, that He is doing all for the best. Unless men can thus confide, they cannot be happy in God and rejoice in Him; for God must often visit the world with severe judgments.

2. This state of mind is indispensable to prevent being disturbed by Satan. God must of course do many things mysterious to His creatures. He is working on a vast scale, consistent with His infinite nature. Much must be unexplained and inexplicable to creatures finite in duration and knowledge. In many cases, doubtless, it would be impossible so to lay before a finite mind the whole scheme of things as to make him see the reason for the

divine conduct. Now, if men cannot feel that God is good in any way, however appearances may be, then they cannot rest in Him and be at peace. Satan will take advantage of all such mysteries, disturbing the mind's repose, throwing it off balance, and sending it headlong down the declivity of infidelity, or if not that, yet greatly harassing and vexing the soul's peace and communion with God. "Ah," Satan will say, "why did God make man as He did, liable to suffer the extremest misery without possibility of escape; and moreover, when He knew certainly that such would be the result? How can God be good and yet permit the world to be as it is—the abode of hate, and war, and suffering inexpressible—to go on as it has these thousands of years in blood and carnage? Why is a good man cut off in the midst of his days, taken from a field of usefulness upon his very entrance thereinto, while a vile and profane wretch, doing nothing but evil continually, is left to live on in prosperity, a sheer curse to the world? Why is one portion of the human race sunk in deep wretchedness, in the profoundest night of ignorance and vice? Could not God have carried the blessed light of heaven to their desolate shores if He had chosen to do so? And can He be good having not done so? "Why," Satan whispers, "should God send parching heat, when drenching rain is needed—and floods of rain, when there should be the warm and genial sun in its mild shining? Why is the holy saint tortured with disease and racked with pain, the faithful martyr bound to the stake, the witness to the truth made to pour out his blood in its defense? Surely the world is sadly out of joint—these are not the dispositions which an all-wise and all-good being would make!" Nothing but the most perfect confidence in God can prevent us from accusing Him of ignorance or impotence, or downright malevolence. In the midst of so much that must be wholly unaccountable to finite minds, what is needed but such a confidence as to say, "Let Him do what He will, I will rejoice in Him continually."

3. Nothing but his confidence can secure the soul against that kind of care and anxiety that restless fear of ill and wrong, which is so destructive of peace and dishonorable to God. Persons are perplexed and anxious because God deals in a particular way with them; they have no confidence in Him, and they cannot be happy until they do have.

4. Nothing short of this state of mind can meet the demands of our intelligence. Reason affirms that we ought to have universal and perfect confidence in God, because He is infinitely wise, infinitely powerful, and infinitely good; and there must be a sense of guilt in the soul where this confidence is not exercised, and the peace of the soul must thereby be destroyed. Nothing else, moreover, is consistent with God's commands. A man does not obey God until he comes into that state—until he can say with the prophet, "Although the fig tree shall not blossom neither shall fruit be in the vines; the labor of the olive shall fail, and the fields shall yield no meat; the flocks shall be cut off from the fields, and there shall be no herd in the stalls: yet I will rejoice in the Lord and I will joy in the God of my salvation." He is an unbeliever and a wicked man who does not thus rejoice, who does not adopt this language as his own with all his heart.

5. It is in this very state of mind that salvation consists. Nothing short of this is salvation. What is holiness here? What is holiness in heaven? What is it but the state in which the mind looks over all God's works and exclaims, "Holy, holy, holy, is the Lord of hosts: the whole earth is full of his glory" (Isa. 6:3). Who shall not praise Thee, O God? Who shall not fear Thy name, O king of saints? No others are saved but those who are thus in sympathy with God. And they are saved no further than they thus rejoice in Him and cry, "Whom have I in heaven but thee? and there is none upon earth that I desire beside thee" (Ps. 73:25). "Thou art my father, my God, and the rock of my salvation" (Ps. 89:26).

REMARKS

1. This state of mind is indispensable to usefulness. A man cannot be truly useful in the world, cannot do what is needed to be done, cannot make the world holy and happy by his influence until he is thus. He cannot truly represent God, promote genuine religion, or enforce the claims of piety on man until he is thus. He may have much zeal, create conviction, produce excitement, but he does not and cannot lead the soul to God. He does not know what true religion is in his own experience, and he cannot tell others what it is, however clear his intellect may be, and sway

their minds under the power of truth. For he is a stranger to that honest, hearty, deep-felt conviction of the truth, and that personal consecration and devotion with its resulting joy—without which all efforts are in vain. His life, conversation, conduct, and preaching will not exemplify true religion without this experience.

2. Anything short of this in one who professes religion is a gross stumbling block. What! Profess religion, declare God to be the all-sufficient and never-failing portion of the soul—profess to rely implicitly on Him, and trust in Him always and forever, and yet practically show the same anxiety and worry, the same distress and perturbation, the same uneasy, restless disquietude that other people have? Is not that a stumbling block? Would it have been honorable to God had the prophet gone on to complain and lament the loss of comforts—to cry out, "What shall I do? I am undone!" What if he had refused to be in sympathy with God, to justify Him in all His doings, to love Him and to rejoice in Him through all? And does it not dishonor God for professedly pious men to distrust His goodness and murmur at His justice? Is it not a stumbling block to those who look on and see their inconsistency?

3. Many seem to be satisfied with nothing else in God but His mercy, without regard to the conditions of its exercise. In so doing, they suppose mercy to be enacted inconsistently with holiness, as if mere fondness, the obeying of the impulses of blind sensibility, could be mercy at all. They are moved to joy and praise only by the compassion of God, and are comforted only by a view of His dealings with His creatures. Instead of rejoicing in *God*, in the great, and glorious, and harmonious whole, which makes up the perfection of His character, they can see Him only in one light—that of compassion and grace. Had the prophet been so, could he have said what he did? Every sustenance of life cut off, the world starving around him, and desolation and desert wastes stretching over the land—how could he rejoice if he had tranquillity only in God's mercy and compassion?

This class of persons seems to have no other idea of religion than a sort of good-natured fondness, a sort of easy disposition, so as not be be angry at sin or sinners, but to exercise a mere blind indiscriminate compassion for sinners and a disposition to treat all, impenitent and penitent, with the same leniency and in just the same way. These men neither know nor worship the true God; the Bible is s stumbling block to them, and Satan keeps them constantly in a worry and fret by pressing on them these points of God's character. Much of the Old Testament—the dealings of God with the heathen, the prayers of David in the Psalms for vengeance—seem to be the spirit of hate and malice. They will not comprehend that a God of love can inflict the penalty of a righteous law; yet, they cannot shut their eyes to the undeniable fact that He does visit the sinner with utter destruction.

4. Holy beings, from the very nature of holiness, rejoice nonetheless in God because He rules the earth in *judgment* and because He visits the world with calamity; love Him nonetheless; confide in Him nonetheless; are no less happy in Him because He sends sinners to hell. They sympathize with Him in *all* He does in the promotion of the highest good of the universe. They love Him nonetheless for His scourgings, for His desolations, for His destruction of men and of nations, than for the pouring out of His Spirit to bring the world to salvation. They know He has the same great end in view in both cases, and they love Him equally in both.

5. Many who profess religion are at heart *Universalists*. They are not thoroughly and truly with God in His administration of government. Universalism has its seat in the *heart*. It is a state of heart divesting God of His holiness, of His justice, of His prerogative to execute terrible judgments, to send the wicked to hell. These things Universalists cannot love. Their God must not do such things as these. Of course not! Is this true religion? To limit God, to say, "Do this or that; don't punish me, my friends, or my race; no matter how rebellious or incorrigible we are, don't destroy us, or we cannot love you"? This is selfishness, and is regarded by Jehovah as such.

6. So many are disturbed by God's providential dealings because they have not the confidence in God which belongs to true religion. Judgments disturb them, throw them off their pivot, and down they go into rebellious murmurings or impious infidelity. If anything goes out of their little channel contrary to *their* marked out path, across their finite judgments, all is wrong.

7. Many seem to have no enjoyment in religion unless the

providence of God seems to favor their particular plans and favorite schemes. "Indeed," they say, "God does just as I want Him to do, all my notions are exactly realized, my ship goes before the breeze with all sails set, in beautiful trim, and therefore, God is good and I am happy!" Their country is blessed, their state is prosperous, their commonwealth is at peace, their family is in prosperity, their circumstances are comfortable. Therefore, God is good, and they are happy! They love God for all this; they rejoice in His love. But let Him thwart them, run across their track, turn upside down their cherished plans, blow to the winds their favorite schemes, and what then? What then? They tolerate God perhaps—perhaps not even that! They by no means rejoice *now* in their God; they do not now joy in the God of their salvation. Oh, no! They cannot help what God has done, to be sure, for He is too strong for them; but suppose they *could*, what would they do? Now what is the matter? They have no true religion. They thought they had religion because God was so good and kind to them. They thought they loved Him, but it was themselves they loved, and Him only because He was subservient to them. They were pleased to have God for an almighty servant. But to have Him on the throne, that was another matter! They are supremely set on their own way, not on God's way. Instead of rejoicing in God's will, whether or not it is like theirs, God must succumb to them, or they are displeased and grieved.

8. To know God as the all-sufficient portion of the soul is the highest knowledge. No man knows anything as he ought to know until he knows this. Until he knows God in this way, he has no knowledge that provides happiness. All other is worse than useless without this. How often have I thought upon the quiet and happiness of ignorance. Ignorance, by its very want of knowledge, avoids much restlessness and anxiety. An increase of knowledge in the same unreconciled state of heart only increases misery and wretchedness. Learning is only a curse without the knowledge of God as the portion of the soul.

9. The happiness of the true saints is secure, because it depends not on external and contingent circumstances but on God himself. They know God, and to know Him is eternal life. As long as God lives and reigns, they know their happiness cannot be disturbed.

President Edwards' wife, at one period, thought she could not bear certain things—she thought certain losses would destroy her peace. She thought she could not bear the alienation of her husband's affection, the loss of her reputation among his people, etc. But when her soul came into communion with God, she was delivered from the fears which had distressed her; she was carried so high above all earthly things, they had no power to affect her happiness. Like the glorious sun, which from its height in the heavens looks down on the earth and rolls rejoicingly on, unmoved by all that passes among us mortals, so the soul whose trust is in God rests in exquisite peace on the bosom of exhaustless love, far beyond all sublunary influences and cares. The martyr at the stake, though in the extremest agony of body, is yet often full, inexpressibly full of glory and joy. Why is this? How can it be? God is the natural and all-sufficient portion of the soul, and it rests in Him.

10. Sinners cannot be happy because of their very state of mind as sinners. If they do not know God, they can find no peace for the sole of their foot—like Noah's dove, on the wing and no place to rest. And why? There *is* no place but in God, and when it does not rest here, it must remain restless, forever seeking peace and finding none. It is thrown from its pivot, and it is naturally impossible for that soul to be happy. It is gnawing upon itself, eating out its own vitals. The soul must return to God, must dwell in God, repose under the shadow of His pavilion, or happiness is out of the question. The home of the soul is the bosom of God. "Thou hast been our dwellingplace in all generations" (Ps. 90:1) is the beautiful and true exclamation of the Psalmist. Until the mind finds its home, its home in God, where can it be quiet? The prophet's soul had reached its home. In this dwelling place rejoicingly he was secure—without care, without anxiety, without fear—with all joy and glory, in unspeakable blessedness.

11. Those who do not know God thus do not know God *truly*.

They have but the outside of religion, the form, the rite, but where is the spirit? Where the filial love, the childlike confidence, the simple unquestioning trust, the artless, heartfelt joy, the soul-absorbing delight in God? Most religion seems to be external—men come to the temple, view the building, the splendor, the sacrifices, the gorgeous apparel, the imposing cermony, and join blindly in the ritual. But the new and living way, into the holy of holies, opened by the great High Priest—that way their foot never trod, that inner glory their eye never rested on. Most have no personal communion with their King, no fellowship with Jesus Christ, or hardly any; but all is distant, cold, hearsay. They have heard of God by the hearing of the ear. But their eyes never have seen Him. Now, the prophet had gone beyond the outward service, inside the veil into the holiest of all, even to the chamber of the King. In view of all that his eye, in the ken of prophetic vision, saw of judgment and calamity, his soul was calm. No, not calm, but intensely wrought up to the most exquisite joy and bliss untold. The prophet knew God and knew His purpose.

12. This is the only reasonable state. This, and this only, answers fully the demands of the intelligence.

13. Sinners can see the necessity of a change of heart. They know this is not their state of mind. Every sinner knows perfectly well he does not feel thus toward God; every sinner knows he cannot be happy unless his own way is followed, his own will gratified. He cannot rejoice in God no matter what he does, and yet who does not know that rejoicing is universal in heaven? How could he be happy in heaven were he to go there? He has no sympathy with God, no delight in His will; he would be alone in heaven. The holiness of that pure place—how could it receive him, or be congenial with his selfishness?

14. If this be true, those who profess religion can see why they are not saved and not likely to be saved. They do not have that spirit, which is the essential element of a state of salvation.

15. Many seem to rest in conviction. They see their sins. They are in agony. There they rest. The agony subsides. But that uneasy state, produced by a sense of present guilt, remains— while they should pass through conviction into a state of conscious consecration, conscious forgiveness and acceptance, and resting their souls joyfully in God. Many do not expect, look for, or labor for anything like continual peace and happiness in God.

16. Those who esteem outward circumstances essential to peace think so because they do not know God. If they only were thus and thus, if they only had this and that, then they could enjoy religion. "If I had some Christian society, if my husband were pious, if I were not so poor, if I enjoyed good health, or were not so

severely afflicted, if the church were only awake and active, if these, and a thousand other things were as I wish they were, I could enjoy religion. But as it is, in my circumstances, I cannot rejoice; I am in distress, in solitude, in persecution, in poverty; how can I be glad?" How can you? How could the prophet rejoice? He could rejoice by having God for his all-sufficient portion and his everlasting home. So could you rejoice. If you knew God thus, no suffering—not the most intense—could shake the fabric of your bliss and throw your soul from its firm resting place on the everlasting Rock.

17. Why sinners seek happiness in vain. They seek it where it cannot be found—everywhere but in God. They strive to attain all sorts of knowledge but the knowledge of God. They push their researches in all directions but toward God. They do everything else but give themselves to God. They seek the world, its pleasures, honors, riches, fame and glory—can these be an everlasting portion? They pass away like a dream. Can the soul say, "If all these pass away, yet is my treasure secure, my happiness unmoved"? Indeed *no*, for these were the sources of his joy, and how can he be happy? He will say, "You have taken away my gods; what else do I have?" So might the Christian's hope be destroyed if God could be dethroned and Satan have full rule. Then the Christian might say, "All joy has fled from my soul." But while the throne of God stands unshaken, the soul who has put his trust in God remains safe. Can riches make a man happy? Is the richest man in this country happy? No, he is one of the most miserable men, and he grows more wretched every day. How could he more effectually become the sport of winds and waves, of every vicissitude, than by placing his heart on riches? His houses burn down, his ships founder at sea, his tenants fail to pay their rent; he is at the mercy of every wind that blows. Can he say, "Let every penny of my wealth be burned up, and still I am happy"? Young man, you are a student. You are talented, ambitious, aspiring—you climb, and climb, and climb the ladder of promotion to the summit of greatness. Are you happy? You are only multiplying incalculably the vulnerable points of your soul, and from the very peak of your fame, you will topple and fall and plunge into the lowest deeps of perdition. Oh, how mad! Why not come back to God, know God, and be able to say, "He lives, and reigns, and I am happy"?

18. The true knowledge of God completely ravishes the soul. Men think they can be satisfied in some object of their choice. This is a mistake with respect to all created things. But with respect to God it is sublimely true! In God is the soul swallowed up, absorbed, hidden, lost, in an ocean of bliss.*

No man should stop short of this knowledge. Do not stop until you reach this high goal. If you profess religion, do not stop until you arrive at this blissful consummation. Be not content until you can rest in God as Habakkuk did. He was no more than in a state of salvation. He was no more than happy. This was not the peculiar privilege of a prophet. And suppose it were *then* so. What did Christ mean when He said, "He that is least in the kingdom of heaven is greater than he"? (Matt. 11:11). You may be able to say not only this, which the prophet did, but everything in the same direction, in the strongest possible manner.

19. Wherever you lack this state, you may know you have unbelief. If there is anything in which you cannot say, "I rejoice in God," you are in unbelief and have no right to stay there a moment.

Most who profess religion know little or nothing of this state of confidence and joy; they therefore represent religion falsely, as a gloomy, sepulchral, deathbed affair, not to be thought of at the same time with joy and gladness.

God deliver us and bring us to the state of joy in Him.

---

*This seems to describe Finney's own experience in 1843 as he drew his lectures on holiness to a close. See "Total Commitment" in *Answers to Prayer*.

17

THE BENEVOLENCE OF GOD*

1 John 4:16

"God is love."

It is not my intention, in commenting upon these words, to prove them true, for I should consider myself poorly employed in attempting to prove the truth of *any* scripture. It is not so much the business of the minister of the gospel to *defend* the truths of the Bible as it is to expound and illustrate them as he finds them revealed, and show their bearing on the relations and responsibilities of men. It would be easy for me to advance any arguments, drawn from the whole range of the created universe, to show that "God is love"; but this I shall not do at this time. I shall merely:

I. *Show the meaning of the text.*
II. *State some things which must be true if "God is love."*

I. *The meaning of the text.*
1. By the assertion that "God is love," I do not understand the Apostle to teach that the *nature*, the *essence* or *substance* of God, is love, for this would be an absurd proposition. Nor do I understand him to teach that God is love in the sense of fondness for His creatures, that His love is merely an emotion, belonging to

---

*Ibid., No. 25, December 6, 1843.

the sensibility rather than to the voluntary faculty of His mind.

2. I *do* understand the text to teach that God is *benevolent*—supremely devoted to doing good—that all His powers are consecrated to the promotion of the highest good of sentient being. The Apostle, by the strong language of the text, surely does not mean to affirm that the nature or substance of God is love, but that His character or voluntary state is infinitely benevolent, that benevolence constitutes the *whole* disposition or state of His will, and that His character is constantly and eternally benevolent—not benevolent at one time, and selfish at another, but *forever*, and without change, benevolent.

II. *Some things which must be true if "God is love."*

1. If it is true that "God is love," it follows that He has been eternally so, or else His character is mutable, which is impossible.

2. If "God is love," He has but one intention or subjective motive for His conduct. He aims at but one thing—consequently, His character is simple, not compound or mixed. In other words, if His ultimate end in acting is a benevolent one, it necessarily follows that He always acts in view of one great consideration: the promotion of the objects of benevolence, or the good of universal being.

3. If "God is love," He never has done, and never will do, anything but in execution of His benevolent intention. There is a difference between the benevolence and the executive volitions of God. His benevolence is one thing, and the action which He puts forth in execution of His benevolence is another. God was benevolent from eternity, but He has not acted in execution of His benevolent designs from eternity—He has not eternally put forth creative power, for if He had done so, there would be created things as old as himself, which is impossible. The will of God has forever been in a benevolent state; the developing, or acting out of that benevolence, is His actions or doings. Now, I say that He never has done, and never will do, anything but in execution of His great design, anything which will not tend to realize the objects of His benevolence, or to accomplish that on which His heart is set. In other words, all the actions of God have been, and will continue to be, in execution of His grand design: the promotion of the highest good of being.

4. If "God is love," it follows, that while He remains benevolent, He can do nothing but in execution of a benevolent intention. He will do only what necessarily results from such a state of mind. Every man knows from his own consciousness that this must be true. Action is caused by design or intention; therefore, it can never be inconsistent with intention. If I plan to go directly home, I cannot go in an opposite direction or loiter by the way. I can relinquish my intention, but so long as the design continues, I must act in obedience to that design. Now, while God remains benevolent, He can only act in obedience to a benevolent design—He *must* act in execution of a benevolent purpose. Since he is a free agent, He can, of course, cease to be benevolent; but while He remains benevolent, He cannot cease to act benevolently.

5. If "God is love," it follows that He has omitted nothing, and can omit nothing, the performance of which would, upon the whole, result in the highest good of being. God is infinitely wise. He can, therefore, make no mistakes. Good men being benevolent cannot act inconsistently with a benevolent design; but having finite intellects, they may make mistakes and err in the path of duty. While intending the highest good of the universe, they may be mistaken as to the means for promoting this end, and so accomplish only mischief by their actions. But not so with God. His infinite wisdom permits Him to make no mistakes. While He remains benevolent, He will and can do nothing inconsistent with His grand design. Hence it follows that He never has, that He never will, and that while He remains benevolent, He never can omit to do anything which would conduce to the highest good of being—it is naturally impossible for Him to do so. He must cease to be benevolent, or else He can do nothing inconsistent with the highest good of being, or leave undone anything which universal good requires.

6. If "God is love," He has allowed, and will allow, nothing to occur that would be injurious to the universe that can be prevented by the attributes of Jehovah. This ought to be perfectly understood. I say, then, that if almighty power, under the control of infinite wisdom and infinite love, *can* prevent the existence of anything which will harm the universe, it *will*, of course, do so. If God is love, it follows as a self-evident truth that He has prevented, and will prevent, so far as He wisely can, the existence of

everything which would work ultimate injury to being.

7. God, being love, has created the universe in obedience to the law of benevolence; for His creative acts result from His benevolence—they are only effects of the benevolent state of His heart. Hence:

(1) He created the universe as early as He wisely could. It would have been a natural impossibility for Him to create *from eternity*, for then His creatures would have been as old as himself. But He did put forth creative power as soon as He benevolently could, taking into account His own character and designs, and the prospective character of those whom He was to create.

(2) He also created the universe as rapidly as He could, consistently with His benevolent design. Not only did He begin His work as early as He wisely could, but when commenced, He carried it on as rapidly as benevolence would permit.

(3) If "God is love," He has created as many worlds as benevolence demanded, and has made no more and no less than the law of benevolence required.

(4) He has created just such orders of beings, and endowed them with just such capacities, as His infinite wisdom saw to be consistent with the accomplishment of His benevolent designs.

8. If "God is love," He has done, and will do, as much to promote the happiness of His creatures as He possibly can. Had He done, or should He do, more or less for the happiness of His subjects than He has done, and will do, He could not be a benevolent being—He would become a wicked one. But being love, no one can accuse Him of neglecting His duty to His creatures. Hence:

(1) He has done, and will do, as much to prevent the misery of His subjects as the good of being will allow. This follows, of course, if He is a benevolent being, or a "God of love." Many persons seem jealous if any limit is imposed on the *power* of God; at the same time they manifest little concern as to whether or not His moral attributes, His justice and benevolence are limited. They seem to think that God might, if He pleased, prevent all misery, regardless of its cause. Now this is a false notion, for if God is a benevolent being, it would have been a natural impossibility for Him not to have done all that He could consistently do to prevent the misery of His creatures. It was, and is, impossible

for Him not to do this and remain a God of benevolence, a God of love. If He had fallen short of it, He would not have been benevolent at all. How can a *man* be benevolent and not do all the good he can? What is benevolence but willing to accomplish all the good that lies in our power?

(2) If "God is love," He has done, and will do, all that He can to prevent the sins of moral beings. He never has allowed sin to be committed which He could wisely or benevolently prevent— which He could prevent without sinning himself. Do you think this a strange assertion? But is it not true? And is it not better that God should permit someone else to sin rather than sin himself? Morever, God has never allowed anything to exist that is inconsistent with the perfect holiness of His subjects which He could wisely prevent. He has never allowed any temptation to draw His creatures from the path of duty which He could prevent without an infraction of the law of benevolence. Now, is not this self-evident? If God is love, is it not certain that no sin or temptation ever existed which He could wisely prevent? Under existing circumstances, if God had done more than He has done to prevent sin, He would have sinned himself. This is self-evident; for if God is a benevolent being, He never could have omitted any exertion to prevent sin which would be consistent with the good of the universe. Therefore, if He had done more than He has done to prevent it, He would no longer be a sinless being.

9. God is love; therefore, He has made every sacrifice on His part which He could benevolently make for the promotion of the highest good of being. "Herein is love, not that we loved God, but that he loved us, and sent his Son to be the propitiation for our sins" (1 John 5:10). Yes, God did not even hesitate to give His Son, His only Son, to die for us. He had no daughters, no other children, only one Son. You who are parents know how strongly a father becomes attached to an only child; while, if he has several children, he does not concentrate his affections with so great intensity upon any one of them. But if he has an only child, he prizes him as his greatest earthly treasure; he will see his property swept away, his buildings torn down, and all his earthly goods destroyed before he will consent to give up his darling child. Now observe. God did not hesitate to give up His only Son to be a ransom for many; and after He has gone so far, will He not be ready

to make any reasonable sacrifice for the good of His creatures? I tell you yes. If it would be wise, He would willingly send His Son to earth to die for us every year. He would himself die a thousand times if it were possible and benevolence demanded it. When He sees that a sacrifice on His part, however great, will be the lesser of two evils, He will not hesitate to make it.

10. If "God is love," He has created all things as well as He possibly could. The question is often agitated—how could God have made such and such a thing, and why did He make it just as He did? Now observe. If God is love, He has done the best He could in the creation of the universe. He has established the best relations and founded the best laws which He possibly could have made for the government of His creatures. We have a beautiful illustration of this truth in our own persons. God made us in the very best way; and if we are ever disposed to find fault with our physical or mental construction, if we will only examine ourselves, we shall be compelled to grant that God has done His best in our creation, having placed all our organs and faculties in just the right place. And if we look away from ourselves, we shall see that in giving laws to the universe, in directing all its movements, in ordering the succession of seasons, of day and night, God has done as wisely and as well as He possibly could. He does not half do His work, nor does He do it slothfully; whatever He sets himself about, He does in the best possible manner.

11. God has *governed* the universe as well as He possibly could. Not only has He created moral beings well, but He has governed them well. Not a single hour, since He first put forth creative power, has He ceased to control the universe in the best possible manner.

12. It does not follow from the fact that God is love that there will not be great, but only incidental evil always existing in the universe. Where there is sin, there must of necessity be misery; there are also many natural evils, which are consequent on the arrangement of the universe. But this misery, and these evils, do not invalidate, nor are they inconsistent with the character of God. They are only incidental evils, resulting from the accomplishment of His great plans of benevolence—the plans, in pursuance of which He created the universe and affixed to it laws for the regulation of its movements. I say that certain incidental

evils have resulted from the creation of the universe, which God made in the best possible manner. But mark, they are only incidental to a benevolent plan. It does not follow, then, that because God is love, great and incidental evils may not exist in the universe, nor that new forms of evil, unknown to us but known to God, will not make their appearance.

13. It does, however, follow from the fact that God is love that as a whole, creation will result in greater good than evil. God was infinitely wise from the beginning. Now, had He seen that creation would result in more evil than good, He could not have ordered it; therefore, we may be certain that the evil will never equal the good which will result from creation, but that it will fall indefinitely short of it.

14. It is also certain that a majority of His creatures will be happy—that the number of those who are happy will greatly overbalance the number of those who are miserable.

15. It is not at all probable that the majority of the inhabitants of any world, except the place of torment, will be finally miserable. I say that it is unreasonable to suppose that more evil than good will result to any world where God has placed moral beings on trial. If it were not true that in every world which God has created, the amount of good resulting will equal or exceed the amount of evil, how, I ask, could God be a benevolent being? What tokens of His benevolence could we have in such a creation?

16. If "God is love," it follows that He abhors whatever is inconsistent with the highest good of being. He of course abhors all sin, and all sinners, and is opposed to all the selfishness in the universe and to whatever is forbidden by His law. If He is benevolent, He is manifestly sincere when He commands His subjects to be holy; and He commands this with all His heart, and soul, and mind, and strength. As a necessity of His character, He is better pleased with holiness than with sin.

17. It follows that He will exercise any degree of needed severity on rebels against His law. He will not hesitate to execute vengeance on the doers of iniquity. We have myriads of instances in this world of the sternness with which God carries out the principles of His government. How often are men and families, yes, even nations, overwhelmed and crushed beneath the mighty

wheels of this vast machine—with *such* firmness does God carry out His benevolent plans. His government of the universe will go on; whoever stands in the way of it will be ground to powder, no matter whether he be an angel from heaven or a fiend from hell.

So, too, in the moral world. If an individual will throw himself in the way of the execution of God's plans, He is sure to let him fall, even though he is a great and mighty king of Israel and though his fall will be the occasion of dire ruin to the church and the world. Yes, God could and did let even David fall. It was better that He should permit the king of Israel to fall and the tale of his crime be told from Dan to Beersheba, through heaven and through hell—I say it was better that He should let the wheels roll over and crush His chosen king rather than that the car of His moral government should be for a moment stopped. And what God did to David, He does in a thousand other instances in the administration of His moral government. Yes, he will let Peter even deny his master, and the whole church apostatize from the true faith, rather than alter the plans of His moral government. He does this because He is infinitely benevolent, because He is firm in the execution of His wise plans, and because He is moving on the great concerns of His government on a vast scale. God will not shrink from sending the wicked to hell, anymore than from taking the righteous to heaven, for both acts are parts of the same great plan. It is indispensable to His peace of mind that He should do this. I repeat, God could never be satisfied with His own conduct if He did not send the wicked to hell as well as take the righteous to heaven. Both acts result from the same great principle of love to being—a principle, which seated in the breast of God, like an infinite volcano, bursts forth on every side—on the one hand scattering death and damnation among the inhabitants of hell, and on the other, casting the smiles of love over the dwellers in heaven. Yes, it is the same thing heaving up from the very depths of Infinite Mind. It is the carrying out of the same benevolent design, which on the one hand consigns the wicked to hell, and on the other, takes the righteous to heaven.

18. If "God is love," He is good and deserving of praise, whatever He does. If there are any cases in which He is more virtuous than in others, they are those in which He is obliged to sacrifice His own feelings—the strong affections of His nature—in order to

inflict merited punishment on the wicked. But being a benevolent being, He always has one intention, and that a benevolent one. He is always guided by the same infinite wisdom; therefore, His virtue is always one and the same; it is never diminished and can never be increased. Strictly speaking, virtue cannot be predicated on His executive volitions, but only on His one eternal consecration to the good of being. It is evident, then, that God is equally worthy of praise at all times and for everything that He does. Hence, He requires us to give thanks at all times. "In everything give thanks," the Apostle says, "for this is the will of God in Christ Jesus concerning you" (1 Thess. 5:18). *They* greatly err who think God must be *praised* when He performs certain acts, and only *tolerated* when He performs others. For instance, He is more merciful under the *gospel* than He was under the *legal* dispensation; therefore, some infer He is more worthy to be praised *now* than He was *then*.

This false notion arises from an ignorance of the fact that God exercises all the attributes of His character in every action; therefore, the different phases of His executive volitions all have the same moral character—for His character belongs solely to His intention, and that results in all His acts, His mercy, justice, etc. His virtue lies behind His executive actions. Virtue is only the outflow of the vast fountain of benevolence within himself.

19. If "God is love," it follows that He will do for every individual of His creatures all that He can wisely do. He will not only do this for the universe at large, but He will also do it for each one of us. Yes, He will do just as much as He possibly can, under existing conditions, for every individual creature in His universe. He *has* done this, and He will continue to do it; and should He do any more or any less for our good than He is doing and will do, He would commit sin. This follows as self-evident if it is true "God is love."

20. If God is benevolent, He will do all the good through us that He wisely can. He will not let a single hair of our head fall to the ground without doing all the good through us that He possibly can, under existing circumstances. What do you think of that? I tell you that not a sinner will go to hell if God can wisely and benevolently employ our instrumentality to save him.

21. What God can wisely do for us and through us must de-

pend mainly on the course we pursue. I did not mean by the preceding remarks that God could not do more *for* us and *through* us if the circumstances were different. I merely meant to affirm that He has done all that He could, considering the course we have taken and do take. If we had acted differently, He would have acted differently. If we had done better than we have, God would have made us wiser and better than we are. So the amount of good which is to be done by us must depend entirely on the course we pursue. God may have done far less for each one of us than He would have done had we acted differently toward Him.

22. God is always doing the best for us and all around us that He possibly can under the circumstances. But by the exercise of our agency, we may so vary the circumstances that He will be compelled to change His conduct, or cease to be benevolent. This is evidently true. It is manifest that God must act differently toward us in the different circumstances in which we place ourselves. Consider the case of a sinner. He repents and believes on the Lord Jesus Christ. Will not God at once change His conduct toward him? Suppose that he lays himself out to do good to others; will not God assist him and make him the instrument of doing infinitely more good than he would have done if he had remained a rebel? The fact is, we may limit the goodness of God to others in a thousand ways; for what He does for the individual subjects of His moral government depends, in a great measure, on the voluntary agency of other free beings.

REMARKS

1. We see why implicit faith and confidence in God is a duty. Faith would not and could not be a duty if God were not a God of love, a God of wisdom—in short, just such a God as the Scriptures say He is.

2. If "God is love," it follows that anything inconsistent with perfect confidence in Him is infinitely wicked.

3. Anything, therefore, like murmuring against His providences, must be very sinful.

4. We see why universal and perfect obedience to God is a duty. If God were not love, obedience to Him would not be a duty. If His laws were not founded on benevolence, we would be

under no obligation to obey them. But as God is love, and as His laws were framed with a benevolent intention, we are bound to obey Him. A rejection of His laws is rebellion against the good of the universe.

5. Our subject gives us a clue to the correct interpretation of the Bible. We must interpret everything in it consistently with the perfect benevolence of God. Once we know that God is love, *everything in the Scriptures must be explained in light of that truth.*

6. We have a key to explain the providences of God. We often hear people say in a complaining way, "Why did God do such and such? Why did He afflict me in such and such a manner?" Now the answer to such questions is obvious. It is because the laws of benevolence demand it. So every movement of divine providence and grace, whether it brings suffering or happiness, is employed for one and the same reason: benevolence requires it.

7. The benevolence of God lays no foundation for the inference of universal salvation. It is no more reasonable to infer from the benevolence of God that misery will not exist in a future world than it would be to infer from the same premise that there will be no more misery in this world. It would be just as reasonable to say that pain does not exist at all as it would be to say that it will not exist through all eternity. But it is correct to say that it will have no power over the holy and the good in a future state. We stand on firm ground when we affirm this, but we have no authority from reason or revelation for saying that great and incalculable evil will not exist in some part of the universe throughout all eternity.

8. To my own mind, a weighty objection to some second advent doctrines is found in the fact that "God is love." I cannot see how it could be consistent with the benevolence of God to destroy the world at the present time. As far as we know, and the fact is not disputed by anyone who believes the doctrines of Christianity, a great majority of those who have inhabited the earth have gone to hell. God saw this from the beginning; could He have benevolently ordained the destruction of the world under such circumstances? It is no answer to this argument to say that men are free and can escape hell if they please, and therefore God is clear of their blood. Suppose there were but one world in the

universe, and that God had peopled it with beings who would certainly be eternally miserable. Assume that their own agency had made them so—assume that God had done His best to prevent their misery—I ask, "Would God have any right to make such a world?" By no means unless He should see that it would offer sufficient happiness to himself to overbalance the misery of the creatures placed in such circumstances. Now, what could be thought of the benevolence of God, if at the present time, under existing circumstances, He should destroy the world? We are to judge the character of God by His dealings with *us*. We are told little of His doings in heaven. We are not told whether the sun, or the moon, or the stars are inhabited; therefore, we must judge the character of God by His doings *here*. Let us remember this, and let us remember that when God created the world, He had full knowledge of all that would result from its creation. And if, foreseeing that nine-tenths of its inhabitants would be eternally miserable, that a vast majority of those who have peopled it would to go hell—if, I say, notwithstanding all this, He had determined to wipe the world out of existence now, when all or most of the results have been evil, could we consider Him a God of love? It is no answer to his question to say that we do not know how much good God will accomplish in other parts of the universe by the destruction of the earth at the present time. As I just said, we are to judge the character of God by His dealings *here*, not by His actions in other parts of the universe. As far as we can judge, greater evil than good has thus far resulted from the creation of the world; and if it should now be swept out of the universe, could we suppose that it was created with a benevolent design? Since God is love, how can it be that the great mass of men will be finally miserable?

9. The fact that God is a benevolent being appears to be a most cogent argument in favor of the doctrine of a temporal millennium, the result of which will be the conversion of the majority of men. No other doctrine, as far as we can judge, is consistent with the benevolence of God. God tells us to reason with Him and judge for ourselves His character. Let us do it. So much does the doctrine of a temporal millennium consist with the benevolence of God that the mere announcement of the fact that He is love seems to tell us with trumpet tongue that He is yet moving in this

world with His great plans of benevolence. His love assures us that He is going on from conquering to conquer, and that the time will yet come when all shall know the Lord, from the least unto the greatest. I love to dwell upon the character of God in this light. I love to think of Him, not merely as Creator of the universe but as the great and good Governor of all things; who can deign to put His mighty hand into the base affairs of earth, and turn, and overturn, until His benevolent design in creating the earth is fully accomplished—until the majority of men come to be His obedient subjects, while those who are damned serve as monuments to warn the universe of the dreadful effects of sin. What! Shall God be defeated in His plans? Is it indeed true, as some assert, that the tendency of things on earth is to go morally backward? If it is, how grievous was Christ mistaken when He compared the kingdom of heaven "unto leaven, which a woman took, and hid in three measures of meal till the whole was leavened" (Matt. 11:33). Some even say that Christianity is dying out on earth, that the meal is killing the leaven, instead of the leaven leavening the lump. God forbid that the tendency of His government should be to surrender captured territory. What! Shall the God of the universe, the creator of all things, because the tide of earthly things is rolling back on himself and thwarting His mighty plans, crush the world, bury it in everlasting destruction, and send its teeming millions off to hell? No, if this be so, we are left to the dim light of conjecturing that for some inscrutable reason, God created such a world as this. I do not say that God could not have a good reason for destroying the world at the present moment, but I do say that if such a reason does exist, He would in some way have made it known to us. But when we open the Bible, we find the truth that God is love standing out on every page, like the sun breaking through an ocean of storms, by its light we can go through all the dark sayings of Scripture and through the mysterious workings of Providence. "God is love" is a key with which we may unlock the designs of God and learn that this world was created to aid in accomplishing the good of universal being, and that it will not be destroyed until its work is fully done.

10. If "God is love," there is no favor too great for Him to bestow. No one need say that He is too insignificant a creature for

God to bless, for He is ever ready to bestow the greatest blessings upon us all, whatever our condition, as soon as He possibly can. He comes close to our side and takes every opportunity to do good to us. We cannot open our mouths before He is ready to fill them. We need not starve, waiting for God to come to our relief. He is always close by. If He withholds spiritual blessings from us, we may infer that the difficulty lies with ourselves, not with Him.

Let me say to you who are impenitent sinners, that if at last you make your bed in hell, you, and not God, will be to blame. And to you who profess to love the Lord, if you have not as much grace as you feel you need, if your experience of heavenly things is cold and barren, be assured that you, and not God, are at fault. *He* is continually crying in your ears, "All things are now ready, come ye in and sup with me." He is ever pressing upon you with all the weight of infinite love, seeking for some nook or corner in your hearts where He may come in and fill you with all the fullness of His Son.

18

REVELATION OF GOD'S GLORY*

Exodus 33:12-23

"And Moses said unto the Lord, See, thou sayest unto me, Bring up this people; and thou hast not let me know whom thou wilt send with me. Yet thou hast said, I know thee by name, and thou hast also found grace in my sight. Now therefore, I pray thee, if I have found grace in thy sight, show me now thy way, that I may know thee, that I may find grace in thy sight; and consider that this nation is thy people. And He said, My presence shall go with thee, and I will give thee rest. And he said, unto him, If thy presence go not with me, carry us not up hence. For wherein shall it be known here that I and thy people have found grace in thy sight? Is it not in that thou goest with us? so shall we be separated, I and thy people, from all the people that are upon the face of the earth. And the Lord said unto Moses, I will do this thing also that thou hast spoken; for thou hast found grace in my sight, and I know thee by name.

"And he said, I beseech thee, show me thy glory. And he said, I will make all my goodness pass before thee, and I will proclaim the name of the Lord before thee; and will be gracious to whom I will be gracious, and will show mercy on whom I will show mercy. And he said, Thou canst not see my face; for there shall no man see me, and live. And the Lord said, Behold, there is a place by

---

Ibid., No. 26, December 20, 1843.

me, and thou shalt stand upon a rock: and it shall come to pass, while my glory passeth by, that I will put thee in a cleft of the rock, and will cover thee with my hand while I pass by: and I will take away mine hand, and thou shalt see my back parts; but my face shall not be seen."

In this discourse I shall show:

I. *What is meant by the glory of God.*
II. *What is implied in Moses' prayer.*
III. *What is implied in God's answer.*

I. *What is meant by the glory of God.*

The original meaning of the term *glory* was brightness, clearness, effulgence. From that it has come to signify honor, renown; and again, that which renders honorable, or demands honor, renown, reverence, adoration, and worship—that which is worthy of confidence and trust. The glory of God is *essential* and *declarative*. By *essential* glory is meant *that in Him* which is glorious—*that in His character* which demands honor, worship, and adoration. His *declarative* glory is *the showing forth*, the revealing, the manifesting of the glory *of His character*—His essential glory—to His creatures, the laying open of His glory to the understanding of intelligence. And this is what Moses meant: God would *reveal* himself to His mind so that he might *know* Him—might have a clear and powerful apprehension of those things which constitute His glory.

II. *What is implied in Moses' prayer.*

1. A desire to know more than he then knew of God. He knew comparatively little of God. Something he had indeed known of Him, but he wished to know more. He desired to know that which makes God worthy of the homage and adoration of His creatures, especially to be so *subdued* by this knowledge and his heart so *fixed* in his confidence as to be prepared for his great work—the work of conducting Israel to the promised land. He desired to be so subdued that his confidence might be perfect in Him so that he might never fail in his trust and leaning upon the Lord. God had called him to an arduous work, and he needed a thorough acquaintance with Him.

2. A sense of the *necessity* of this knowledge of the glory of God—that he greatly needed it.

3. He was *disinterested* in his desire entirely for God's glory and the people's good—that he might succeed in the great work of emancipating God's people and of glorifying His name by their establishment in the land of Canaan.

4. He had a sense of his responsibility, of the necessities of the people, and of himself.

5. The prayer of Moses implies that he had a right to expect this revelation since God had called him to lead Israel from Egypt. God had called him to a work. He saw he must have a clearer knowledge of God to sustain him in his difficult position and to uphold him under discouragement. He seems to have thought he had a right, therefore, to expect that God would not deny him this requisite to success.

III. *What is implied in God's answer to Moses.*

"I will make all my *goodness* pass before thee," He said. God's glory consists in moral attributes—in His *goodness*.

1. The answer implies Moses' disinterestedness in his request—that his motives were right. If it had been mere curiosity that induced Moses to ask, God would not have granted it. God saw the sincere and earnest consecration of Moses' soul to the one object of his aim: to know the fulfillment of the work which God had given him.

2. He recognized the necessities of Moses and the people, and testified that He thought it necessary to give what Moses asked.

3. God saw the reasonableness to Moses' expectation—that Moses had a *right* to expect grace equal to his circumstances.

4. There was willingness on the part of God to make himself known to Moses for the purpose for which Moses desired it.

5. God had regard for the frailties of Moses and the people: "Thou canst not see my face and live." It was as though He said, "The glory of My ineffable presence is too much for mortal eye to behold; it would overwhelm you and separate soul from body. But I will hide you in a cleft of the rock, and will cover you with My hand as I pass by. And I will take away My hand and you shall see My back parts, but My face shall not be seen. You may see as much as you can bear, but no more. You will have as clear

a revelation of My character as you can sustain; as vivid an apprehension of My holiness as your powers can endure and bear up under."

6. The revelation to Moses implies that God considers His *goodness*, His *moral* attributes, as making up His essential glory. His glory does not consist in His natual attributes—His power, His wisdom, His omnipresence, His eternity—these are awesome, fearful for us to behold. But His glory lies in His *goodness*, His moral character, His justice, holiness, mercy. All these are but so many forms of His benevolence. God respects himself and demands respect and honor of others for His holiness, because He is voluntarily subject to the law of love, of universal and impartial benevolence. His glory consists not merely in one attribute but in *all* combined and balanced in due proportion. Mark what He says, "I will make all my goodness pass before thee." And what a beautiful and awesome revelation it was! "And the Lord passed by before him, and proclaimed, The Lord, The Lord God, merciful and gracious, long-suffering, and abundant in goodness and truth, keeping mercy for thousands, forgiving iniquity, transgression and sin, and that will by no means clear the guilty [the impenitent]; visiting the iniquity of the fathers upon the children and upon the children's children, unto the third and to the fourth generation of them that hate me" (Ex. 34:6, 7). This was all of it, the *goodness* of God—forgiving the penitent, rewarding the obedient, bearing with the rebellious, fulfilling His promise for good to the faithful and confiding, and pouring the vials of fiercest wrath on the incorrigible. This is the *goodness* of God, His benevolence under different phases, and all of this is the essential glory of the living God.

7. God's answer shows His sovereignty in the disposal of His mercies. "I will have mercy on whom I will have mercy, and I will have compassion on whom I will have compassion" (Rom. 9:15). By God's *sovereign* grace, I do not mean that He acts arbitrarily, or without a good reason, but that He acts independently of all but himself—that He obeys the dictates of His *own* infinite benevolence and asks no being but himself for permission to do what He sees best to be done. "I will consult My own unsearchable wisdom, and that which to *Me* seems best, I will do," is His declaration to the universe.

REMARKS

1. The *circumstances* and the *prayer* of Moses were the conditions of the revelation which God made to Him. His circumstances—he *needed* to know more of God. His prayer—he made *supplication* to be taught. The circumstances alone were not enough, nor the prayer alone, but both united. *He had subsequent and frequent manifestations of God's presence and power as circumstances required*—sometimes alone, sometimes in the full presence of all the people. On awesome Sinai, He moved in thunder and fire, and the congregation quaked at the terror of the Lord. God dealt with Moses and the people according to their needs, and showed His glory to them.

2. *A principle of the divine administration is here developed; God will furnish such grace and manifestation of His goodness as the circumstances demand and their needs require.* He is unchangeable. In the same circumstances His dealings are the same. He who gave to His ancient servant an overwhelming view of His glory so that in unspeakable awe, "he bowed his head and worshiped," will grant the same or greater manifestations if it be requisite to strengthen for His own work.

3. He will be *inquired* of to do the things that need to be done for you for His glory. The Bible everywhere insists on this. Moses prayed and prayed with great earnestness and importunity: "O God, show me thy glory." "Lord, if thy presence go not with me, carry us not up hence." The universal example of Bible saints is one continued stream of prayer flowing onward in a broad and deep current, with a strong and relentless tide, to the great ocean of God's boundless mercy and compassion.

4. We are to persevere in this asking. Was Moses to be put off? No indeed. He cries, "Show me now thy way, that I may know thee, that I may find grace in thy sight." God answers, "My presence shall go with thee, and I will give thee rest." But a mere promise was not enough for Moses. He knew God would go up with them, but he pleaded, "Show me thy glory." He wanted to know God, to understand His character so that God would wholly control him. He reminded God that He had called him to bring up the people; yet he was not prepared: "Thou sayest unto me, Bring up this people; and thou hast not let me know whom

thou wilt send with me." Moses persevered and he gained his request. God did for him what he asked. It is exceedingly important that we continue to *press* upon God, so to speak, for any grace which we need. Let us learn our duty from the Bible, and the relations we sustain, and then, having settled the question that we are in the work to which God has called us, let us come to God with a full assurance of faith that He has *promised* to be with us always, and that what He has promised, He is able also to *perform*. Press upon Him your wants. Say to Him, "Lord, You have placed me here. You have made me what I am, and I don't have strength for the work. I don't have knowledge for the labor. Lord, arm me for the contest, harness me for the battle, fit me for the work. Lord, Your name will be disgraced if I fail, for You have set me here, Your honor is at stake. What will become of Your great name? O God, show me Your glory." Whatever we find ourselves in need of for the success of *His work* to which *He* has called us, we have a right to go and ask for, with perfect confidence and complete assurance, and we should not give up until the request is granted. We should come with importunity.

See how Moses speaks to God, with what confidence and holy familiarity he addresses his heavenly Father! When God was angry with the rebellious Israelites and said, "Let me alone, that my wrath may wax hot against them, and that I may consume them" (Ex. 32:10), Moses sought the Lord. He came, seizing His hand as it were, "Lord," he cried, "why doth thy wrath wax hot against thy people, for whom thou hast done so much? Why should the Egyptians say, For mischief did he bring them out to slay them? Oh, turn from thy wrath and repent thee of this evil." Moses was so persistent, it seemed as though God *could* not deny him.

And thus may we come to God and cry, "Are not all your promises yes and amen in Christ Jesus? Haven't you promised, and will your word fail?" Brethren, isn't this the point? May we not come to God and ask at all times? Is He not able to save to the uttermost? Will not our strength be equal to our day? Oh, how strongly my experience testifies to this truth. Many times I would have given up all for lost and sat down in despair had it not been for such a revelation of God's glory, which strengthened me for the work I had to accomplish. *Always, yes always*, when I have gone to God, as Moses did, with the prayer, "Show me Thy glory," He has never denied me, never, *never*. [Italics are Finney's own.]*

5. It is reasonable to understand a *call* of God to any station as God's virtual pledge of *everything* that we need to stand in that place and meet those responsibilities. If God calls us to do a thing, it can be done. What is needed to accomplish is available. God is not a pharaoh, commanding to make brick, yet withholding straw. If God requires something, the requirement itself is assurance that the necessary means are provided.

6. The people always need *one* thing. *Every child of God is called to represent God, to be a teacher of God, to show the world around him the character of God.* Every saint is called of God to do this. Every Christian has a right to *insist* that God give him grace to do that—to do it fully and successfully. He may say to God, "Lord, You have made me a Christian, put Your spirit within me, called me to represent You, and show the world who You are, and what Your character is; but how can I do this unless You show me by Your grace, unless all Your goodness pass before me and melt me into contrition and love?" How long will it be before Christians, feeling their weakness, will go to God and ask Him thus for what they need and must have, or perish?**

7. Many persons seem to have exceedingly narrow, partial, obscure views of God. So shadow-like and dim is their notion of Him, or so partial and one-sided and distorted, that it is more like anything else than God. Perhaps Moses was *somewhat* in this condition. He had seen God in the burning bush; he had heard His voice, saying, "Go, lead my people Israel." He had seen the rod of Jehovah's wrath on wicked Egypt. He had stood on Sinai and seen God in fire and smoke and lightnings. But he could not be satisfied—he must know more. And Moses had to ask for new revelations continually.

---

*When we read his *Autobiography* or *Answers to Prayer*, we find that Finney had many refreshing baptisms in the fullness of the Sprit to fit him for greater tasks.

**The experience of Finney in the chapter "Total Commitment" in *Answers to Prayer* was but another example of how Finney was seeking new revelations of God continually, so that he could better represent His character. He fulfilled the conditions. God understood his need, and He blessed him mightily in 1843. The experience of Moses was exceedingly similar to that of Finney's, throughout their lives in relation to God.

Many know God only as a lawgiver and judge. They comprehend His law, and they sink in terror and fear; that is all they know of God. Others know nothing of Him but what they call His mercy and love—nothing of justice, and holiness, and righteous indignation against sin. Neither of them have any confidence in His word and promises. Now Moses, after seeing God's glory, trusted firmly and unwaveringly in God's truth. God had shown him His truth, and Moses did not forget it. He always felt the impress of that hand pressing on him; that sight was ever present in his mind. He had confidence in His mercy after this. When God said, "Let Me destroy this rebellious and stiff-necked people, and I will make of thee a great nation," Moses had such trust in God's mercy, he cried, "O Lord, save Thy people, or blot out my name from Thy book." "O God, what will become of Thy great Name?" What a savor and relish the revelation had left on his mind—a sweet and controlling sense of God's mercy and goodness.

God's justice, too, rested with awful distinctness upon Moses' apprehension. He was the great and terrible God, visiting the iniquities of them which hate Him upon their own heads and upon the heads of their children. It is vastly important that men should have just and symmetrical views of God's character; for where the revelation is partial, they do not possess a well-proportioned piety—they show a want of balance in their character. If they have not seen the *justice* of God, His holiness, they have no apprehension of the guilt of sin, of its required punishment, of God's infinite hatred of it. They have no proper sense of the condition of sinners, have no compassion, no ardent zeal, no burning love for them. So, if men have not a revelation of the mercy and love and compassion of God, they will be legalistic, have very little confidence to pray for sinners; instead of laying hold of God, as they should do, even in the most desperate cases, they slacken and give up in despair. So it is with all His attributes; if men have not sought and obtained a just view of God's character, they will be like their views of God—ill-proportioned and unbalanced in their own character.

8. It is of the greatest importance that men should *realize* that *all* God's character is made up of His *benevolence*, His *goodness*. See how He says, "*All* My goodness"; not My mercy, My

love, but *all* My mercy, My justice, My holiness, My hatred of sin and My settled purpose to punish it, My tender compassion and pity, and My righteous vindictive justice. Ministers, especially, should thus know all His goodness, and be duly affected by every attribute. If they do not have such a revelation, they will induce and foster an unnatural and ill-proportioned piety in their congregation and the people with whom they associate—either an antinomian or a legal spirit, just as the bent and cast of the minister's own mind is.

9. Nothing but a revelation of God's glory can make us stable Christians. No excitement, no intellectual acumen, no strength of logic—nothing can secure us but a revelation of God to our souls. We should therefore persevere and insist that this be done for us, that we see God's glory and be fixed on Him. The church should pray for *ministers* and for candidates for the ministry. The church should pray that God would reveal to them the deep secrets of His love and mercy, that He would open to them the ever-flowing fountains of exquisite and perennial blessedness from which to drink and thirst no more. Oh, do the churches think and feel how much they can do for their ministers by praying the heavens open to let down on their hearts rays of glory that will forever enrapture and hold them in aweful apprehension of God's presence and character, so that the Spirit of the Highest will come upon them and the power of God overshadow them, transforming them from men of clay to angels of mercy and power to a fallen world? Why do they not pray? Brethren, why do *you* not pray? Pray that God would show you, would show the students, the community, the whole church in the land and in the world His glory. Pray and give God no rest until He will glorify His people before the nations!

10. It is easy to see what made Moses' face shine so when he came down from the mount. The manifestation of God's glory has the same effect always and everywhere. There was such a clearness, a glory, a brightness in his countenance that the people could not look upon him. Christ was transfigured on the mount when the glory of God appeared to Him. His raiment was white as the light, and His face was like the sun.

11. Many cannot bear much of the revelation of divine glory to them. They are babes and must be fed with milk and not with

meat, for they cannot take meat. How it affected Isaiah to behold the glory of the Lord! Isaiah, that man of God! Who could behold, if he could not? One would think *his* views of God were high and exalted. But see his vision. . . . "I saw also the Lord sitting upon a throne, high and lifted up, and his train filled the temple. Above it stood the seraphims. . . . And one cried unto another and said, . . . Holy, holy, holy, is the Lord of hosts: the whole earth is full of his glory" (Isa. 6:1-3). Think of it! It overcame Isaiah. He cried in despair, "Woe is me, for I am undone; because I am a man of unclean lips, and I dwell in the midst of a people of unclean lips, . . . for mine eyes have seen the King, the Lord of hosts" (Isa. 6:5). He saw the holiness of God as he had never seen it before. He was completely overcome; he seemed unable to recover from it until one of the seraphims came with a live coal from the altar and laid it on his lips, saying, "Thine iniquity is taken away, and thy sin purged" (Isa. 6:7). Oh, how much do we need such revelations—new revelations—great and mighty things which we have not known! And then we shall be humbled, subdued under His mighty hand. Mark how Isaiah was subdued to the will of God. When he heard the voice crying, "Who will go for us?" with meek boldness he answered, "Here am I, send *me*." And so shall we be humbled, and say, "Lord, glorify Thy name in us."

But often God must hold back. He covered Moses in the cleft of the rock and hid His face from him. Often must Christians say, "Hold Your hand. O Lord, it is enough; draw the curtain and veil the glory from my fainting, reeling sense."

12. Sometimes young converts get proud and think that they know much of God, and imagine that all which *they* never experienced is fanciful and cannot be true. If just what they know of God is not presented, they think it is not the gospel. They are poor, blind men; they know just one part, and a very small part. They must not think *they* know the whole of God, all that may be known of Him. Many cannot bear to hear of God's justice, of His sovereignty, of His holiness. We should desire to have *all* the character, *all* the goodness of God pass before us—to have Him let in upon the mind as bright and glorious a vision as it can bear.

Brethren, is it not true that we need new manifestations of God! One revelation brings need of new and more glorious revelations. Do we not need it? My soul from its depths, my heart from its very bottom, cries out, "O God, I beg You, show me Your glory. Let me see and know more of God!" Will you pray for your minister? Will you pray for yourselves? Do we not need it? I ask again. Have we not high responsibilities? Who has higher? Now pray in view of your circumstances; besiege the throne; give God no rest; let Him have no peace until He comes and revives His work and makes His name glorious.

19

REST OF THE SAINTS*

Hebrews 4:3

"For we which have believed do enter into rest."

The following is the course of thought to which I wish to direct your attention. I shall endeavor to show:

    I. *What is not the rest spoken of in the text.*
    II. *What the rest is.*
    III. *When they who believe do enter into this rest.*
    IV. *How to come into possession of this rest.*
    V. *That all sin consists in, or is caused by, unbelief.*

I. *What is not the rest spoken of in the text.*
1. It is evidently not a state of inactivity in religion.

The Apostle who wrote this was himself very far from being inactive in religion, or from encouraging it in others. Those of whom he spoke, including himself, where he says, "*We* which have believed, do enter into rest," would know at once that it was not true, that they had entered into the rest of supineness.

2. Neither are we to understand that the perfect rest of heaven is the rest here spoken of.

He speaks of it as a present state—we "do enter"—which is

*Lectures to Professing Christians, Lecture XXIV, pp. 276-285.

not consistent with the idea that heaven is the rest here spoken of. The perfect rest of heaven includes an absolute freedom from all the pains, trials, sufferings and temptations of this life. The rest of the believer here may be of the same nature, substantially, with the rest of heaven. It is that rest begun on earth. But it is not made perfect. It differs in some respects, because it does not imply a deliverance from all trials, pains, sickness and death. The apostles and primitive Christians had not escaped these trials, but still suffered their full share of them.

II. *What the rest is.*

1. It is rest from controversy with God.

In this sense of cessation from controversy, the word rest is often used in the Bible. In the context, it is said the children of Israel rested when they were freed from their enemies. It is cessation from strife or war. Those who enter into this rest cease from their warfare with God, from their struggle against the truth, their war with their own conscience. The reproaches of conscience, which kept them in agitation, the slavish fears of the wrath of God under which men exert themselves as slaves in building up their own works are all done away. They rest.

2. It implies cessation from our own works.

(1) Cessation from works performed *for* ourselves.

Much of the apparent religion in the world is made up of works which people claim as their own, in this sense. They are working for their own lives; they have this end in view, and are working for themselves as absolutely as the man who is laboring for his bread. If the object of what you do in religion is your salvation, whether from temporal or eternal ruin, it is for yourself, and you have not ceased from your own works, but are still multiplying works of your own. Now the rest spoken of in the text is entire cessation from all this kind of works. The Apostle, in verse 10, affirms this: "He that is entered into his rest, also hath ceased from his own works." And in the text, he says that we who believe do enter, or have entered, into rest. It is plain that this rest is ceasing from our own works—not ceasing from all kind of works, for that is true neither of the saints on earth nor of saints in heaven. We have no reason to believe that any saints or angel, or that God himself, or any holy being is ever inactive. But we cease to perform works with any such design as merely to save our own souls.

It is ceasing to work for ourselves that we may work for God. We are performing our own works just as long as the supreme object of our works is to be saved. But if the question of our own salvation is thrown entirely on Jesus Christ, and our works are performed out of love to God, they are not our own works.

(2) In entering into this rest, we cease from all works performed *from* ourselves as well as works performed *for* ourselves.

Works are from ourselves when they result from the simple, natural principles of human nature, such as conscience, hope, fear, etc., without the influences of the Holy Spirit. Such works are universally and wholly sinful. They are the efforts of selfishness under the direction of mere natural principles. Amid such works conscience convicts, hope and fear come in aid, and under this influence, the carnal, selfish mind acts. Such acts cannot but be wholly sinful. It is nothing but selfishness. Multiply the forms of selfishness by selfishness forever, and it will never come to love. Where there is nothing but natural conscience pointing out the guilt and danger, and the constitutional susceptibilities of hope and fear leading to do something, it comes to nothing but the natural workings of an unsanctified mind. Such works are always the works of the flesh, not the works of the Spirit. To enter into rest is to cease from all these, no more to perform works from ourselves or for ourselves. Who does not know what a painful time those have who set about religion from themselves; painfully grinding out about so much religion a month, they are constrained by hope and fear, and lashed up to the work by conscience, but without the least impulse from that divine principle of the love of God shed abroad in the heart by the Holy Spirit? All such works are just as much from themselves as any work of any devil is. No matter what kind of works are performed, if the love of God is not the mainspring and life and heart of them, they are our own works, and there is no such thing as rest in them. We must cease from them, because they set aside the gospel. The individual who is actuated by these principles sets aside the gospel, in whole or in part. If he is actuated only by these considerations, he sets aside the gospel entirely; and just as far as he is influenced by them, he refuses to receive Christ as his Savior in that relation. Christ is offered as a complete Savior; He is our wisdom, righteousness, sanctification, and redemption. And just so far as anyone is making efforts to dispense with a Savior in any of these particulars, he is setting aside the gospel for so much.

(3) To enter into rest implies that we cease from doing anything for ourselves.

We are not even to eat or drink for ourselves! "Whether, therefore, ye eat or drink, or whatsoever ye do, do all to the glory of God." The man who has entered into this rest has ceased from doing it. God requires it, and he who has entered into rest has ceased to have any interest of his own. He has wholly merged his own interest in that of Christ. He has given himself so perfectly to Christ that he has no work of his own to do. There is no reason why he should go about any work of his own. He knows he might as well sit still until he is in hell rather than attempt anything of his own to try to save himself. When a man fully understands this, he ceases from any efforts in this way. See the convicted sinner: how he strains himself and puts forth all his efforts to help himself, until he learns that he is nothing; then he ceases from all this and throws himself, helpless and lost, into the hands of Christ. Until he feels that he is in himself without strength, help, or hope, for salvation or anything that leads to it, he will never think of the simplicity of the gospel. No man applies to Christ for righteousness and strength until he has used up his own, and feels that he is helpless and undone. Then he can understand the simplicity of the gospel plan, which consists in *receiving* salvation by faith as a free gift. When he has done all that he could, in his own way, and finds that he has grown no better, that he is no nearer salvation, but rather has grown worse, that sin is multiplied upon sin, and darkness heaped upon darkness until he is crushed down with utter helplessness, then he ceases and gives all up into the hand of Christ. See that sinner trying to get into an agony of conviction, or trying to understand religion, and finding all dark as Egypt, and cannot see what it is that he must do. "Oh," he says, "what must I do? I am willing to do anything. I can't tell why I don't submit. I don't know how to do anything more. What am I to do, or how shall I find out what the difficulty is?" When he is fully convinced, he turns his eyes to the Savior, and there he finds all he needs—wisdom, righteousness, sanctification and redemption. Christ the Life of the world, the Light of the world, the Bread of life—he needs nothing but what is in

Christ. All he wants and all he can ask is in Christ to be received by faith; then he ceases from his own works and throws himself at once and entirely upon Christ for salvation.

(4) To cease from our own works is to cease attempting to do anything in our own strength.

Everyone who has entered into rest knows that whatever he does in his own strength will be an abomination to God. Unless Christ lives in him, unless God works in him, to will and to do of His good pleasure, nothing is ever done acceptably to God. To set himself to do anything in his own strength, independent of the spirit of God, is forever an utter abomination to God. He who has not learned this has not ceased from his own works and has not accepted the Savior. The Apostle says we are not able of ourselves to think anything concerning ourselves. The depth of degradation to which sin has reduced us is not understood until this is known and felt.

3. To enter into rest also includes the idea of throwing our burdens upon the Lord Jesus Christ.

He invites us to throw all our burdens and cares on Him: "Come unto me, all ye that labour and are heavy laden, and I will give you rest" (Matt. 11:28). "Casting all your cares upon him; for he careth for you" (1 Pet. 5:7). These words mean just what they say. Whether your burden is temporal or spiritual, whether your care is for the soul or body, throw it all upon the Lord. See that little child, going along with his father; the father is carrying something that is heavy, and the child takes hold with its little hand to help, but what can he do to help such a load? Many Christians make themselves a great deal of trouble by trying to help the Lord Jesus Christ in His work. They weary and worry themselves with one thing or another as if everything hung on their shoulders. Now, the Lord Jesus Christ is as much pledged to the believer for *all* that concerns him as he is for his justification. The Lord has promised equal help for the believer's temporal and eternal interests. There is nothing that concerns the Christian which he is not to cast on the Lord Jesus Christ. I do not mean to say that the Christian has no agency in the matter. Here is a man who has cast his family upon Jesus Christ; but he has not done it in such a manner that he is not to do anything for his family. But he has so cast himself upon God for direction, for light, for strength, for success that he has yielded himself absolutely to God to guide and to sustain him. And Christ is pledged to assure that everything is done right.

4. To enter into rest is to make the Lord Jesus Christ our wisdom, our righteousness, our sanctification, and our redemption, and to receive Him in all His offices as a full and perfect substitute for all our deficiencies.

We lack all these things absolutely, and are to receive Him as a full and perfect substitute to fill the vacancy and supply all our needs. We must cease expecting, or hoping, or attempting anything of ourselves to fill the vacancy. We must receive Christ as all.

5. Entering into this rest implies the yielding of our powers so perfectly to His control that henceforth all our works shall be His works.

I hope you will not understand anything from this language to be more mystical than the Bible. It is a maxim of the common law, that what a man does by another, he does by himself. Suppose I hire a man to commit murder; the deed is as absolutely my own as if I had done it with my own hand. The crime is not in the hand which struck the blow any more than it is in the sword that stabs the victim. The crime is in my mind. If I use another's hand but my mind is the moving cause that influenced him, it is my act still. Suppose that I had taken his hand by force and used it to shoot my neighbor; would that not be my act? Certainly; but it was in my mind. And it is just as much my act if I influence his mind to do it. Now apply this principle to the doctrine that the individual who has entered into rest has so yielded himself to Christ's control that all his works are the works of Christ. The Apostle Paul says, "I laboured more abundantly than they all: yet not I, but the grace of God which with was with me" (1 Cor. 15:10). And he frequently insists that it was not himself that did the works, but Christ in him. Do not misunderstand it now. It is not said and it is not to be understood that the believer acts upon compulsion or that Christ acts in him without his own will, but that Christ by His Spirit dwelling in him, influences and leads his mind so that he acts voluntarily in such a way as to please God. When one ceases from his own works, he so perfectly gives up his own will and places himself so completely under the guidance of the Holy Spirit that whatever he does is by the impulse of the Spirit of Christ. The Apostle describes it exactly when he says, "Work out your own salvation with fear and trembling. For it is God which worketh in you, both to will and to do of his good pleasure" (Phil. 2:12, 13). God influences the will, not by force, but by love, to do just what will please Him. If it were done by force, we should be no longer free agents. But it is love that so sweetly influences the will and brings it entirely under the control of the Lord Jesus Christ.

Our agency is not suspended, but it is employed by the Lord Jesus Christ. Our hands, our feet, our powers of body and mind are all employed to work for Him. He does not suspend the laws of our constitution, but He so directs our agency that the love of Christ constrains us to will and to do of His good pleasure.

Thus, you see that all works that are really good in man are, in an important sense, Christ's works. This is affirmed in the Bible, over and over again, that our good works are not from ourselves, nor in any way by our own agency without God; God directs our agency, and influences our wills to do His will, and we do it. They are in one sense our works, because we do them by our voluntary agency. Yet, in another sense, they are His works, because He is the moving cause of all.

6. Entering into this rest implies that to the extent we yield our agency to Christ, to that extent we cease from sin.

If we are directed by the Lord Jesus Christ, He will not direct us to sin. Just as far as we give ourselves up to God we cease from sin. If we are controlled by Him so that He works in us, it is to will and to do of His good pleasure. And as far as we do this, so far we cease from sin. I do not need to prove this.

III. *When they who believe do enter into rest.*
It is in this life.

1. This appears from the text and context. The Apostle in connection with the text was reasoning with the Jews. He warns them to beware of failing to enter the true rest, which was typified by their fathers entering into the land of Canaan. The Jews supposed that was the true rest. But the Apostle argues with them, to show that there was a higher rest, of which the rest of temporal Canaan was only a type and into which the Jews might have entered but for their unbelief. If Joshua had given them the

real rest, he would not have spoken of another day. Yet another day is spoken of. Even as late as David's day, it is spoken of in the Psalms as yet to come: "Today, after so long a time; as it is said, Today if ye will hear his voice, harden not your hearts. For if Jesus [that is Joshua] had given them rest, then would he not afterwards have spoken of another day. There remaineth therefore a rest to the people of God." He therefore argues that the rest in Canaan was not the real rest which was promised, but was typical of the true rest. What then was the true rest? It was the repose of faith in Christ, or the gospel state, a cessation from our own works. And believers enter into that state by faith.

I know it is generally supposed that the rest here spoken of is the heavenly rest, beyond this life. But it is obviously a rest that commences here. "We which believe *do* enter into rest." It begins here but extends into eternity. It is the same in kind, but made there more perfect in degree, embracing freedom from the sorrows and trials to which all believers are subject in this life. But it is the same in kind, the rest of faith, the Sabbath keeping of the soul, when it ceases from its own works and casts itself wholly upon the Savior.

2. It is manifest that this rest must commence in this world if faith puts us in possession of it. This is the very point that the Apostle was arguing, that faith is essential to taking possession of it. "They could not enter in because of unbelief" (Heb. 3:19). The writer tells the Hebrews to beware that they do not fall prey to unbelief, and thus fail to enter into rest. He warns them not to indulge in unbelief, because by faith they may take immediate possession of the rest. If this rest by faith ever commences at all, it must be in this world.

3. The nature of the case proves this. Nothing short of this taking possession of rest is fully embracing Jesus Christ. It is a spiritual rest from the conflict with God, from the stings of conscience, and from efforts to help ourselves by any workings of our own mind. Nothing short of this is freedom from the law, or full entrance into the gospel.

IV. *How to come into possession of this rest.*
From what has already been said, you will understand that we take possession of it by faith.

The text, with the context, shows this. You will recall also what the Lord Jesus Christ says in Matt. 11:28, 29: "Come unto me, all ye that labour and are heavy laden, and I will give you rest. Take my yoke upon you, and learn of me; for I am meek and lowly in heart: and ye shall find rest unto your souls." Here this same rest is spoken of, and we are told that if we will only come to Christ, we may find it. If we will take His easy yoke, which is love, and trust Him to bear all burdens, we will find rest. The Psalmist speaks of the same rest, "Return unto thy rest, O my soul" (Ps. 116:7). What Christian does not know what it is to have the soul rest in Christ, to hang upon His arm and find rest from all the cares and perplexities and sorrows of life?

Again, it is evident that faith in Christ, from its own nature, brings the soul into the very state of rest I have described. How instantly faith breaks up slavish fear and brings the soul into the liberty of the gospel! How it sets us free from selfishness and all those influences under which we formerly acted! By faith we confide all to Christ—to lead us, and sanctify us, and justify us. And we may be just as certain to be led and to be sanctified as we are to be justified if we only exercise faith and leave ourselves in the hands of Christ for all. As a simple matter of fact, such faith brings the soul into a state of rest. The soul sees that there is no need of its own selfish efforts, nor any hope from them if they were needed. In itself, it is so far gone in sin that it is as hopeless as if it had been in hell a thousand years. Take the best Christian on earth, and let the Lord Jesus Christ leave his soul, and where is he? Will he pray or do anything good or acceptable to God without Christ? Never! The greatest saint on earth will go right off into sin in a moment if abandoned by Jesus Christ. But faith throws all upon Christ, and that is rest.

Again, faith makes us cease from all works for ourselves. By faith we see that we have no more need of doing works for ourselves than the child whose father is worth millions needs to work for his daily bread. He may work from love to his father, or from love to the employment, but not from any necessity to labor for his daily bread. The soul that truly understands the gospel sees perfectly well that there is no need of mingling his own righteousness with the righteousness of Christ, or his own wisdom with the wisdom of Christ, or his own sufferings with the sufferings of Christ. If there were any need of this, there would be so much temptation to selfishness and to working from legalistic motives. But there is none.

Again, by faith the soul ceases from all works performed from itself. Faith brings a new principle into action, entirely above all considerations addressed to the natural principles of hope and fear and conscience. Faith brings the mind under the influence of love. It takes the soul out from the influences of conscience, lashing it up to duty, and brings it under the influence of the same holy, heavenly principles that influenced Christ himself.

Again, faith brings the mind into rest, inasmuch as it brings it to cease from all efforts merely for its own salvation, and puts the whole being into the hands of Christ.

Faith is confidence. It is confidently yielding all our powers and interests to Christ to be led, and sanctified, and saved by Him.

It annihilates selfishness, and thus leaves no motives for our own works.

In short, faith is an absolute resting of the soul in Christ for all that it needs or can need. It is trusting Him for everything. For instance, although a little child is wholly dependent on his father for house and home, food and raiment, and everything under the sun, that little child feels no uneasiness, because he confides in his father. The child rests in him, and gives himself no uneasiness, knowing that he will provide all he needs. He is just as cheerful and happy all day long as if he had all things in himself, because he has such confidence. Now the soul of the believer rests in Christ just as the infant does in the arms of his mother. The penitent sinner, like a condemned wretch, hangs all on Christ, his only help and hope. Christ alone does all that is needed.

If faith does consist in thus trusting absolutely in Christ, then it is manifest that we take possession of this rest when we believe; for it is in this life that faith is to be exercised.

V. *All sin consists in, or is caused by, unbelief.*

I do not mean to imply by this that unbelief is not itself a sin, but to say that it is the fountain out of which all other sin issues. Unbelief is distrust of God, or lack of confidence. It is clear that it was this lack of confidence which constituted Adam's real crime.

It was not the mere eating of the fruit but the distrust which led to the outward act that constituted the real crime for which he was cast out of paradise. That unbelief is the cause of all sin is manifest from the following considerations:

1. The moment an individual lacks faith, and is left to the simple impulse of natural principles and appetites, he is left just like a beast, and the things that address his mind through the senses alone operate on him. The motives that influence the mind when it acts right are discerned by faith. Where there is no faith, there are no motives before the mind except those natural inclinations confined to *this* world. The soul is then left to its mere constitutional propensities, and gives up itself to the minding of carnal things. This is the natural and inevitable result of unbelief. The eye is shut to eternal things, and there is nothing before the mind calculated to beget any other action but that which is selfish. It is therefore left to grovel in the dust and can never rise above its own interest and appetites. It is a natural impossibility that the effect should not be so; for how can the mind act without motives? But the motives of eternity are seen only by faith. The mere mental and bodily appetites that terminate on this world can never raise the mind above the things of this world, and the result is only sin, sin, sin—the minding of the flesh forever. The very moment Adam distrusted God, he was given up to follow his appetites. And it is so with all other minds.

2. Suppose a child loses all confidence in his father. He can thereafter render no hearty obedience. It is a natural impossibility. If he pretends to obey, it is only from selfishness and not from the heart; for the mainspring and essence of all real hearty obedience is gone. It would be so in heaven, it is so in hell. Without faith it is impossible to please God. Without faith it is a natural impossibility to obey God in such a manner as to be accepted by Him. Thus, unbelief is shown to be the fountain of all the sin in earth and hell, and the soul that is destitute of faith is left to work out its damnation.

REMARKS

1. The rest which those who believe do enter into here on earth is of the same nature with the heavenly rest.

The heavenly rest will be more complete; for it will be a rest from all the sorrows and trials to which even a perfect human soul is liable here. Even Christ himself experienced these trials and sorrows and temptations. But the soul that believes rests as absolutely in Him here as in heaven.

2. We see why faith is said to be the substance of things hoped for.

Faith is the very thing that makes heaven; therefore, it is the substance of heaven, and will be throughout all eternity.

3. We see what it is to be led by the Spirit of God.

It is to yield all our powers and faculties to His control so as to be regulated by the Spirit in all that we do.

4. We see that perfect faith would produce perfect love, or perfect sanctification.

A perfect yielding of ourselves, and continuing to trust all that we have and are to Christ, would make us perfectly holy.

5. We see that just as far as any individual is not sanctified, it is because his faith is weak.

When the Lord Jesus Christ was on earth, if His disciples fell into sin, He always reproached them for their lack of faith: "O ye of little faith." A man who believes in Christ has no more right to expect to sin than he has a right to expect to be damned. You may startle at this, but it is true.

You are to receive Christ as your sanctification just as absolutely as your justification. Now you are bound to expect to be damned unless you receive Christ as your justification. But if you receive Him as such, you have then no reason and no right to expect to be damned. Now He is just as absolutely your sanctification as your justification, and if you depend upon Him for sanctification, He will no more let you sin than He will let you go to hell. And it is as unreasonable and unscriptural and wicked to expect one as the other. And nothing but unbelief, in any instance, is the cause of your sin. Some of you have read the *Life of Mrs. Hester Ann Rogers* and recall how habitual it was with her to throw herself instantly upon Christ when any temptation assailed her. She testifies that in every instance He sustained her.

Consider the case of Peter. When the disciples saw Christ walking upon the water, and their fright was over, Peter requested permission to go to Him on the water. Christ told him to come, a promise on the part of Christ that if he attempted it, he should be sustained. Without this promise, his attempt would have been tempting God. But with this promise, he had no reason and no right to doubt. He made the attempt, and while he believed, the energy of Christ bore him up as if he walked upon the ground. But as soon as he began to doubt, he began to sink. So it is with the soul; as soon as it begins to doubt the willingness and the power of Christ to sustain it in a state of perfect love, it begins to sink. Take Christ at His word, make Him responsible, and rely on Him, and heaven and earth will sooner fail than allow such a soul to fall into sin. Say, with Mrs. Rogers, when Satan comes with a temptation, "Lord Jesus, here is a temptation to sin, see Thou to that."

6. We see why the self-denying labors of saints are consistent with being in a state of rest.

These self-denying labors are all constrained by love, and have nothing in them that is compulsory or hard. Inward love draws them to duty. It is so far from being true to say that the self-denying labors of Christians are hard work, that it would be vastly more painful to them *not* to do it. Their love for souls is such that if they were forbidden to do anything for them, they would be in agony. In fact, a state of inaction would be inconsistent with this rest. How could it be rest for one whose heart is burning and bursting with love for God and souls, to sit still and do nothing for them? But it is perfect rest for the soul to go out in prayer and effort for their salvation. Such a soul cannot rest while God is dishonored and souls destroyed, and nothing done for their rescue. But when all his powers are used for the Lord Jesus Christ, this is true rest. Such is the rest enjoyed by angels, who cease not day or night, and who are all ministering spirits to minister to the heirs of salvation.

The Apsotle says, "Let us therefore fear, lest, a promise being left us of entering into his rest, any of you should seem to come short of it" (Heb. 4:1). And "Let us labour therefore to enter into that rest" (Heb. 4:11). Do any of you know what it is to come to Christ and rest in Him? Have you found rest from all your own efforts to save yourselves, from the thunders of Sinai, and the stings of conscience? Can you rest sweetly in Jesus and find in Him everything essential to sanctification and eternal salvation? Have you found actual salvation in Him? If you have, then you have entered into rest.

APPENDIX

Two Testimonials About Finney and Holiness

An Interesting Letter from a Member of Congress
for the *Oberlin Evangelist*

Washington, Feb. 24, 1843

To the Editor, *Oberlin Evangelist:*

Since I am about to leave the city, to return to private life, I would like to say a word to stimulate your subscribers to an effort to increase the circulation of your paper. I know of no other paper so well calculated to promote *holy living*, and I believe its doctrines will abide the test of time and the judgment day. Mr. Finney's sermons, so plain, pungent, logical, and so eminently practical, are worth many times the price of the paper. They can hardly fail to sweep away a variety of loose and false ideas which have collected in the minds of many who profess religion, ideas in relation to what constitutes inherent, indwelling sin, the new birth, and a change of heart. These sermons can convince of the efficacy of faith for sanctification as well as justification—of the practicability as well as the obligation of perfect obedience. They can expose the injurious tendency of that heresy, which affords no encouragement to the young convert that he can never exist a moment in this life without sinning against God, and yet may have a sure hope of heaven; thus, in some inexplicable way, the Son of God is made a *justifier in*, rather than a *Savior from* sin!

The recent excellent articles on the "Libertine's Code of Morals" ought to be read by every man, woman, and child in the nation, and I hope they will be extensively republished.

I entreat the readers of the *Evangelist* not to be alarmed at *threatened discipline* for circulating this paper, but, while they exercise great Christian forbearance, patience, and brotherly love toward those brethren who do not see things this way, to be fearless in the dissemination of truth, to make constant efforts to procure new subscribers for the paper, and after reading their own paper, always to place it in the hands of others who may benefit from it. I know of many instances where great good has been accomplished in this way.

Your late remarks on "The Progress of the Anti-Slavery Cause" were timely and true. I have now for four years carefully watched the progress of events and the providence of God in respect to American slavery, from this elevated point of observation, and I have not a lingering doubt that this infernal system must soon come to an end. I am not, however, so bold as to predict the exact process by which it is finally to be accomplished, but the moral power of the civilized world and the most marked providences of the Most High are bearing down upon it with irresistible force! Whether it be the lynch law of the mob, or the Gag Rule[1] of Congress—the unrighteous and retaliatory enactments of southern legislatures, or the subservient and black enactments of northern legislatures—the escape of the *L'Amistad*,[2] or the insurrection of the Creole captives—the murder of a Lovejoy,[3] or the imprisonment of a Torrey[4]—the attempted expulsion of an Adams[5] or the censure of a Giddings[6]—*all, all things* tend to *expose the enormity, weaken the power*, and *hasten the overthrow of slavery*. The escape of Clark into Ohio sends an eloquent missionary from Ashland over the free states, making hundreds of converts to abolition; and the arrest of a Latimer in Massachusetts rocks the old "cradle of liberty" and sends up to an expresident in Congress a petition signed by *fifty-one thousand persons,* demanding to be relieved from all participation in the sin and shame of slavery!!

That petition, rolled upon an iron crank, in the form of a cylinder about two feet wide and two feet in diameter, resting on a suitable wooden frame, stood for two days upon Mr. Adams' desk in the House, while the *veteran champion of the right of petition stood entrenched behind the embodied voice of fifty-one thousand freemen, demanding its reception!* It was higher than his head when he was on his feet, and during the two days it remained upon his desk, attracted great attention, hundreds flocking to the House to see it. Only some eighty members voted to suspend the rules to permit him to present the petition, and he was obliged to take it privately to the clerk's table, and have it referred, under the general rule of the House, adopted to avoid the utter denial of the right of petition under the gag.

Elder Knapp has been preaching several weeks in this city and has baptized some sixty converts. This week he has commenced in the Presbyterian church, and the pastor, Mr. Rich, and his congregation join in the meeting. The Rev. Ezra Styles Ely is also conducting a protracted meeting in another part of the city, and both meetings are increasing in interest.

The hope of our country, after all, is in the spread of the gospel. When the masses become imbued with the principle of pure practical religion and sound morality, the mere partisan, the noisy declamatory politician, must give place to men who fear God and work righteousness. Then, and not until then, will we as a nation become truly exalted.*

New York

A Letter from a Minister Who Was Converted to Finney's View on Holiness

"We give this letter to our readers as an example of the working of truth upon the conscience when the mind becomes truly honest and consequently open to the Holy Ghost."—*The Oberlin Evangelist,* May 22, 1844.

Dear Brother _____,

I am probably the last person from whom you would expect a letter like this. My views and feelings regarding the doctrine of holiness greatly changed since I said that wicked "No." The first

---

*Published in the March 15, 1843, issue of *The Oberlin Evangelist.*

emotion I recall after my change of mind was to write to Bro. _____ and confess the wrong I did in voting to exclude him from a seat in the synod. By so voting, I thought I certainly did what was according to the name of Jesus of Nazareth. But I am now thoroughly convinced to the contrary. If I was not like Saul, a "blasphemer and a persecutor," I was certainly injurious in that act. But as he has, I trust I have, "obtained mercy, because I did it ignorantly in unbelief."

I can truly say that I never saw or heard of anything in you which I thought wrong, except that you held the heretical doctrine that it was not only possible to be a wholehearted servant of God, but that you yourself were one of these strange beings. But this is saying little. I saw much in you to esteem highly and love, and even regarded you with the warmest emotions of friendship. You might well exclaim, "Oh, consistency!" as you did the first time you took me by the hand after I voted to exclude you from a seat in a deliberative assembly. I feel deeply pained to think that I could ever have been so inconsistent and wicked as to do such a thing. I know you will forgive me, but I could not feel forgiven of God until I had asked pardon of you.

What is the history of this remarkable change? I can now state it only briefly. I have been trying by God's help for several years to learn, do, and practice the truth. And I can now clearly see, as I retrace my steps, that I have been constantly, though almost imperceptibly, gliding toward the point where I now stand. I have always felt a difficulty in bringing home the law of God to my own and to my hearers' consciences, while I taught them that they must not expect success in their endeavors to obey it. I have several times examined the arguments of the advocates of entire sanctification with great interest. The truth sometimes flashed in my face with irresistible force, and there were always points which I could not clear up to my satisfaction. But the old objections would soon return, and I would settle down in my old belief that I must struggle on in despair of triumphing over sin except in death.

I have long preached the attainableness of entire sanctification in the present life and the duty of men now to be perfect, but at the same time I have preached that the attainment was so exceedingly difficult that it would be the height of presumption for one to know it, even if he should succeed, or long to *retain* that giddy height, if he should *attain* it. But I have recently found myself dwelling less and less on the difficulties and more and more on the encouragements to expect entire success. Before I was aware of it, I found myself unable to reconcile my preaching with my old views of imperfection. Just at that point, as providence would have it, the *Oberlin Evangelist*, of April 26, 1843, fell under my eye. I read it with the greatest interest. It contained President Mahan's sermon, "Perfect Love Attainable." My heart responded amen to every word. I saw at once, as I never had seen before, that the provisions were complete and were now as available for entire sanctification as for repentance, faith, or any single duty of religion. All pleas of ignorance and weakness were swept away by the glorious promises of divine aid—but stop!

This will make me a perfectionist, I thought—can I bear to be called by that hated name—a name everywhere spoken against—one against which I myself have so recently spoken? What will my friends say? Can I endure ecclesiastical proscription? What will my people say? If I believe it I must preach it. I can have no mental reservation. Can I endure all this? *Yes, I will.* Come life or come death, I will share the fate of God's truth. I will follow it, though it be to the stake. I immediately felt a calm reliance on God, which I do not know that I ever felt before. I felt that He was my all, and that in Him I had enough for all emergencies. I have since felt no anxiety as to what disposal He would make of me. But I feel sure that all will be well.

I now feel that I can preach the whole truth without any drawback. It feels like a two-edged sword in my hand, and I preach it as I see it, frankly and fearlessly. I hear no objections yet, and if I do, it will make no difference, except to fill my heart with sorrow that men will love darkness rather than light. I have procured the last volume [1843] of the *Oberlin Evangelist*, and read it with greater interest than I ever felt in the perusal of any other similar amount of reading, save the Bible itself.[8] I mourn that I so long practically made void the law of God. But I intend the rest of my life to redeem the time by preaching the whole truth.

Yours in Christ, _____

Notes

1. Law enacted in 1837 to suppress antislavery debate.

2. A slave ship mutineered by its captives. When brought to port, a lawsuit followed, which freed the Africans.

3. A newspaper editor shot in 1837 because of his antislavery views.

4. A congregational minister imprisoned in 1843 for his report of a slaveholders' convention.

5. John Quincy Adams proposed abolitionist legislature in Congress.

6. Censured from the House in 1842 for introducing resolutions.

7. Published in the March 15, 1843, issue of *The Oberlin Evangelist*.

8. He is obviously referring to the lectures and sermons in this book, especially to the series, "Holiness of Christians in the Present Life."

If you desire to learn more about Charles G. Finney, his minstry and his writings, write:
Christian Life Study Center
P. O. Box 7024
Rochester, MN 55903